Working for Change

Working for Change:
Making a Career in
International Public Service

Derick W. Brinkerhoff
Jennifer M. Brinkerhoff

Kumarian
Press, Inc.

Working for Change: Making a Career in International Public Service
Published in 2005 in the United States of America by Kumarian Press, Inc.,
1294 Blue Hills Avenue, Bloomfield, CT 06002 USA

Production and design by Rosanne Pignone, Pro Production
Copyedited by Lynne I. Lipkind
Proofread by Beth Richards
Index by Barbara DeGennaro

The text for *Working for Change: Making a Career in International Public Service*
   is set in Janson 10/12.
Printed in the United States of America on acid-free paper by McNaughton &
   Gunn, Inc.
Text printed with vegetable oil-based ink.

♾ The paper used in this publication meets the minimum requirements of the American National Standard for Information Sciences—Permanence of Paper for printed Library Materials, ANSI Z39.48-1984

Library of Congress Cataloging-in-Publication Data
Brinkerhoff, Derick W.
Working for change : making a career in international public service /
   Derick W. Brinkerhoff, Jennifer M. Brinkerhoff.
      p. cm.
   Summary: "This book focuses on development management positions in international service employment and offers guidance on finding the right mix of service objectives, degree programs, job opportunities and personal lifestyle choices. For students considering careers in public service and mid-career professionals looking for a change in direction. It is also for university career development officers and faculty advisors"—Provided by publisher.
      Includes bibliographical references.
      ISBN 1-56549-203-X (pbk. : alk. paper)
   1. Vocational guidance. 2. Career development. 3. Economic development projects—Developing countries—Management. I. Brinkerhoff, Jennifer M., 1965– II. Title.
361.2'6'0231724—dc22
                                                                    2005001044

14 13 12 11 10 09 08 07 06 05   10 9 8 7 6 5 4 3 2 1

*This book is dedicated to members of the
Development Management Network who, in addition to their own
commitment to social justice in the world, have shepherded
and continue to shepherd others into careers in
international development management.*

Contents

List of Acronyms

AAAS	American Association for the Advancement of Science
ACVFA	Advisory Committee on Voluntary Foreign Aid
ADRA	Adventist Development and Relief Agency
AIPT	Association for International Practical Training
AKRSP	Aga Khan Rural Support Program in Pakistan
APEC	Asia Pacific Economic Cooperation
ARD	Associates in Rural Development
ASPA	American Society for Public Administration
BATNA	the best alternative to a negotiated agreement
CEIP	Carnegie Endowment for International Peace
CG	Consultative Group
CIA	Central Intelligence Agency
CIDA	Canadian International Development Agency
CV	curriculum vitae
DAC	Development Assistance Committee
DAI	Development Alternatives Incorporated
DANIDA	Danish International Development Agency
DAWN	Development Alternatives with Women for a New Era
DFID	Department for International Development
DMN	Development Management Network
DR	Dominican Republic
EI	emotional intelligence
ESSD	Environmentally and Socially Sustainable Development
FAO	Food and Agriculture Organization
FS	Foreign Service
GS	General Schedule
GW	George Washington University

HBCUs	historically black colleges and universities
HSI	Hispanic Serving Institution
IAEA	International Atomic Energy Agency
IAESTE	International Association for the Exchange of Students for Technical Experience
IAP2	International Association of Public Participation
IDI	International Development Intern
IDMC	International Development Management Center
ILO	International Labour Organization
IMF	International Monetary Fund
IPC	Implementing Policy Change
IQC	Indefinite Quantity Contract
IR	intermediate result
IRIS	Institutional Reform and the Informal Sector
ISS	Institute for Social Studies
IYF	International Youth Foundation
JPA	Junior Professional Associates
LAC	Latin America and the Caribbean
MCA	Millennium Challenge Account
MDG	Millennium Development Goal
MI	Masters International
MIIS	Monterey Institute of International Studies
MSH	Management Sciences for Health
MSI	Management Systems International
MSIs	Minority Serving Institutions
NDI	National Democratic Institute
NEP	New Entry Professionals
NGO	nongovernmental organization
NIPA	National Institute of Public Administration
NRSP	National Rural Support Program
NSEP	National Security Education Program
OD	organizational development
OECD	Organization for Economic Co-operation and Development
OPF	Overseas Pakistani Foundation
PASA	participating agency service agreement
PECC	Pacific Economic Cooperation Council
PID	project identification document
PMF	Presidential Management Fellow
PP	project paper
PRSP	Poverty Reduction Strategy Paper
PSC	Personal Services Contractor
PVO	private voluntary organization

RAP	Rutgers Arts Program
R4	Results Review and Resource Request
RFP	Request for Proposal
RPCV	Returned Peace Corps Volunteer
RSSA	resources support services agreement
RTI	Research Triangle Institute
SAIS	Johns Hopkins' School of Advanced International Studies
SICA	Section on International and Comparative Administration
SID	Society for International Development
SO	strategic objective
SOW	scope of work
SPRITE	Social Policy Reform in Transition Economies
SWOT	strengths, weaknesses, opportunities, and threats
T&M	time and materials
TCUs	Tribal Colleges and Universities
TDY	tour of duty
TO	Task Order
TOR	terms of reference
UC	University of California
UNDP	United Nations Development Programme
UNESCO	United Nations Education, Scientific and Cultural Organization
UNFPA	United Nations Fund for Population Activities
UNHCR	United Nations High Commissioner for Refugees
UNICEF	United Nations Children's Fund
USAID	United States Agency for International Development
WHO	World Health Organization
WMO	World Meteorological Organization
YMCA	Young Men's Christian Association
YP	Young Professionals
YPIC	Young Professionals for International Cooperation

Acknowledgments

This book is a labor of love. To a large extent it represents fulfillment of our own service vision, to facilitate others in exploring career options in international public service, and in becoming as true to themselves and to their service as they can be. Our frameworks and the structure for the book are the product of our years of practice, teaching, advising, and research. But the book would not be complete without the voices and input of so many who have chosen service careers and lifestyles. We thank our support networks of family and friends, and those who mentored us on our career paths in international public service.

More specifically we thank our profiled practitioners, Jef Buehler, Jennifer Butz, Sarah Newhall, Najma Siddiqi, Aaron Williams, and David Yang, for sharing not only their career paths, but also their life stories and insightful advice, which we pass on to you.

The Section on International and Comparative Administration (SICA) of the American Society for Public Administration has had a long and fruitful relationship with Kumarian Press. We acknowledge support from SICA for the publication of this book.

We benefited from several opportunities to test and refine our frameworks and to collect additional input for the book. Among these was a roundtable at the 2003 American Society for Public Administration Conference. We thank Tara Hill, Susan Holcombe, Marcus Ingle, and Phil Morgan for their prepared remarks and input, as well as others who participated in the discussion. The frameworks were further tested in Jennifer's Fall 2003 Development Management Processes and Tools class at George Washington University. We took inspiration from these discussions and shared experiences. The class agreed to allow us to share some of their thoughts and struggles with you. Since to a large extent they represent our primary audience for this book, we thank them for helping us to understand our readers better and for permitting this book to be a vehicle through which they could "talk" to you. We also thank the members of our focus group of young professionals, several of whom are former students of Jennifer's, including Alec Bardzik, Ana Bilik, Christina del Castillo, Ashley Miller, Brendon Miller, Tom Sinclair, and Natasha Wanchek. As Jennifer has often said and Derick concurs, it's been a privilege to work with you.

We would also like to acknowledge the participants of the Fall 2003 and Spring 2004 Development Management Network workshops, who contributed to our brainstorming on the necessary skills for effective international public service careers. We received additional input from other practitioners, colleagues, and friends including Ana Bilik, Bruce Douglas, Sarah Gavian, Susan Holcombe, Marcus Ingle, and Adam Schumacher. Finally, we wish to acknowledge the many conversations we have had with students and job seekers over the years. They taught us a lot about the issues they struggle with and helped us to explore how we might assist them in this process.

CHAPTER **1**

Introduction

Our increasing recognition of interdependence in a globalized world challenges us to think more broadly about both the context and the options available for service-oriented careers. People of all ages are exploring new, creative pathways to service and civic engagement, not always acknowledged or counted among researchers and practitioners of traditional voluntary efforts and service professions. The creation of the World Social Forum, the increases in Peace Corps enrollment, and the popularity of Americorps are testament that not only do people want to serve; they also want to be empowered to lead change for the better, both at home and abroad. However, few guideposts exist to mark the paths and opportunities for careers in service. The purpose of this book is to introduce the field of international development management and to explore potential career paths in international public service—whether these are based overseas or here at home, whether they involve working for change from outside systems, from the inside, or some combination. We define public service as service in the interest of others. It encompasses work in all three sectors: government, nonprofit, and business, depending on one's particular role. Public, in this sense, refers to an action arena where the benefits derived serve to contribute to widely distributed social goods, as opposed to private individual gain.

Psychology tells us that we make rational sense of our careers after the fact; looking backwards, it all seems to be part of a grand plan. While that may be true in some cases, the image of career planning as a set-the-goal, plot-the-steps process misses both the reality and the richness of the what, where, and how of people's career choices. There are many paths to careers in international public service. Some of us are inspired to reach out into the world, engage, and, when we perceive deprivation, injustice, or inequity, look for ways to work for a better global community. Others come to international public service in a more incremental way, perhaps through the accumulation of particular

1

international experiences and personal and professional contacts. State Department kids may be one example. Still others come from an academic disciplinary perspective, studying economics, anthropology, health, or education, for example, but wanting to move beyond the academy to apply their knowledge for the benefit of those who are disadvantaged. Most of us come to this field through some combination of the above. We may come from developing-country institutions, government or nonprofit; from US-based nonprofits; federal government agencies; academia; or the private sector.

This book offers some concrete guidance and some conceptual career "signposts" to inform both students curious about international or domestic public service, and mid-career professionals looking for a change in their search for meaningful careers and lifestyles. The book is mainly targeted at those who share the values orientation of public service and poverty alleviation but who are not certain how to pursue such careers. This includes graduate students already attracted to public service who may need additional guidance in channeling their energies, and participants in service programs such as the Peace Corps and Americorps. We also hope this book will be helpful to those who teach and advise these audiences.[1]

Contents of the Book

This is not an international development or a public management textbook, although we touch upon these topics. Our intention is to introduce to those who are interested in or curious what a career in international public service is all about. But it is not a step-by-step "how-to" guide. We outline some issues for you to think about and to reflect upon in order to come to your own—perhaps evolving—conclusions. We, the authors, have thought about these issues for our own careers, as have the people you will read about, and we encourage you to do the same. This is the spirit of development management: to understand and commit to a life and career of service, you must decide what these mean for you.

We weave personal stories of service throughout the book so you can see how others have responded to these issues. These are stories about real individuals and their service careers and life choices. We selected them to represent diversity on a number of fronts, including gender, ethnicity, age (thirties to fifties), and, most importantly, career choices. They are perhaps a bit biased towards slightly older and more experienced people, in order to benefit from the full range of their careers and experience to date. In early conversations about the book, some colleagues and friends suggested we profile people like Kofi Annan and Jimmy Carter. Our intention, though, is to present to you some examples of people in their careers who were once just like you. Our profiled practitioners are remarkable people for what they have become. But no one starts out that way. And they're not finished yet!

Later in this chapter, we talk about the broad aims of public service that focus on promoting development, a term whose definition is debated. In Chapter 2, we look at a particular subset of international public service activity that in our view is highly relevant to what people actually do in public service positions: development management. We argue that development management is much more than simply a set of skills and tools. Among other things, it embodies a continuous tension between our ideals and how they get enacted, especially through the industries of international and community development. These tensions encourage us to question and clarify what development, empowerment, and service mean.

We then introduce our conceptual signposts: what we call the service-choice spiral. The service-choice spiral hones in on the personal pathways, capacity building, and choices we make, consciously or otherwise, as we pursue service careers. By making this process more conscious and strategic, you can enhance the contributions of your service choices both to yourself and to others. The bulk of the book is dedicated to describing the components of this framework—self-awareness, serving in community, skills and knowledge, and job choices. In elaborating these topics, we offer suggestions for how to deepen each of these, including how to begin to cultivate your own service vision, participate in and nurture communities of service, identify and acquire skills and knowledge, and consider the range of work options available in international public service careers. We provide more specific tips and starting points for your own exploration in the appendices.

We also discuss how careers progress and evolve, including advice for advancing on your career path, and how you can navigate particularly challenging career transitions, from getting the first job, to advancing to increasing responsibility and technical expertise, to moving from domestic to international work. Finally, we turn to how it all fits together, not just with respect to your career, but also with regard to a service lifestyle. We touch on the challenges of finding a mate and contemplating family options while pursuing international work, and we explore the difficulties of maintaining balance in your personal and professional life while avoiding burnout and sustaining your motivation for service.

The Many Voices in the Book

Throughout the discussion of development management, the service-choice spiral, and sustaining motivation for service, examples and quotations from those we profile highlight key points and personalize the discussion. We also include the voices and experiences of some of our students. These include the George Washington University's School of Public Policy and Public Administration Fall 2003 international development management class. We occasionally quote from their reflections and struggles to understand and cope with the challenges of development management in practice. We include insights from young professionals we have trained and worked with. We build upon our respective teaching, mentoring new entrants to the field and offering employment advice. The book draws upon our previous research, which seeks to define the field and explore its many actors and organizations. And, of course, it builds on our personal experiences in international public service. So from time to time we may mention portions of our own career paths, and in such cases we'll simply refer to either Derick or Jennifer.[2]

In thinking about the issues addressed in the book, we benefited from the input of several colleagues and friends. We first tested our service-choice spiral at a roundtable at the American Society for Public Administration Conference in March 2003, where we profited from the insight of other teachers and practitioners of development management, as well as a student discussant. Our resulting expanded model was first published in the *Journal of Public Affairs Education*. We twice brainstormed with our colleagues from the Development Management Network, to whom this book is dedicated. Finally, we benefited from a focus group of young professionals, as well as less formal conversations and e-mail with a broader range of colleagues and friends. We hope you will benefit from this collective wisdom and the range of voices and experience reflected in these pages as you join us in a global community of service.

What and Where Is Development?

Public service tackles the greatest challenges, with the highest expectations—due, in part, to the dire needs disadvantaged people face, and the scarcity of resources available for the effort. The needs are most evident in countries of the developing world, and many choose a path of international public service specifically focused on "development." But what is that?

International development as both an analytic and academic discipline and a career option is largely the product of American politics after World War II. In his inaugural speech in 1949, and building on the Marshall Plan, President Truman proposed a new component to US foreign policy: technical assistance beyond Europe and Latin America. Truman's Point Four provided the impetus for the expansion of the UN structure to include a series of special agencies specific to international technical assistance.

Since then, the international development field has evolved as a discipline, marked by changed understandings of how to address development challenges.[3] A primary change has been increased recognition of the complexity of what makes development happen. Early models from the 1950s, with their notions of economic "take-off" or a "big push" toward modernization, implied that, first, all countries followed the same path to development, and, second, that once a country launched itself on the path by pushing the right buttons, progress was automatic. These early models proved inadequate to explain what observers on the ground saw, namely that development was neither simple nor easy. Theorists and practitioners began to explore the role of culture, institutions, local knowledge, values, and behaviors. Development definitions moved away from Western-centric modernization towards an image of "development with a human face," "people-centered development," "development as freedom," and a host of other characterizations that have sought to capture the idea that development is more than simply a question of economics.

Today, definitions compete with each other. Among the arguments is whether development is an end or a means. If it is an end, this implies that someone knows what the destination should look like, and that how to get there can be determined in advance (for example, by the International Monetary Fund or the World Bank). If, on the other hand, development is a means, then it looks more like a process of social mobilization or social learning. Development, then, involves learning and evolution; no end point exists at which someone can determine that he or she has "arrived."

Arguments over terminology mask a range of agendas, some technical, some political. The multilateral development banks lean in one direction on definitions, NGOs (nongovernmental organizations) in another. Yet you are likely to find different, sometimes conflicting agendas coexisting inside the same organization. The broad distinctions commonly used—between "developed" and "developing" countries; among first, second, third, and fourth worlds; and between the global "North" and "South"—are the subject of fierce debates, and it can be hard to separate the content from the politics.[4] Our perspective is that development terminology, while laden with political baggage, is nonetheless descriptive both of societal patterns and processes found in many countries around the world (poverty, economic and social deprivation, lack of capacity) and of aspirational goals (having more and being more). Many see "international" public service—and development work, in particular—as encompassing all countries of the world. The drive to expand people's choices and quality of life is universal, whether we pursue these aims as Westerners entering alien cultures, as Southerners working in Northern countries, or in addressing poverty and marginalization in our own backyards.

The point to recognize is that there exists no simple answer to the question of what development is or is not. Engaging in public service requires pondering the question, not coming up with a definitive answer. And the latter is not possible anyway. Working to promote development means that you, together with others, will always be learning what it might mean, as will be more fully discussed in Chapters 2, 4, and 5. Public service, whether international or domestic, shares a significant amount of overlap and commonality.

In the stories interspersed among the book's chapters, you'll read about mobilizing citizens in Camden, New Jersey, working with refugees in Portland, Oregon, organizing citizen focus groups in Fresno, California, promoting a greater understanding of Asia in the United States, helping Pakistani women in Scandinavia, building the capacity of village women in Nepal, mobilizing village associations and training community activists in Pakistan, fostering economic development in Latin America, brokering partnerships between nonprofits and multinational corporations, and educating voters in Mongolia and citizens in Albania. And you'll read about working for city and federal government (with the US Agency for International Development [USAID], the State Department, and the Federal Main Street Program); for domestic and international nonprofits, small and large; for private consulting firms; and for the World Bank, International Labour Organization, and United Nations. These profiled personal tales are among the many options for international public service, but they represent only a few of the possibilities. They emphasize that each person's path to service is unique. At the same time, they demonstrate the range of opportunities, challenges, and rewards of international public service.

Notes

1. While we did not set out to write a book for international pre-service and mid-career students who intend to serve in their home countries, the general frameworks introduced in the book are still relevant to this audience.

2. References to Jennifer in the text refer to Jennifer Brinkerhoff. When referring to our profilee, we use Jennifer Butz.

3. For an informative overview of the history of international development see Rist (1997). See recommended reading on international development, Appendix 4.

4. While it does not accurately describe geographical characteristics, for simplicity we retain the use of the North and South terminology to distinguish between relatively more or less advantaged places. We actually prefer the distinction inclusion-exclusion (referring to dominant economic, social, and political systems whether at the national or global level), though this terminology is more familiar in Europe than in North America, and North-South remains the most commonly understood classification.

CHAPTER 2

What Is Development Management?

The range of activities involved in international public service is vast. Engaging in public service can mean teaching and training, both children and adults; providing health services, from medical emergencies to primary care, to family planning; building houses, schools, clinics, or roads; handling money, for example, raising funds, issuing grants, preparing budgets, or monitoring spending; doing scientific research, for example, developing new vaccines or conducting field trials of new seeds for better agricultural production; or facilitating economic development, for example, helping communities organize to obtain resources or to start businesses, or lobbying legislators for new policies. We could go on—the list would be nearly endless—and what you end up doing will depend upon the unique combination of your interests, skills, and background, and the opportunities that present themselves. But one thing we can promise you is that whatever type of international public service you become engaged in, you won't be doing it alone.

This common feature of all public service, whether international or domestic, leads to the topic of this chapter. Public service takes place in some kind of organization, formal or informal, and it involves people. So achieving success in public service means being able to navigate effectively within an organizational setting and to achieve results through the collective effort of groups of people. A more succinct way of saying this is that engaging successfully in public service means being a good manager. We see management as the umbrella concept that informs public service, and in this chapter we provide a way of thinking about the subset of the broad public management field that is specific to international development—development management.

Along with the evolution of the concept of development, and what its goals are or should be, have been significant changes in thinking

9

regarding how to achieve it. Early notions of what to do concentrated on government leadership, where development would be the result of centrally planned, state-dominated strategies. The failure of the state to deliver, in most cases, provoked new thinking, which led to the familiar strategies of today's international development policy agenda. These emphasize market-led approaches to growth and poverty reduction with the state as a supporter and regulator of private and community efforts and investments rather than as the sole or predominant actor. Currently, the Millennium Development Goals (MDGs), established in 2000 and endorsed by 189 countries of the United Nations, describe a widely accepted international development agenda.[1] The goals include halving poverty, achieving universal primary education and gender equity, reducing maternal and child mortality, combating HIV/AIDS and other major diseases, and ensuring environmental sustainability. Opinions vary on how achievable the goals are within the proposed time frame.

If we accept the MDGs as a shorthand statement of development that will improve poor people's and communities' assets and quality of life, then development management refers to managing the service/technical inputs, operational systems, processes, and capacity-building necessary to achieve these goals, including understanding and dealing with the array of constraints that impinge upon their achievement: political, institutional, social, cultural, and so on. Although the need for development management is greater in the global South, it is also applicable to poor communities in the North. As Jef Buehler's (Profile 5) experience confirms, community organizations in New Jersey confront the need to identify needs, mobilize constituencies, engage poor and marginalized citizens, obtain resources, design and implement programs, deal with politicians and officials at various levels (municipal, state, federal), and demonstrate results. All of these issues face community organizations in developing countries, such as Burkina Faso in West Africa or the rural highlands of Guatemala in Latin America.

Development management as an applied discipline has evolved along with changes in international development strategies and in the way people think about management. From its initial focus on institution building for central-level public bureaucracies and capacity building for economic and project planning, development management has gradually expanded to encompass reforming and "loosening up" bureaucracies at all levels to make them more effective at reaching the poor. Moving beyond just applying technical tools, development management integrates politics and culture into organizational improvement, and introduces participation and performance-based approaches to service delivery and program management. It also pays attention to building community and NGO capacity, and to implementing policy reforms, which involves large numbers of people and organizations.[2]

Changes in management theory and practice have also influenced development management. Among the clearest examples is the impact of the public management-reform movement—begun in the United States, Australia, New Zealand, and the United Kingdom—to graft private sector-management approaches onto public agencies to emphasize performance and attention to the public sector equivalent of the "bottom line." The reform strategies and management tools from this movement have been widely applied in developing countries. In some cases, they have been part of World Bank or other donor-supported public sector-assistance programs.

Other advances in management thinking that have percolated into development management, just to name a few, include new models of motivation and incentives that look beyond simply salaries, culturally based theories of leadership and organizational behavior, the emerging importance of ethics and values (especially related to fighting corruption), new learning about how to introduce and sustain change, and greater understanding of how to manage across organizations and in partnership structures. In sum, and to oversimplify a bit, the trend in development management has been away from:

- Sole reliance on the technical-rational "fix": concentrating on improving so-called hard systems (for example, budgeting/accounting and personnel) and structures, to the exclusion of "soft" systems (people).
- Universalist solutions: one size fits all, good for any situation.
- Focus on reactive administrative models: fulfilling routine functions and paying attention to day-to-day routine.

Development management has moved toward:

- Context specificity: while solutions in various settings will share some features, they must be adapted to the particular features that make each context unique.
- Recognition that any change is politically infused: even if a change appears to be just a technical modification, somebody wins and somebody loses.
- Multi-sectoral solutions: no single discipline or perspective has a corner on "the truth"; the best solutions emerge when the insights of many viewpoints and sources of expertise are brought to bear.
- Strategic perspectives merged with operational administration: it is necessary to pay attention to the "big picture" and long-term direction while not neglecting the details of how to get there.
- Multi-organizational models: the complex problems of development almost always require the attention and intervention of

numerous agencies, even if one organization is nominally "in charge."

To help explain what being a development manager means, we define four related facets that comprise development management. First, and most commonly understood, development management means working to improve the efficiency and effectiveness of foreign assistance programs and to further international agencies' policy and program agendas. Second, development management is a toolkit; it promotes the application of a range of management and analytical tools adapted from a variety of social science disciplines, including strategic management, organization development, psychology, and political science. Third, development management is process intervention, where the application of tools in pursuit of objectives is undertaken in ways that self-consciously address political issues and values. Fourth, development management incorporates a values dimension that emphasizes self-determination, empowerment, and an equitable distribution of development benefits.

Because for many "management" is associated with efficiency and simply getting the job done, some are surprised at the complexity of development management as we define it here. This led George Washington University (GW) student Tara Hill to conclude that development management is *more a philosophy of action as opposed to any one given job, assignment, or place.* Each of the facets we identify represents one essential aspect of development management, and taken together they constitute a whole. However, there are some inherent tensions among them, which can lead to contradictions and dilemmas for you as a development manager. For example, managing a development project to carry out an international assistance agency's desired agenda may not necessarily promote the values of empowerment and self-determination; and the donor agency's procedures may not be flexible enough to support a genuine process approach. The four-faceted definition explicitly recognizes that development management can mean different things to different people. We'll look at each of these four facets of development management in more detail and illustrate their interdependencies. We return to these facets in later chapters, because they relate closely to the critical steps along career paths in public service.

Development Management
as a Means to Institutional Agendas

Development management is most often sponsored by international aid agencies, all of which have their own priorities and corresponding agendas.

Typically, international public service is funded by one or another aid agency, such as USAID, the British and Canadian bilaterals, Department for International Development (DFID) and Canadian International Development Agency (CIDA), the World Bank, or one of the regional development banks. So you, as a development professional, enter "the scene" at the behest of a donor agency for a predetermined task. It is not always clear if the need for, and the design of, this task represent priorities of someone in a developing country—for example, rural women seeking health care for themselves and their families, or urban slum-dwellers who need improved infrastructure and access to jobs. To be fair, most donor agencies make some effort to consult with project beneficiaries, or their representatives, to assure that the projects and programs they design fit with people's needs and wants. However, that fit is mediated by the priorities the donor agency establishes, which determine how funding is allocated.

For example, in the case of USAID, when Congress provides the agency with its annual budget, it tells USAID that certain line items must be spent for particular purposes (earmarking). So if USAID is seeking to program money earmarked for child survival in, say, Zambia, and country officials indicate that agricultural production or HIV/AIDS in copper-mining communities is a higher priority, then USAID either has to look to other budget sources to respond to the Zambians' preferences or seek to convince them to want a child survival program. To continue this example, say you're working for an NGO in Zambia that emphasizes community-led development and USAID wants to contract with your NGO to manage the child survival program. The contract will engage you to do your best to achieve the child survival objectives, and will not allow you to pursue some other set of objectives, even if in your view these are more in line with what the community wants. In this sense, development management is a means to enhancing the effectiveness and efficiency of projects and programs determined and designed by donor agencies. This is what Alan Thomas calls management of development, as opposed to management for development.[3]

Institutional agendas encompass more that what should get done. They also dictate, in part, how programs and projects should be implemented. For example, the emphasis on performance measurement and results orientation, noted above, is built into calls for proposals, requiring implementing actors—NGOs and private sector consulting firms—to identify measurable indicators of progress and results and associated timetables. In practice, this can skew incentives, sometimes blurring the big picture—the why of a particular program. It can also reduce the emphasis on responding to community needs and changing contextual factors.

Many of us may be reluctant to accept this facet of development management. But it is the reality of the international development industry—and of much of domestic service as well. As Jennifer Butz (Profile 6) puts it, *development is an extension of foreign policy. It's a cheaper way of building nations so that they can become partners rather than opponents, even if that doesn't work out sometimes. Actually, it's taken me a long time to finally accept this. It would be nice to say, "Oh, it's about helping people." Well, that may be what drives individuals to contribute, which is great. But that's not why governments and multilateral institutions exist.*

Whether you accept these agendas or not depends on your own orientation. This includes the values dimension discussed below, as well as your personal vision for development, explored in Chapter 4. One of our GW students describes herself as *a person who often places ideals above practicality. However, I have quickly learned that in this industry, most of the money lies in initiatives that clash with my values. I have no desire to push the US foreign policy agenda. Yet I do understand the need to work with power structures to achieve change. After all, I have found many small creative initiatives that adhere closely to a set of values with which I am comfortable, but how much change are they actually achieving?* Not all of these agendas are "bad," even if they are politically motivated. It is difficult to argue with the spirit of child survival earmarking, even though we may disagree with its practice.

Institutional agendas are often the subject of our decision making with respect to working for change inside or outside of systems, discussed in Chapter 7. David Yang (Profile 2) offers the following advice: *I would invite everyone to act their conscience in whatever institution they are serving in. At the same time, I'm very pragmatic. If a person has the will towards a reformist agenda, one can always find opportunities to pursue it. It might be frustrating and it might be limited, but if you recognize the limits of political action, I think there's always satisfaction to be gained. And that's not to say if one is antiwar and one's institution goes to war that one shouldn't resign. But short of those monumental questions, I've always found in my career great opportunity to make real progress on what I was trying to do.*

This facet of development management can be perhaps the most problematic to reconcile with its other facets. First and most obviously, as the above hypothetical Zambia story makes clear, foreign assistance agendas at a minimum compromise some degree of self-determination in pursuit of socioeconomic reforms. Second, donor programming requirements and incentives—such as loan disbursement schedules, project timetables, and compliance with predetermined indicators—can further inhibit the ability of groups in the recipient country, whether inside or outside of government, to play an active role in tailoring the assistance provided to their needs and their pace of change. These limitations can make it difficult to allow room to accommodate political realities, or to change course during implementation. What if, for example, the implementation process leads to identified priorities and targets that significantly modify or contradict the foreign assistance package funding the effort?

Third, these same pressures and incentives can also lead to superficial commitment to reform and pro forma meeting of targets. In other words, development clients may go through the motions of complying with requirements and making changes without internalizing them. As a hypothetical example, the Zambian government signs on to a World Bank public sector–reform project that requires downsizing government staff. They might let go the targeted number in the short term, only to hire them back in another capacity. In recent years, development management specialists have had an impact on how international donor programs are designed and implemented to take more account of the need to build in flexibility both to gain more buy-in or political will from host governments, and to modify designs during implementation, particularly for programs with long life spans.

Development Management as Toolkit

Development management promotes the application of a range of management and analytical tools adapted from a variety of disciplines, including strategic management, public policy, public administration, organization development, psychology, anthropology, and political science. These tools assist in mapping the terrain in which policy reforms, programs, and projects are designed and implemented, that is the political, sociocultural, and organizational contexts of interventions. For example, in his work on USAID's Implementing Policy Change project (IPC), Derick and his colleagues drew upon strategic management to help developing-country reformers decide what to do. They might begin with SWOT analysis (identifying internal strengths and weaknesses and external opportunities and threats), which would then be followed by other tools to assess the important characteristics of the actors involved. These latter tools include stakeholder analysis, political mapping, and various tools for needs assessment, such as the capacity enhancement-needs assessment. The results of these exercises would feed into the elaboration of potential response strategies that incorporate flexibility and adaptation.[4]

Development management tools merge policy and program analytics with action. The blending of the process and values facets with the tools accounts for the distinctiveness of development management as toolkit. On the analytic side, this means tools that explore the institutional and organizational incentive aspects of achieving results, and that examine the psychology of change efforts, focusing on individual incentives and motivation. For example, why would various actors choose to champion this particular development effort? What's in it for them? Answering these questions leads to others. How can the interests of reluctant actors be factored into program design so they are more likely to commit to and sustain the effort? On the operational side this means tools and approaches that focus on data gathering, such as participatory rural appraisal; flexible and adaptive design and planning; and action-learning and experimentation. For example, the US Federal Main Street Program's methodology is one of both process and the application of specific tools, such as goal setting, work planning, and cost-benefit analysis. Jef Buehler (Profile 5) and his clients use these for the projects they design and implement. Aaron Williams (Profile 4) has always emphasized the importance of team building, but also applies economics, budgeting, and market analysis in his work.

Tools may not be the most exciting of the development management facets, but they are a prerequisite to becoming an effective doer. As GW student Jason Berry puts it, *it is not sufficient to just have a desire to change the world. It is necessary for one to possess the skills and tools (policy analysis, project planning, evaluations, etc.) to be able to get the work done. We would never say it is okay for someone to want to be a carpenter but say they don't need to learn how to use a saw or read blueprints.*

Development managers acquire these tools in a variety of ways from a range of sources. We talk more about the what, how, and where of tools and skills acquisition in Chapter 6. Some can be obtained through professional degree programs and academic study; others are available through specialized non-degree training and seminars. Still others will be picked up on the job, learning by doing, and through experience. For example, Jennifer Butz (Profile 6) created a civic engagement index to enable her to monitor program success and to respond to USAID's requirements for results reporting.

An important consideration in the connection between this facet of development management and the other facets is the issue of who is acquiring the toolkit. Both the process and values facets are explicit in their attention to assuring that tools and expertise do not remain the sole province of outsiders, donor agencies, international NGOs, and consulting firms. Acquiring the appropriate tools and expertise is important, but so is transferring them to others. You've probably heard the repeated-to-the-point-of-corniness adage, "give a person a fish and he eats that day, teach a person to fish, and he'll eat forever." Like many corny sayings, there's some truth to this (more on this one below).

Development Management as Process

Development management as process means, in essence, paying attention to how things are done, not just what gets done. Development managers care about achieving results, but they do so not by stepping in and doing everything themselves according to how they think things should be done. Instead, they start with their client's priorities, needs, and values, and help them to solve today's problems in a way that gives them the capacity to learn to solve tomorrow's problems as well. In a nutshell, this is what is called process consultation. Through enacting this facet of development management, you help to 1) empower people to assert and maintain control over what they want to do and 2) build their capacity to sustain the process into the future and apply it in other situations.

Supporting these two outcomes—empowerment and sustainable capacity—is not as straightforward as you might think. Sometimes even if the client has specified the need and invited the help, the way the helper provides assistance serves to maintain dependence. And the creation of dependency is the opposite of the intent of process consultation. International public service to promote socioeconomic development is not like a doctor-patient interaction, where the power and responsibility of diagnosis and of prescribing the solution rests solely with the doctor/expert. In addressing these complex problems, all parties bring some level of expertise to the table and no one has a monopoly on the "truth" by virtue of "superior" understanding.

Najma Siddiqi (Profile 3) makes the distinction between two change models. *There are people who try to change action first. They say, "If you change action, then it will change your thought processes, and then your perception." For example Shoaib Sultan Khan of AKRSP* [the Aga Khan Rural Support Program in Pakistan] *has this approach: "Start meeting, start saving. I'm telling you it's good for you, do it. And then you will come together, and you can do this, that, and the other." But to me, perception comes first. Maybe that's my psychology hat—perception, and then thought processes, and then action. I don't try to change action. My approach is completely different: Understand your situation. It's probably slower. So it's not adopting as much as internalizing. I believe in organizing the people, not in forming organizations. If you can show people that the desirable is possible, then they will be motivated and they will try to get the skills, the knowledge, and the assertion that they need to bring about a change. If you say, "I am here to help you change. I'll tell you how to change," then you're also encouraging a dependency on you, which I totally don't believe in. You offer the knowledge and experience that you have. You don't hold it back. You can say, "These guys did this. I have done that." Share your learning, but don't tell them what to do.*

This raises a dilemma for the language we so often use to describe service. It calls into question the very meaning of helping. Listen to Ram Dass and Paul Gorman on this issue: "The more you see yourself as a 'helper,' the more need for people to play the passive 'helped.' You're buying into, even juicing up, precisely what people who are suffering want to be rid of: limitation, dependency, helplessness, separateness." Emphasizing "helping" can actually alienate us from those with whom we seek to connect. "What otherwise could be a profound and intimate relationship becomes ships passing in the night. In the effort to express compassion, we end up feeling estranged. It's distressing and puzzling."[5] Think for a moment how you feel when some authority figure tells you what you should think and do, and how that differs from when you are problem-solving with a team. Technical expertise has its place, but it is only one component of problem solving. We will return to this theme in Chapter 5.

Development management, as Alan Thomas says, means doing things with people, not for them. This statement encapsulates three core principles of process consultation:

- Clients know more about their own situation than the consultant will ever know.
- The consultant-client interaction needs to engender the client's psychological ownership of the activities, plans, objectives, etc. that results from the relationship.
- The consultant should use the interaction to seek to develop the clients' capacities to solve their own problems in the future.

Just because clients know more about their own situation does not mean a process consultant has no expertise to offer. The delicate balance between being an expert and a facilitator is an issue all development managers face, and one the GW students grappled with. Given criticisms of the development industry, many were reluctant to label themselves experts even when considering their future professional development. Jennifer Swift-Morgan provides a typical response: *I definitely see myself more as a facilitator than an expert, in that I, a young white woman from America, am not likely to have all of the answers or understand any given situation in the field better than the people who are from there. It is easy to see the facilitating role as superior to that of the "expert" if one intends on trying to bring about sustainable development based on and with the goal of empowering people to use their own agency to make positive change, to realize development as freedom. . . . At the same time, there are times when a certain amount of "expertise" is requested by the host country or community itself, and may be what is needed.* As Najma Siddiqi put it, *share your learning, but don't tell them what to do.*

Navigating the balance between expertise and facilitation is indeed a challenge. Acquiring expertise can feel daunting, as described by GW student Jennifer Villemez: *I do not consider myself an expert in development. (In fact, I would be afraid to misspeak or mislead by claiming to be such an expert.) I recognize that being an expert at something is often necessary to "getting your foot in the door" in this field; however, I do not feel that I have, as yet, had the experience to be considered an expert in a specific facet of development. I join my classmates in feeling that this term is especially daunting, weighted with a responsibility I fear I cannot carry.* We encourage you to develop both technical and process expertise. While the facilitation may fit more closely with your values, it is often the technical expertise you can demonstrate that gets you hired.

You don't always have to develop the technical expertise yourself. Sometimes you can work as part of a team that combines process and technical experts. For example, Derick worked in West Africa with a team to assist African entrepreneurs to organize advocacy networks to lobby government officials for more pro-business policies. He relied upon his teammates for expertise in private sector issues, while he provided help to the groups of entrepreneurs in defining their objectives, planning their advocacy activities, and tracking their progress.

Paying attention to process doesn't just involve how you interact with the people you're working with in your service activity or project. The organizations where you and your clients, beneficiaries, partners (whatever term you feel fits best) work—whether in an individual agency or across multiple organizations—also affect how things happen. So you as a development manager need to be concerned with how organizational structures and procedures either help or hinder you in implementing plans and achieving objectives. What you'll find is that the best managerial solutions will emerge from a process of matching what you want to get done with the organizations you work with and the larger environment in which the work takes place. Sometimes you'll need to adjust the work to fit the organization and the environment; other times you'll be able to make changes in the organization (and sometimes in the environment) to accomplish your original plan. You won't know ahead of time exactly what kinds of adjustments will be needed, so this process is an ongoing one, and you'll get better at it as you gain experience.

Among the adjustments that development managers often need to make is to use the tools and procedures that the organizations they work in have adopted. Particular tools may be required or standardized in ways that have implications for process. For example, the Logical Framework (and its variations) is a tool designed by the international development industry for program design, performance measurement, and evaluation.[6] It has been criticized on several fronts, most of which are really about the process of its implementation rather than the tool itself. It was originally intended to be a tool for building participation and consensus, to be used to foster collaborative problem solving and dialogue. Instead it is often applied as a blueprint, usually with a top-down specification of what to do that locks implementers into specific activities, results, and sometimes timelines. In fact, one development scholar has warned that it can be a "lockframe" rather than a logframe. In that sense, it has become more of an auditing than a learning tool. In their application, these types of tools confirm one of the universal features of life in organizations: what gets measured gets done.

At the sector level—public, civil society, and private—the process facet of development management moves you into the realm of "big picture" issues, such as: how and where participation takes place, how public agencies are held accountable (if at all), information availability and transparency, and government responsiveness to what local people want and need. These issues bring in empowerment in its societal and political dimensions, and push you to ask questions about how various sociopolitical groups interact in the policy and program implementation process. Who has a place at the policy table? What process mechanisms allow which groups to play a role, and/or exclude others? What managerial practices and capacities are required for effective democratic governance and socioeconomic development? How can public sector agencies and NGOs best cooperate to achieve joint objectives?

As these questions imply, the process facet of development management links with the tool and foreign assistance agenda facets. An important place in the toolkit is accorded to process tools, those that facilitate consultation, joint problem and solution identification, ownership and commitment building, participatory strategy development, and so on. Further, many of these questions arise in the context of evolving international assistance agendas. For example, USAID has struggled with its civil society-promotion agenda when confronting contexts where such promotion might lead to empowering religious fundamentalist groups.

They also hold implications for the application of tools like the Logical Framework. Who gets to decide what the objectives and activities of a program will be? Who gets to participate in the process of identifying indicators for what success means? And if beneficiaries are consulted, which ones? Can we assume that community leaders represent the aspirations of the community as a whole? In practice, consultative processes often suffer from what has been called "tarmac bias." This refers to the donors (or their designated implementers) flying into a country and consulting or contracting only with those actors who are the easiest to reach.

Aaron Williams (Profile 4) emphasizes the importance of development management's process facet in terms of building bridges both among sectors—business, government, and civil society—and between host country actors and USAID. *You need to understand how you bring in all the players in any particular sector, so you have a broad picture of what the development problem is, the issue you're trying to focus on. You need to listen to the people in the host country, because this is their country, and if there's no buy-in to what's being done developmentally, it's not going to work anyway— and even if that seems to be at odds with what the US Government seems to think needs to be done. I always saw myself as being the broker between those two sides, trying to find a way to walk down a common road.*

Development Management as Values

Development-promoting activities of any sort constitute interventions in the status quo, and any intervention advances someone's particular set of interests and objectives at the expense of others'. So if you're helping to implement a policy reform or a development project or you're building managerial capacity in a particular agency, then—whether you're aware of it or not—you're engaging in a values-driven endeavor. Development management as values is expressed in two ways. First, development managers acknowledge that managing in the world of public service is infused with politics. Part of this acknowledgment means that you, as a provider of technical or managerial assistance, are a "carrier" of values. However, providers of international technical assistance often don a mantle of neutrality, assumed as a function of their scientific and professional expertise. Our experience tells us, though, that knowledge and expertise cannot be separated from the values context in which it is developed and applied. We explore this more fully in Chapter 5 in our discussion of communities of understanding.

Second, development managers take a normative stance on empowering and supporting groups, particularly the poor and marginalized, to play an active role in determining and fulfilling their own needs. Development managers should enhance the capacity of development actors to effectively pursue their own development: it should be people centered. This is desirable not simply because it works, but because it's right. This stance recognizes that empowerment is more than skills and capacities; it involves accessing, creating, and exercising political power as well.

Remember the "teach a person to fish" story? Giving people the ability to catch fish is not enough. We need to be concerned with who has rights to the ownership of the fish and the fishing equipment, who controls access to the bodies of water where the fish are found, and who is responsible for assuring the quality of the water so that the fish caught are safe to eat. Unless the people fishing have some influence on these other factors, all of which have to do with empowerment, then the feel-good fishing story is incomplete.

There is another more subtle aspect of the values facet: whether we intend to or not we bring our own values to the work and they inform the decisions we make, including whose view counts, how resources are allocated, and what we choose to do and why. Values cannot be avoided. This aspect of being a development manager is closely linked to ethics. Scholars and promoters of development ethics argue that because our values inevitably inform our behavior and interactions with others (including those with whom and for whom we perceive we are working), we have an obligation to make those values explicit.[7]

All that said, in reality, values are most often discussed only in terms of how they relate to programmatic objectives. For example, implementers may link to values when discussing political feasibility and winners and losers of policy and program initiatives. Or, initiatives targeted to capacity building may specifically refer to empowerment and participation. Beyond that, values may not often be openly discussed, as GW student Kipp Efinger discovered in his work to date in the development industry: *I currently work in a setting that is modeled after private industry. It is very efficient; however, values are never discussed. I think that this should be remedied through dialogue at staff meetings. Understanding the values of the organization builds an employee connection with the organization. It brings pride and care to your work.*

It is the values dimension that most often attracts people to development management as a career, as confirmed by GW student Joanna Ramos: *What attracts me to development is the prospect of empowering people to take control of their lives and realize their own potential. I want to facilitate human development and take action to change, oftentimes slowly, the structures that contribute to oppression and poverty.*

Combining the Facets of Development Management

Now that we've "unpacked" the four facets of being a development manager, we want to remind you before you leave this chapter that the full picture of development management emerges only from combining them. We separated them to better explain development management to you. You may be asking, is one facet more important than another, and if so, which one? Our answer, which you might not find very satisfying, is that it depends. Some facets may emerge as primary in a particular situation, or in the eyes of a specific actor. For example, some people may not see, or prefer not to see, the values aspect. Donors may be primarily concerned with your role and expertise in managing their projects and programs. Trainers and capacity builders may highlight managerial toolkits. Political activists may stress empowerment. So development management can look very different depending on who is doing it and where.

In our view, all the facets are intimately connected. Development management as values is closely related to development management as process. The values orientation also links to tools and the donor-funded provision of external assistance. Management tools and technologies are meant to combine external expertise with local knowledge and skills in a process that employs outside resources in the service of indigenously directed endeavors. Thus, as we've mentioned, development management blends indigenous knowledge and norms as it seeks to promote sustainable change, whose contours are developed through a participatory dialogue incorporating multiple perspectives.

Notes

1. See http://www.developmentgoals.org.

2. For those who want to learn more about development management and its evolution, see the references in Appendix 4.

3. See recommended reading on development management, Appendix 4.

4. Part II of *Managing Policy Reform* describes these tools and others. See the recommended reading on development management in Appendix 4.

5. This is a classic book that we highly recommend. It raises a lot of questions, such as, "are we really 'helping?'" It also addresses burnout, as we will discuss in Chapter 9. See the recommended reading on service in Appendix 4.

6. Most donors continue to use the Logical Framework, or logframe, but USAID has modified it into what it calls the Results Framework. The underlying program logic is the same, and both tools have faced similar criticisms.

7. To learn more about development ethics, visit the International Development Ethics Association Web page at http://www.development-ethics.org.

CHAPTER **3**

The Service-choice Spiral

Now you can begin to grasp the complexity of what it is you need to do once you become a development manager. But how do you become one? How can you begin this career path for international public service? To answer this question, we developed what we call the service-choice spiral, illustrated in Figure 1. As with any schematic framework, this simplifies the much messier reality of people's public service careers; but we find it helps to capture the notion that a career path is more than a linear progression of one job choice after another. We see career development as a spiral, not a ladder, because moving through the steps leads to new combinations of the various components, rather than simply transferring existing competencies to different situations in a linear way. The cone shape of the spiral illustrates the enhanced depth and breadth you achieve as you accumulate experience, build skills, and grow in your understanding of yourself and others, expanding your career options along with your personal growth. The cone shape also conveys another important element of our conception of career development: although you can think of your career as following some sort of path, there is not an ultimate "destination." Unlike a ladder, there is no "top." The value and satisfaction in your public service career will come from the accumulation of your skills and experience, their application to important problems, your expanded understanding and growth, and the doors to new opportunities that may open as a result.

So, what are the signposts, or components, along the career path of a development manager? The service-choice spiral 1) begins with self-awareness (values and skills), 2) continues with finding meaning in community and dialogue as 3) you acquire skills and knowledge (the tools and process dimensions of development management), and 4) leads to decisions about where to work, including the relative emphasis of working for internal organization change and/or advocating for broader systems change. As you progress along the spiral, the four steps are mutually

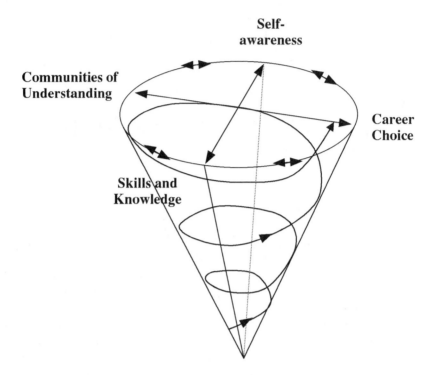

Figure 3.1. The Service-choice Spiral

reinforcing, leading to an expansion of personal and professional development, and career options. The spiral promotes continuous learning as well as socialization into the profession. Each of the components will be discussed in its own chapter (4–7). Here, we offer a brief overview of what they entail and how they fit together.

Self-awareness

Self-awareness begins with a keen understanding first and foremost of your values, and also of your strengths, and relative weaknesses. This understanding provides the foundation for the integrity and genuine concern for others that inform effective public service. Given development management's values dimension, it can be said that development managers are the "hands and feet" of those values—and it is our task to foster their enactment. As we discovered in Chapter 2, this is not straightforward, and each of us will interpret that responsibility differently, depending on how we emphasize each of the facets relative to the others. For some, the "duty" will be to implement the institutional agenda, period. Here the operating values concern responsibility and accountability to one's employer. Others may interpret their responsibility as ensuring that development management's values of empowerment and participation are integrated into that agenda, or at least in its implementation.

Awareness of your values can help you determine your own vision for what service is, what development means, and how to balance those four facets accordingly. Of course, this is not a one-time plan or decision. Just as we discovered with development more generally, the range of alternatives and their relative feasibility will vary from situation to situation. But having an initial understanding of your own position is the best starting point for navigating each context. This requires actively reflecting on these questions and knowing clearly why you are pursuing international public service in the first place (more on this in Chapter 4). To the extent that you can articulate your own values, you can facilitate understandings with your colleagues and counterparts, develop mutual expectations around professional relationships, and help to bridge cultural gaps.

Self-awareness also informs your choices regarding where to serve, and your decisions with respect to how you want to work for change— the fourth step of the spiral. For example, will you work for a public service contractor (e.g., Academy for Educational Development), a faith-based voluntary organization (e.g., World Vision), a government agency (e.g., Department of Commerce or US Agency for International Development)? Will you join the ranks of antiglobalization advocates or donor watchdog groups? Engage in labor organizing in the assembly factories on the US-Mexican border? Work for a human rights non-profit organization? Clearly, you will make these choices many times during your career. As your path evolves, new opportunities emerge, you develop new skills, and perhaps your vision for service changes.

Knowing your preferences, innate strengths, and evolving skills and expertise will help you match these with the appropriate options for public service. For example, some people are more skilled in organizational processes and the consistent application of standards for equity and fairness; others are more equipped to work through social interaction, cultivating trust and understanding. Similarly, some are better at facilitating and improving the efficiency and effectiveness of others who are more skilled at and comfortable working on the front lines of direct service delivery. All of these roles are important and necessary for the expression and enactment of compassion and service, and there are many more than those discussed here.

Of course, how effective you are in your chosen role will depend on your awareness of your strengths and weaknesses and how well these fit with that role. This is a continuing process of self-awareness that informs all of the steps along the service-choice spiral. You cannot fully grasp your strengths and weaknesses without the benefit of the "mirrors" others hold for you, the feedback you receive, and the understandings you develop together with others for what is necessary for a given role. Seeing your "reflection" (that is, seeing yourself as others see you) and hearing their feedback are necessary prerequisites to building your self-awareness, and to growing, both professionally and personally.

As you discover your strengths and weaknesses, you may decide to pursue a particular job possibility precisely to build upon your strengths and/or to address your weaknesses. All of these efforts will combine to continuously inform how you will work for change—either inside or outside of systems, depending upon your personal vision for service. The more you cycle through the spiral, the more your capacity to self-reflect and self-critique will grow, as will your effectiveness and self-esteem.

Communities of Understanding

The second step in the spiral, finding meaning in community and dialogue, sheds more light on why you choose to serve. Community refers to the collection of people (defined geographically or according to some other criterion, for example, poor mothers) whom you are serving, and to the professional community of development management scholars and practitioners, including the coworkers and clients who comprise your community of work. Communities of understanding encourage organizational learning, innovation, teamwork and shared norms, and the achievement of synergistic results—where the whole is greater than the sum of its parts. Creating meaning through community and dialogue is the subject of Chapter 5.

Operating in community means that you accept you are not out to change the world as an individual. You need to be humble, recognizing that you can't save the world on your own. Community is also a source of mutual empowerment and learning as you identify shared understandings and synergies in skills and approaches. The motivation is not the ego, but the helping, and the helping is shared in the sense of working together, and being transformed together. Many in public service will tell you that they feel they have learned and benefited far more than they can imagine their "beneficiaries" have. This is true of many Peace Corps experiences. Derick certainly felt that way about his service in Chad, teaching English-as-a-second-language.

So communities of service include your own teams and organizations and especially those with whom and perhaps for whom you perceive you are working. Building on development management's values and process facets, communities of understanding ideally reduce the barrier between service provider and beneficiary, helper and helpee. Ultimately, communities of understanding represent the very connection that many seek through service, whether you are conscious of it or not.

Skills and Knowledge

Clearly at the heart of effective public service, whether international or domestic, is a relevant toolkit and knowledge base. We do not intend to present to you an exhaustive list of the skills and knowledge necessary to effective international public service, either here or in Chapter 6. There are too many options and associated skills and knowledge for any one book to cover. In Chapter 6, we present an overview of general skills necessary, and discuss how you can go about acquiring them. In terms of career development, our focus on skills and knowledge moves beyond the orientation of most college career advisors: we want to set the stage not just for getting your first job, but also for your next job, and the one after that, as you advance to increasing levels of responsibility and influence. This progression requires expanding your skills and knowledge into new areas and greater depth, depending on the path you've chosen. We discuss some of the challenges to career evolution generally and with respect to the most challenging transitions in Chapter 8.

The skills and knowledge component of the service-choice spiral relates directly to development management's tool and process facets, introduced in Chapter 2, but encompasses far more. It confirms that a desire to help and an interest in service are not enough. To be effective in your career, you also need concrete management and technical skills, and accumulated international and technical experience. This is obvious to most of us, but it is surprising how often students may have an aversion to acquiring "hard" technical skill sets, such as economics, financial management/budgeting, trade relations, and policy analysis. And while some of you readily embrace these types of skills, you may be the very ones who find distasteful the so-called "soft" skills necessary to effective public service. The latter, often referred to as emotional intelligence, are usually the hardest to learn. You may aspire to be leaders of change efforts and service programs. The theory and practice of leadership and organizational change emphasize the importance/necessity of mutual inspiration and collective leadership. So leadership and team skills cannot be viewed separately, and this is particularly true in public service (international or otherwise), where effectiveness depends upon working in community.

Career Choices

The combination of self-awareness, finding meaning in communities, and skills and knowledge leads to choices about where to work. One of your communities of understanding is the organization you work for. So one aspect of your work for change is the continuous definition and transformation of that organization and its agenda. Most of you will prefer to work for organizations and agendas consistent with your values, but this fit is never perfect. Some of you may choose to work for organizations with an intention to influence and change them from within. In either case, since meaning is created in dialogue, you are likely both to transform and to be transformed by your workplace.

At different stages in your career, perhaps in different contexts, you may decide to work for change from inside—or from outside—the system you target for transformation. Some of you may seek to work for large powerful bureaucracies, such as the World Bank or government agencies, with the intention of promoting new understandings and change from within. Others may choose instead to participate in civil society-advocacy organizations and networks to improve the workings of these institutions through pressure from the outside. Some may opt for direct service provision by working with community groups and/or nonprofit service delivery agencies. Many see themselves as simultaneously working for change from the inside and from the outside of organizational systems.

You are likely to have several careers, or at least a number of different jobs along your path. So you will make the decision of where to work for change not once, but many times over the life of your career. Since careers in international public service are so dynamic, you will need a broad range of skills and a high degree of flexibility to respond to changing job responsibilities, organizational contexts, and emerging development challenges. And as your values and competencies evolve over time, your job preferences and choices are likely to change as well.

Traveling the Service-choice Spiral

Finding your place in public service through development management begins with your self-awareness and builds on humility in continuously contributing to and benefiting from communities of understanding through dialogue—as you apply your knowledge and skills, and ultimately transform the organizations and broader systems in which you choose to work. This process is not a one-time sequence. Your accumulated work experience and personal development will lead to new levels of self-awareness, provoking further progression through the steps of the spiral (not necessarily in the original order), which in turn leads to acquiring more skills and knowledge, and perhaps making new choices about where to work. In this sense, the service-choice spiral depicts an expanding array of personal growth and professional development as you advance on your career path. Through successive iterations of the spiral, your career path balances your personal interests and career aspirations with the larger idealistic goal of serving others to enable them both to have and to be more. How you will accomplish this is rarely clear from the beginning, as Sarah Newhall's experience attests.

Profile 1. Sarah Newhall:
Going International Mid-career

Sarah Newhall has lived her life and pursued her work by the motto of Gloria Steinem, that where your time and energy goes is what you become. No aspect of her career was consciously planned, though her core values were always absolutely clear. *Probably in utero*, she says, *because of my upbringing, because of the family I was born into.* These core values create a clear logic for Sarah in terms of the issues she has pursued throughout her career, though not necessarily the strategies and finite goals for pursuing them. *I could not have told anybody that at age 55 I would be living in Washington, D.C., president of a $23-million nonprofit that was doing capacity building globally. But I could have said I would probably always spend my life on issues related to social justice, always having an educational orientation, always working on issues of economic equity, and always with a progressive-to-left-leaning political outlook. I just knew these were my core social values.* Sarah is currently the President and CEO of Pact, a US-based international NGO.

Sarah was born into a family of social activists. Her father was a professor of philosophy at Portland State University, where he taught peace and Gandhian studies, Greek philosophy, and ethics. Her mother was a social activist/volunteer, who after raising five children became a well-known community leader in local government and public education in Portland, Oregon. Social justice was a frequent topic of conversation around the dinner table, and discussions were often driven by Socratic questioning in search of ideas. Sarah's parents didn't just read her bedtime stories; they asked her what she thought of them. From this experience she learned how to think for herself and to use literature as a way of understanding human nature. These roots, combined with her coming of age during the Civil Rights Movement, emphasized the importance of social justice and a humanities orientation to education.

Sarah completed her undergraduate studies at Occidental College in California and immediately left for a kibbutz in Israel to pursue her interest in intentional communities. This was formative for her understanding of human nature and issues of war and conflict. *Having grown up in a pacifist family, this was very important for me to see that I wasn't a pacifist at that point—that I would fight for these types of things, but I wouldn't fight for those types of things.* It also deepened her understanding of competition. *Even if you had a social system that was supposed to be socialist or built on equity—natural leadership, natural pecking orders, and natural power struggles exist in any community. So the glow that there was a right way to live disappeared before the age of twenty-five.*

Upon returning from Israel, Sarah went to work in domestic human services programs. After five years of progressively responsible positions, and with her undergraduate degree in English literature in hand, Sarah thought, *Okay, I know how to think, and I have a good understanding of human nature. But now I'm going to be underqualified credentially for the rest of my life if I don't catch up with the situation here.* Sarah was fortunate to have good advisors, one of whom told her she was ideally suited for a master's degree in public administration. *Bingo! I'd never heard of such a thing before then. And it was exactly right for me.* Sarah earned her MPA at Portland State University.

For the next twenty years, she worked in Portland, either for city government or in nonprofit organizations, always in leadership roles. She started in youth services, where she founded a neighborhood family counseling center that was tied into the juvenile justice system, and was later asked to coordinate all of the youth service centers in the city. She then took a job as the director of the Office of Neighborhood Associations, a city bureau. This office became a nationally recognized model for citizen participation in local government. The office's charge included community policing, neighborhood mediation, and commissions on youth, aging, and human relations. *It was an interface zone, a mediating structure within the city government to bring citizens, politicians, and public officials into better sync with one another. Interestingly, this is exactly what Pact is all about. I learned a lot there and I think that all I've been doing is just taking it to the global arena.*

Sarah also served on the Portland school board, promoting a platform of bringing the community and the schools together. She sought to encourage a better understanding of the purpose of public education: to make communities healthy. Also in her early career, Sarah worked for the Ecumenical Ministries of Oregon as the Refugee Services Coordinator and as Associate Director of their Center for Urban Education. Her task was to build programs for 25,000 South East Asian refugees who were resettling in Oregon. *That was the beginning of my interest in becoming a global citizen.*

All the jobs I had in those twenty years were within five miles of the office, within five miles of each other. So at age forty, I had the freedom, the resources, and a willing partner to launch another part of my life and career. So we moved to Thailand with the goal of having a two-year sabbatical from Portland and to work for local NGOs there. The goal was to go and learn something, do something different, and break even financially. Sarah went in search of the most activist organization in Bangkok, where she could learn something and do some good. One of Sarah's mentors suggested she visit Mechai Viravaidya, and made some calls on her behalf. *Mechai was a luminary in the development field, known by the nickname, the "Condom King." He ran the largest NGO in Thailand, Population and Community Development Association. He was the champion of putting community-based family planning systems on the map in Thailand and is the reason why their population is under control.* Sarah arrived just as Viravaidya was mounting one of the best examples of a successful HIV/AIDS prevention campaign. *So I had a front row seat with a mentor, from whom I feel I got my graduate degree in international development.* (Sarah has no formal education in international development.) *It would have been as if I'd gone to South Africa and ended up in the headquarters of the ANC at the feet of Nelson Mandela, just learning from a master.*

After two and a half years, Sarah had the opportunity to come full circle. She was interested in exploring Vietnam, but a friend and Pact employee handed her a job description for the Pact country representative position in Cambodia. *"Sarah,"* she said, *"this job has your name written all over it."* *I thought, "That's very interesting, but I'm going to Vietnam."* *But I read the job description and it literally started making my heart beat fast, my blood coursed, that adrenaline rush. . . .* Sarah had been working with leading Cambodians who had resettled in Portland through the South East Asian Refugee Federation. *I had had this rare opportunity to work with leaders of Laos, Cambodia, and Vietnam, who would have been fighting each other in Southeast Asia. But in Portland they were building a coalition together to survive. I was their American strategist, grantwriter, networker, facilitator. So in Cambodia, I'd get to see the other side of the equation.*

Sarah flew to Bangladesh for what turned out to be a four-hour interview with Lou Mitchell, then President of Pact. She left that interview thinking, *I know I'm going to get this job offer. I guess I'm going to Cambodia.* In February 1992, Sarah flew into Phnom Penh, as Pact's country representative, with a fifteen-page concept paper outlining what she was to do to set up the program. It was shortly after the signing of the Paris Peace Accords, and Sarah was to launch a large-scale democracy and governance capacity building program. What started as a two-year sabbatical turned into a new career. Sarah left a situation where she had worked for the mayor, was a known person, and knew the scene. Now she was in Phnom Penh, an international novice, starting a program from scratch.

Only a year and a half later, Lou Mitchell contacted Sarah asking her to become his deputy. At that time, Sarah resisted. *I told him, "I don't want to be your deputy this year. I want to finish my work in Cambodia. If you don't find somebody that you want, let's talk again. But I really can't drop this. I'm right in the middle of what I need to do here."* A year later, he still hadn't hired a deputy. By then Sarah had undergone changes in her personal life. With invitations and persuasion from both her new partner and potential new boss, she decided to come to Washington to become the Deputy Director of Pact. Three years later she was promoted to Executive Vice President. Then in 2000, Sarah was surprised by an offer of a senior position at the US Agency for International

Development (USAID). The Pact board of directors countered quickly with an offer of president and CEO. *I'm not really sure I wanted to be the CEO. I'm not sure I felt I was going to be capable of being the CEO—that's probably a girl thing. When I was making the decision, I figured I'd feel worse if I didn't try than if I did and failed.* After four years on the job Sarah says with enthusiasm that she is finding it the most challenging and rewarding position of her professional career.

CHAPTER 4

Self-awareness

Self-awareness initiates the service-choice spiral and informs the choices you will make on your path. It includes knowing what your current skills and knowledge are. This can help you identify areas you might want to invest in for further development. Self-awareness also refers to knowing your preferences in at least two areas. The first set of preferences is about your job. For example, what type of work interests you? What roles might you play? And where will you work? What kind of organization will offer you the opportunity to pursue your service preferences? Will you serve domestically or overseas? At your organization's headquarters or in the field? We further explore options in answer to these questions in Chapter 7. The second type of preferences concerns the quality of life you have in mind, including salary requirements, and issues concerning personal and family life (more on this in Chapter 9). These two sets of preferences are obviously related.

Together, your awareness of your skills and knowledge, and your preferences inform your career choices. Along the way, as noted in Chapter 3, the communities with whom you work will assist you in better understanding your relative strengths and weaknesses in terms of skills and knowledge, and will help you to understand trade-off decisions with respect to your preferences. A less tangible, but fundamental component of self-awareness concerns your values and associated vision for what service and development mean, and where you, in the role you see for yourself, fit in that vision. These considerations get to the core of why you're interested in and committed to service, and will help you to clarify the best option for how you will do it. Remember that the best option is not going to be a "once and for always" choice. As the service-choice spiral illustrates, you will revisit your choices over the years, and they will be different at different phases in your career. Further, some choices come with built-in time limits, for example, serving as a Peace Corps volunteer, so you'll need to answer the questions we've listed above not just once, but multiple times. We start first with brief discussions of skills and knowledge, and lifestyle preferences. Then we turn to the values and vision issues.

Self-awareness and Your Skills and Knowledge

When thinking about yourself in action, on the job, what excites you? What are you good at? What do you enjoy? What do you not enjoy? While these questions are related to initial preferences, how you choose to act on the answers may lead you to become good at something you were not originally interested in. For example, are you right handed or left handed? What would happen if you lost the use of your preferred hand? You may know of people, or at least have heard stories of them, who lost the use of a limb, and yet, they have taught themselves to compensate with their alternate limb. It's not that they were incapable of writing with their other hand, for example. It's just that they never needed to try, since their preferred hand was perfectly accommodating. You prefer something, you use it, you get better at it, and so on. Such patterns can lead you to misinterpret where your true abilities lie. It may be that you will never write equally well with your alternate hand, and you certainly may not enjoy it as much at first, but with practice you can come pretty close.

So, let's return to one of our questions: What do you not enjoy? Now ask yourself, of that, what do you still believe may be necessary to accomplish what you want to do? Jennifer teaches a public management course at GW that includes a managerial profile, where students use a series of diagnostics to self-assess their preferences and potential strengths and weaknesses as public managers. Students' reactions to the findings vary. In identifying implications, some focus primarily on building on their strengths. Others become fixated on their identified potential weaknesses and incorporate specific action and skill-building agendas to address these. We believe that without attention to both of these components, you cannot reach your full potential on the path of the service-choice spiral.

We will discuss skills and knowledge in Chapter 6. For now, we want to emphasize that to begin to identify priorities and create strategies for growth and development, you need self-awareness.[1] All knowledge is acquired through interaction, whether it's with another person, a book, or both. This means that what you learn depends fundamentally on what you bring to that dialogue. As professors, in every classroom, we are conscious that we have a shared experience together with our students, but in addition to that, there are as many experiences and realities of the course as there are people in it. When you are more aware of where you are starting from, you can focus on those areas where you know you need to grow and learn. You can also begin to be more conscious of your reactions to new knowledge and why you react the way you do.

What's the point of this? Let's face it, learning something we're good at is easy. But learning something totally new, something that may not come naturally . . . well, that can be very challenging. You may choose to avoid those areas, moving on to other things before you've fully applied yourself. You may have gotten good at these skills if you had just given yourself more of a chance. Some of us are so terrified of failure we end up cheating ourselves of opportunities to be the best that we can be. We encourage you to move beyond your comfort zone. As Aaron Williams (Profile 4) puts it: *Sacrifice, because you need to find out who you're really all about.* On the other hand, maybe that particular skill area is not what excites you. There's nothing wrong with that. Move on. Try something else. If you're passionate about something, you're likely to make a significant contribution. The opposite is also true: if you are not passionate about something, you're probably more likely to do a lousy job and maybe suffer from burnout.

Self-awareness can help you to distinguish when you're choosing to avoid some subjects because you're frustrated when they aren't coming easily, or when you're choosing another path because this one just doesn't click for you. For example, accounting can be an important skill set to have. As an undergraduate business major, Jennifer recognized this and decided to take an additional year of accounting. *I had earned good grades the previous year, so I knew it was something I could do if I chose to. But even though I told myself the added course was a good idea, I hated it; I was too depressed even to look at the book. This experience helped to confirm for me that I wanted to work with people-centered organizational systems and concepts, not the numbers-based details of financial management.* Knowing when something is right for you, or simply doesn't resonate, often requires that you try it out, not simply think about it.

Job and Quality-of-life Preferences

As the accounting example shows, practicing the kind of self-awareness suggested above can help you to discover your job preferences. This is usually a long process—it doesn't just come to you all at once. These preferences are likely to be refined and to change throughout your career, as you progress along the service-choice spiral. Job preferences start with exploring what you get excited about, where your passions lie.

You are likely to discover these with experience and through interaction with your communities of service. This seems very straightforward, but you might be surprised how many people do not actively listen to themselves. You may be driven by the "shoulds" instead of the affirmations of who you are and what you want to be. Why shouldn't you be happy in your service job? Your passions can enhance your commitment and effectiveness. We encourage you to reflect on your motives when exploring which job parameters are right for you.

The same holds true with quality-of-life preferences. These are informed by our values and personal preferences, but to a large degree they are also influenced by others' expectations of us. For example, your family may be disappointed or worried if you decide to live overseas, far away from them. But what do you feel is right for you? What is your heart telling you? We often joke with colleagues and students about the difficulty of explaining to our families and friends what we actually do. In crafting her answer, Jennifer Butz (Profile 6) says *it depends on who they are. Sometimes I just say, "I'm in international development." "Oh, what do you do?" "I live in Albania." "Oh!" End of conversation. It was the same reaction when I was living in Mongolia. If it's a more thoughtful answer, then I say, "I'm working to support the democratic transition that Albania began eleven years ago. I'm working with citizens, so they can understand both their rights and their responsibilities in the new system, so that they can become involved in the process." And people usually respond, "Oh. That's nice," because they have no idea what I just said.*

Sometimes the choice to pursue a career of service is not necessarily what others had in mind for you. We hear from our students the familiar story of when they informed their parents that they wanted to pursue a master's degree in public administration. "Public administration? Why would you want to do that? You should be getting an MBA!" But these stories are told with pride—we have yet to meet students who were disappointed with their decision to follow their hearts despite deviations from what their families thought was best for them. And sometimes, even when you have the wholehearted support of your family, you may still be challenged to justify your path to others. Witness GW student Jennifer Swift-Morgan's passion in articulating this struggle: *I've had many people ask me why I am in international development. "Who are those people to you?" Or, "Why can't you just help people in your own community?" Who is to say that the people of the village in Lariabhé, Guinea, are not my community too? I believe that we are responsible for all of humankind, and that any action I take will be felt by the rest of humanity—as does the action I did not take. . . . When people ask, "Why do you care what happens in Africa? What connection can you possibly have to Africa?" I respond: "How am I not connected to Africa, just as all life is connected?"*

External pressures can be difficult enough. And it's often hard to know what your true preferences are apart from others' expectations. The real challenge, though, is maneuvering around your own competing preferences. For example, you may want to travel a lot, but you also want to be able to meet someone with whom you might start a family. What if you find you are spending too much time on airplanes, in too many places to even meet someone let alone date? At what point do you say, "Enough is enough. I need to make some investments in a community and some relationships"? And maybe the travel is great. Maybe you're getting the kind of experience you need to get to where you want to go in your career. Maybe you see it as a short-term option. If, after awhile, you don't meet someone on the tarmac, you may decide to take a different job. The worst-case scenario would be if you wake up one day and realize that you never made that decision. And by not making a conscious choice, you did in fact decide. We take up this issue and others related to balancing life priorities in Chapter 9.

Knowing your priorities in advance will help you to recognize when you need to make a change in one area of your goals that is jeopardizing your other aims. In some respects, the way careers are now structured makes these trade-off decisions much easier. You are no longer expected to choose one path and stick to it. In fact, it's just the opposite. Most employers value a variety of experience. So, whether it's the pursuit of particular skills and knowledge, your choice of what kind of job to take and where, or what kind of family life you aspire to, we encourage you to practice self-awareness. Know what you want; it can save you a lot of heartache.

Values and Vision

Of course, what you want is ultimately based on your values, and the vision for service that they inspire. People are most motivated by internalized interests or concerns. It's not really about a carrot and a stick; those will only get you so far. What motivates the most is that sense of fulfillment that can only come from your ability to express your values and to fulfill the vision you have created for yourself. A career can be magical when you have a particular view of what it means for you to be the best that you can be and you are given an opportunity to play that out. Especially in service fields, values inspire and sustain. Success is not always easy to identify or achieve in terms of measurable outcomes. Values can give you a sense of personal success because it is satisfying to live and work by them, even when you don't know what impact you've had. We will discuss sustaining your motivation for service in Chapter 9.

As a senior administrator with the Port Authority of New York and New Jersey, Mark Duffy accounted for all personnel and maintained the delivery of critical services in the intermediate aftermath of September 11, 2001. Here's what he said when he received George Washington University's Public Administration Department's 2002 Distinguished Alumni Award:

> I am honored to be chosen by you as a distinguished public servant in a year when we are revisiting some simple values—to simply celebrate people who do their jobs with a sense of pride, who have a strong work ethic, who genuinely care about their community and try to do the things needed to make it a better place. While I may never be famous or celebrated in the media, to the extent that I have exemplified those simple values, I feel distinguished. And I encourage all of you to focus on simple core values as you pursue your careers. While that approach will not guarantee you recognition or elevation to a high position of prestige, it will lead to a career marked with a sense of integrity and it will improve your chances of doing something that really makes a lasting difference. In the end, no one can destroy that.

Values are central to another component of self-awareness and service: knowing why you want to serve and making sure your motives and behavior are consistent with your values. In his *Guide for Grassroots Leaders*, Si Kahn recommends thinking about the following questions (which we've slightly modified) in order to uncover and clarify your values:

1. Why are you willing to put in the enormous time and trouble necessary to be a leader and/or work for change?
2. Why is it important to you that people stand up and fight for their own justice as well as justice for others?
3. What is it about the things that you believe that makes you willing to take the risks that you take, to spend the time that you spend?
4. What is it in how you feel about yourself that gives you the self-confidence and pride to be able to step forward?
5. What is it in your beliefs about others that makes you work with them, trying to foster their skills, abilities, and self-confidence?[2]

Most of us don't walk around every day spelling out our values like a checklist, but we do tend to have some sense of what we believe. Sadly, some people only recognize their values when they feel they have been violated, whether by themselves or by others. So your values can guide you in behaving ethically, and can also help you to be strategic in living out your priorities in terms of what you want to accomplish. Maybe your religion is a starting place for thinking about your values. Back in the 1980s a group of people at the World Bank met every Friday morning to discuss their spiritual and religious beliefs and how they informed their work in development. Some of these perspectives are summarized in a book they compiled.[3] It includes statements on Hinduism, Christianity, faith in science, and Islam. From the Christian tradition, some development activists are finding support in Micah Network.[4] Micah Network includes regional and international workshops to enhance capacity and understanding of poverty issues, and the Micah Challenge, a global advocacy campaign in support of implementing the Millennium Development Goals. Jubilee Congregations, a component of the Jubilee 2000 movement that successfully advocated for debt relief, similarly seek "to grow the voice and moral presence of faith communities in the struggle to break the chains of debt in the developing world."[5] These movements are largely inspired by liberation theology.[6] In the Islamic world, new efforts and organizations are emerging to encourage the application of *zakat* (tithing) to sustainable development and related personal engagement, as opposed to its traditional emphasis on charity and welfare programs. For example, in Egypt a group of students from the American University in Cairo founded an all-volunteer NGO called Fat'het Kheir. The organization supports community and economic development in a poor community on the outskirts of Cairo. Volunteers work as micro-loan counselors to families and their businesses. The emphasis is on empowerment as opposed to charity.[7] If you ground your values in religion, we encourage you to explore the philosophies, organizations, and activities from your own faith. Not everyone grounds their values in faith and religion. You may prefer to reflect on and articulate your values from a more secular perspective.

Those we profiled identified the following motivating values: justice, honesty, integrity, respect, dignity of life, trust, hard work, teamwork, flexibility, humility, transparency, empowerment for all, personal growth, learning, curiosity, faith that things can get better, joy, and righteous indignation. We were not surprised to find a lot of overlap among the six. And these aren't just words or ideas. They are drivers that help them interpret their surroundings and shape their behavior and vision for development. For example, Jennifer Butz talks about righteous indignation: *There's just so much injustice at the most basic level. Often, I see people just taking it, rather than getting angry. Or, they have so-called leaders who drive them to the streets to demonstrate, march, and sometimes kill their enemies. That's not righteous; that's just anger. Righteous indignation is an anger that's sufficiently controlled so that it's motivating toward a goal of more justice or more dignity.* This understanding of righteous indignation helps Jennifer Butz recognize injustice, and also determine the parameters of what she sees as appropriate responses. Najma Siddiqi stresses the importance of transparency and justice in all that she does. As you will see in Profile 3, she didn't just work for justice in Denmark and Pakistan; she tried to embody it. And when you live by your values, the work benefits. Not only are you able to fully commit to service, but others also have a more difficult time preventing you from doing your work. The Pakistani Prime Minister's Inspection Commission tried to harass the National Rural Support Program, which Najma was leading, in order to seize its funding. But after six months they could not find any grounds for impropriety.

Greater awareness of your values can also help you withstand others' expectations of you (including society's) and navigate trade-off decisions. Sarah Newhall (Profile 1) reflected on various values and drivers: *The political science world says the drivers in life are money, power, status, and sex. When I was learning that, I thought, "Gee, that doesn't speak to me very clearly," because that wasn't my value system. Do I like money? Yes. Do I want to have economic viability? Yes. Power? Yes. But my orientation to power is not to have it and hold it, but to share it. Status? Yes, recognition is a good thing in life. As for sex, you see all the ways that sex drives people and gets them into huge amounts of trouble and scandals. So in my mind, I add service. I think there is a whole other way of being and a type of person that is driven by a service orientation.* Sarah had to address some trade-offs when she decided to do her sabbatical in Thailand. She forfeited her creature comforts in the United States, as well as her American salary. She was willing to invest her time and energy but wanted at least to break even financially. This is not an easy thing to do when you are working for a local NGO. Such negotiations can be uncomfortable, especially when you know you will still be paid richly in comparison to your colleagues. Jennifer Butz (Profile 6) has similarly wrestled with salary trade-offs, sometimes taking a cut in pay in order to pursue work she believed in and was excited about, but always at the risk of jeopardizing her salary for the next contract. This is a particularly prickly dilemma for independent consultants who need to plan for their own health benefits and retirement.

Our students also wrestle with their drivers and how they are enacted in their service. Rachel Surkin reflects on how a sense of responsibility can lead to behavior that is less than flattering in terms of her intentions: *If my passion stems from a feeling of responsibility for other people with whom I am in contact, would I, as a white, privileged outsider in a developing country context, become patronizing? Yes, I think so, if I'm not careful in continually reflecting on not only my goal but also my process.* Joanna Ramos similarly emphasizes the importance of values in guiding her service path. Her statement on values is typical of a lot of our students, perhaps reflecting some of your own motivation for service. *Although I am still a novice, it seems to me that in order to make a difference in this field,*

I have to let my values guide me, as well as respect and tap those of the communities with whom I will work. My values have brought me to the field of development and have helped shape my vision of development, which involves empowering others, helping them recognize and realize their own dignity, knowledge and talents, and sharing and learning together.

Vision for Service and Success

As Joanna's quote illustrates, values inform what our vision for development is and, together with preferences, help us to envision our service role. For example, Aaron Williams (Profile 4) resonated with International Youth Foundation's mission "to improve the lives of young people wherever they live, learn, work, or play." His personal vision for his service role has been to promote partnerships among the private sector, government, and NGOs. David Yang (Profile 2) started with a vision of human rights. His service vision is to join political action with development programming. Some of you may be further along in thinking about your service vision than others. GW student Oriana Gusmão Bonfim's vision for development encompasses human rights, empowerment, and self-determination. Her service vision is to *work with governmental agents, dealing with their individual personalities, behaviors, expectations, and culture, in order to: 1. Understand their behaviors and make them accept that they contribute to the creation of problems (promote self-awareness); 2. Encourage these professionals to propose their own solutions to tackle institutional problems (promote self-confidence and ownership); and 3. Induce their accountability to implement changes (promote sensitivity and public commitment). . . . Working with public servants on these three fronts can contribute to reforming governments and further promoting and sustaining development.*

Part of thinking about your vision for development and for your personal service is also to consider what success will look like. Having some sense of what success means for you is critical to sustaining your motivation for service. Otherwise, it's too easy to become overwhelmed by the need, frustrated by the scale of what you're capable of contributing, and eventually demobilized and depressed. Beware the person who sets out to save the world! As a Peace Corps Volunteer, Jef Buehler (Profile 5) organized an empowerment workshop; if he had defined success as the realization of a planned demonstration, he would have been sadly disappointed. It may have been a blow to his ego that the approach he championed never came to fruition. However, his understanding of success was that the people recognize they could do something and that, ultimately, their needs would be met. On that score the community effort was a great success.

Sometimes how we define success may be different from the institutional agenda we are serving. In reflecting on his Peace Corps experience, GW student Kipp Efinger notes, *as an English teacher I set out to teach as many children to speak English as possible. Later I realized that some of my students had no motivation to learn English since they would be farmers all of their lives and probably not leave their village. What those children needed most of all was self-esteem. If I could have taught them to respect themselves and their classmates, I would have met with greater success, in my opinion, than I would have by trying to force grammar down their throats. Increasing their self-esteem and opening their eyes to possibilities in life would have increased their freedoms.* What Kipp's experience tells us is that we shouldn't limit our service vision to the roles of our job description. This doesn't mean we ignore our prescribed role. In fact, you may be driven by a value of responsibility, and hopefully, your professional ethics will bar you from taking a job and then ignoring your side of the contract. However, you can broaden your technical role to encompass the full range of your service vision. The process of meeting your job obligations can be an important vehicle for expressing your values. For example, Sarah Newhall self-consciously includes mentoring younger staff in her role as president of Pact, reflecting her personal commitment to capacity building.

How you define success depends on your personal view and the context. As we said, here we are not talking about the formal criteria by which successful job performance is defined, but about your own definition. For example, Najma Siddiqi (Profile 3) distinguishes her deepest and broadest satisfactions. *The deepest satisfaction I have experienced is when I worked with people who were labeled mentally disabled. My expectation was only that this one person use his right hand. I was teaching him murals and batik. And he started painting. I can bring a catatonic person to use his hand! That's fantastic. It's unbelievable. It gives you a high. But then when you see groups of 10,000 to 30,000 people actually practicing what you have talked about, that's unbelievable as well.* Not all of us are capable of reaching an individual to such depth. Can we be satisfied with influencing someone to do something they have never done before, if it is not as dramatic as regaining the use of a hand? Jennifer takes inspiration from Buddhism, which emphasizes the connectedness of all things. If this connectedness is true, then each of us can be seen to embody the world. Change yourself, change the world. Exercise compassion toward this one person before you, and you have expressed your humanity, you have contributed to all beings.

As with Najma, your service vision and associated definition of success may change as your career evolves and with each new job. For example, one member of our focus group shared, *my definition for how I effect social change has gotten way bigger than seeing a kid go to school for the first time. That's why I came home from Peace Corps. Now I think of change on a macroeconomic policy level. Anything short of that doesn't feel big enough to me. I'm not in a grassroots arena anymore. I have a new definition of change and that's what I'm now working for. And I may go back. At different points in time, I may say, one woman at a time, or one Baltic country at a time.*

In addition to understanding what success means in each context, you also need to take success where you can get it, and celebrate those smaller successes along the way. Jennifer Butz (Profile 6) was asked to go to Kosovo for the National Democratic Institute, to help them package their survey data into some public relations material to convince the donors of the need for continued funding. *My role was to help them get the funds so they could do their job. It wasn't about me going into the villages and doing their work. I made the most impact I could in that context. I've learned over the years that you can't be superhuman and do everything. You have to really say, "Okay, this is what I'm going to do," and then just do that piece. Because you're part of a system. The Kosovars always treat me like a good-luck symbol because I helped them keep their jobs for another year.*

You are very lucky when you can directly attribute success to your own effort. It is a rare occurrence. As we will discuss in Chapter 5, success is never the result of one actor alone. Well beyond that, working for socioeconomic development means striving towards visions that require long-term processes with contributions from multiple actors, for results that are often unobservable, let alone measurable. And in order to remain motivated, you have to have faith in possibilities for change, and you have to believe that you can make a contribution. You have to believe in your own effectiveness.

This is a good place to remind you, though, that it isn't about you or your individual success. To expect that you can save the world or even a single community is, after all, very egotistical. It's important to remind yourself from time to time that the success of this or that effort has little to do with how you feel about it. You can put yourself out there and do your best, but to expect a return on that effort assumes that you are somehow in control. Sorry, but none of us is. So at some level, you need simply to take satisfaction from being and doing, not necessarily accomplishing. This requires faith, and validation that can only come from you. Especially in the applied side of development management, there are many times when we are asked to "parachute" in for two weeks and somehow work miracles. Obviously, there are a lot of issues with this practice. What we want to emphasize here is that whatever influence you may have in that short time, you are likely never to see it. You often have to gauge your success according to your own measure of whether or not you did your best.

How to Start Thinking about
Your Vision of Development and Service

In Chapter 1 we illustrated how development can have many different meanings. In fact, you may not even choose to use the term in defining and talking about your profession. (Jennifer Butz doesn't refer to the term when she describes her work in Albania.) It's important that you develop your own interpretation of what development means to you. What does it look like? What are you striving for?

You might start with these questions: Do you believe that poverty and inequality are inevitable? Is some degree of each tolerable? Is it feasible to eliminate poverty and inequality completely? Within the international donor community, in recent years more attention has gone to targeting the "poorest of the poor" or the "most vulnerable" with specific policies and investments instead of assuming that the resources generated by economic growth will automatically trickle down. For example, the Millennium Development Goals (MDGs) aim to halve poverty by 2015, and establish targets to provide services and benefits to children and women, among other objectives. There is a lively debate among development professionals about the feasibility of the MDGs, and how best to achieve them. At the same time, the George W. Bush Administration has launched the Millennium Challenge Account (MCA), which seeks to make strategic investments in those countries most likely to "take off" economically. Implicitly, the policy behind the MCA accepts that in some cases poverty is inevitable, and absent significant changes in the actions of national leadership and considerable institutional reforms, additional foreign aid will not help. Using efficiency criteria in determining foreign aid programming—that is, getting as much bang for your buck as possible—is very different from a strategy of targeting the poorest of the poor.

Beyond these fundamental questions, we encourage you to give serious thought to whether you believe development is an end, a means to other things, or both. Such reflection can help you to set some parameters for the way you believe development should be pursued. If you see development as a process, or a means to broader fulfillment, then you need to consider what the process (not just the result) looks like and how you should participate in it. So start with what you think "development" looks like. How do your values set the parameters for what you will work towards, whatever the scale?

In thinking about what your development vision is, you might consider exploring alternative models to those of the mainstream development industry. For example, Amartya Sen emphasizes human development, rather than material wealth, arguing that development relates to people's ability to generate for themselves the real opportunities of good living.[8] Here, too, you will find models inspired by various religious traditions. For example, in addition to the Christian orientations noted above, there are several interpretations of the Buddhist vision of development. Sulak Sivaraksa, a Thai Buddhist monk and social activist, outlines a Buddhist interpretation of development in his book, *Seeds of Peace*.[9] It includes attention to the four requisites of food, clothing, shelter, and medicine, but also heavily emphasizes quality of human life, with attention to the questions, "What is a human being, and what should a human being be?" He presents proposals for how we can reform our current economic and political structures to begin to address these concerns. A. T. Ariyaratne built on the work of Gandhi and his follower Bhave to establish the Sarvodaya Shramadana movement in Sri Lanka. Sarvodaya means all awakening; Shramadana means giving labor. The movement, founded in 1958, is rooted in Buddhist religious values that redefine the nature and purpose of development. It mobilizes participation broadly, including not only the targeted villages, but also volunteers from throughout society.[10] Other alternatives derive from indigenous cultures, such as native Americans, or the Maori of New Zealand.[11] Still others draw on the viewpoint from the grass roots, or approach the challenge from women's perspective.[12] What these alternatives tend to have in common is a holistic view of development that is community based and community engaged, with attention to compassion in each moment.

Once you've considered that bigger picture of what development means to you, is there a particular piece that you prioritize? Is it a specific population or human need? Girls' education perhaps? Or indigenous people's right to live sustainably off the land? The possibilities are endless and take us back to the beginning of this chapter: What excites you? What strikes your heart's chord? The answer may not sound all that exciting to others, but your service vision should resonate with you and feel right to you. For example, you might not feel a strong connection to Oriana Gusmão Bonfim's vision to work to improve governments, but perhaps the idea of bridging political action and development programming inspires you, as it has David Yang (Profile 2).

Given your self-awareness with respect to skills, knowledge, and preferences, is there a particular role you see for yourself in pursuing your vision of development? Crafting your personal service vision is a lifelong process, with inevitable changes of course along the way. In beginning this process, think about what technical area you would like to work in (for example, health, education, governance, environment, human rights), the population you see yourself working with (for example, governments, communities, indigenous people, those with disabilities, children), and your particular role in sharing technical expertise with this population (for example, training and education, process consultation, community mobilization, policy influence, service delivery).

In Chapter 2 we defined development management according to four facets (institutional agendas, tools, process, and values). Your service vision—the role you see yourself playing in advancing development—should incorporate some reflection on these facets and their trade-offs. What values inform your priorities among these four facets and how? Where are your limits in navigating trade-offs among these? For example, at what point will you say no to an institutional agenda that contradicts the values of empowerment and participation, or your own personal values?

We encourage you to talk with people who are doing the kinds of things you might be interested in. Visit the Web sites of organizations that spark your interest. Read about current events in other countries and see if the challenges inspire you to work for change on the issues described. Learn more about development generally. Perhaps you will identify some of the new challenges facing the field. Aaron Williams (Profile 4) broke new ground in promoting a greater and more cooperative role with the private sector in the development industry. Derick focused on advancing the practice and theory of management as applied to international development problems. David Yang (Profile 2) and Jennifer Butz (Profile 6) benefited from new policy agendas related to democratization. Several of our students are thinking about how to work on the relief-development continuum; that is, how can emergency services be provided in ways that contribute to rather than undermine sustainable development?

A Final Word on Self-awareness

Self-awareness encompasses so much and serves several purposes. It can enhance your effectiveness. By knowing your relative strengths and weaknesses, you can maximize their use, as well as set the stage for continued growth and development. It is the foundation for satisfaction. By knowing who you are, what you bring, and what you want, you can better ensure that you will find fulfillment in your service life, your career, and your lifestyle.[13] Ultimately, self-awareness is a responsibility. Its role in the service-choice spiral makes explicit your personal responsibility as you pursue a career in international public service. Much of what you do and how effective you will be depends on what you bring and how self-conscious you are in identifying and expressing your values and choices. Self-awareness can guide your responsible participation in communities of understanding, inform your continuous growth of skills and knowledge, and help you to determine the path for working for change that is most appropriate for you.

Most importantly, don't wait until you are doing the work to begin crafting your vision for development and your particular service vision. By the time you are doing the work, there is rarely opportunity to fully process all that you are experiencing and learning and to place it in this broader vision of what it's all about. But that doesn't mean that you stop thinking about these things when you're in the work—only that it can be more difficult. GW student Kipp Efinger quotes Leo Tolstoy in considering the importance of practicing continuous self-awareness: "In the name of God, stop a moment, cease your work, look around you." This is a good reminder of how you can get so wrapped up in what you are personally doing that you may forget its meaning, and its impact on others. He also draws from Leo Tolstoy to underscore the ultimate responsibility concerning self-awareness: "Everyone thinks of changing the world, but no one thinks of changing himself."

Just as changing the world takes time, and occurs through a long-term sequence of small steps—forward (for the most part, we hope), sideways, and backward—so does increasing self-awareness and effecting personal growth. Our sense of who we are, what values we enact, what we are willing and able to do, and what we want from work and life evolve with experience and maturity. Who we are at twenty-five will not be a complete picture of who we are at fifty. One of Derick's and Jennifer's core values is openness to learning; in this chapter we encourage you to explore your preferences, values, vision, and understanding of development so as to provide a foundation for your service choices. However, this foundation does not mean casting the answers to the questions we pose "in concrete" and enshrining them as some sort of fundamental "truth" about yourself or about the world. Just as the proverbial bending reed provides a more enduring base for connection to the earth than does the inflexible tree in the face of the storm, the foundation of your self-awareness will serve you more effectively if you remain open to ongoing reflection, revisiting and refining your answers to the questions over time.

In terms of a service career, we are not talking about giving up the ideals that you believe in (what Derick's baby-boomer undergrad classmates in the 60s used to call "selling out"), but reaching a deeper understanding of how you can act upon your ideals in an imperfect world—where not everything that may be desirable is feasible, where sometimes the "right" things get done for the "wrong" reasons, and where the ideological certainties of "black and white" give way to the practical ambiguities of "shades of gray." Our hope is that as you embark on a career to create change with the world, you include yourself as one of the targets for change. This is implicit in David Yang's experience and is the topic of Chapter 5.

Notes

1. For cultivating self-awareness about your skills and preferences, Shea and Mattson recommend creating a two-by-two matrix, categorizing your interests and skills as follows: things you do well and enjoy, things you do well but dislike, things you don't do well but enjoy, and things you don't do well and also dislike (pp. 28-29). See recommended reading on service, Appendix 4.

2. See recommended reading on community development and empowerment, Appendix 4.

3. See recommended reading on service, Appendix 4.

4. Micah Network seeks to promote "a biblically-shaped response to the needs of the poor and oppressed," which includes collaboration and advocacy. See http://www.micahnetwork.org.

5. See http://www.jubileeusa.org. For the United Kingdom and Australia counterparts see http://www.jubilee2000uk.org and http://www.jubilee2000.org.au.

6. Liberation theology, a movement that emerged in Latin America in the 1960s, has global implications today. Consistent with Paulo Freire's conscientization, liberation theology seeks to liberate the poor and oppressed through Christian teachings and an emphasis on poverty as the product of societal structures. Liberation theology became more popularly known through the movie *Romero*, which chronicles the life and assassination in 1980 of El Salvador's Archbishop Oscar Romero.

7. See http://www.fathetkheir.org/.

8. Amartya Sen won the Nobel Peace Prize in Economics, in large part for the ideas he articulates in *Development as Freedom*. See recommended reading on international development, Appendix 4.

9. See recommended reading on selected biographies to explore, Appendix 4.

10. See Joanna Macy's book referenced in recommended reading on community development and empowerment and selected biographies to explore (A. T. Ariyaratne), Appendix 4.

11. See, for example, Terence M. Loomis, "Indigenous Populations and Sustainable Development: Building on Indigenous Approaches to Holistic, Self-Determined Development," *World Development* 28, no. 5 (2000): 893-910.

12. For the grassroots perspective, see *The Post Development Reader*, referenced in Appendix 4. For an articulation of women's priorities and associated proposals, see the Web page of Development Alternatives with Women for a New Era (DAWN): http://www.dawn.org.fj.

13. Carol Straub offers some helpful guidelines for thinking through what you bring and what you may be seeking through your service. See reference in Appendix 4.

Profile 2. David Yang:
Joining Political Change with Development Programming

David Yang received an unlikely response from his Chinese father when he was arrested for occupying the Chancellor's Office at University of California (UC) Santa Cruz in 1977: "That's great. Stand up for what you believe in. Good for you!" Perhaps equally unlikely was that this young activist, from a Chinese refugee family living in California's Central Valley, would one day end up as a political appointee working for the US State Department and eventually become the Senior Advisor on democratic governance, poverty reduction, and conflict prevention for the UN Development Programme (UNDP) in Washington, D.C.

David's path to international public service cannot be separated from those of his parents. David's Cantonese mother originally intended to complete a PhD in social work at Catholic University and return to China to work on antipoverty programs. While she was in Washington in the early 1940s, the Japanese occupied Hong Kong, cutting off her funding, and she went to work for the Chinese Embassy, where she met David's father, who was a military attaché. David's father later became the military director of a US-backed anticommunist movement called the Free China Movement, whose aim was to train guerillas who would be sent back into China to mobilize resistance to Mao Tse Tung. *My mother was more of the pure social worker reformer. My father was always the more "get involved in politics, that's how you change the world" kind of influence. I think they were complementary. My mother was almost too saintly, and my father was too Machiavellian. So the hybrid was a good mix.*

The family eventually applied for refugee status in the United States and settled in Stockton, California. *We grew up with very little money. Both my parents came from fairly comfortable upbringings in China, but as refugees, they gave it all up when we came to this country.* David remembers having two record albums in the family as he was growing up. One was of Spanish bullfighting music, won at a school raffle, and the other was the greatest speeches of John F. Kennedy. *We played it endlessly. What I remember most is the inaugural speech: "Ask not what your country can do for you. Ask what you can do for your country."*

It was difficult to find role models within my ethnic community in the 1960s and '70s, people doing something different. But I always knew I would do some service-oriented thing, and more internationally focused than domestically focused. In high school, David became politically active, following presidential campaigns and doing public opinion polls of his high school population. In college at UC Santa Cruz, David became a student leader of People for a Free South Africa, whose agenda it was to promote UC divestment from US corporations that operated in South

Africa at the time. Just prior to the occupation of the Chancellor's Office, David had served with Volunteers in Asia in Taiwan, where he taught English at a YMCA. *I got exposed to the student underground movement in Taiwan, where they were fighting for Taiwanese democracy and independence. So when I came back to Santa Cruz I was all the more politicized, both in an international and a domestic sense.*

After graduating from college and completing a research internship at the Carnegie Endowment for International Peace (CEIP) in Washington, D.C., David applied to Johns Hopkins' School of Advanced International Studies (SAIS). *I wanted to get a quick master's at SAIS and then to just go off into the world.* It was now the late 1970s and his former group, Volunteers in Asia, was trying to sustain American interest in Southeast Asia as the United States withdrew militarily and politically. They had received a grant to start a publication on Southeast Asian affairs. *Since I was interested in Asian politics and the media, I thought I'd just defer SAIS for a couple of years and go to work on this fledgling newspaper. I felt inspired to do what I could to keep Americans engaged in a developmental sense in Southeast Asia.*

David spent one year at the newspaper, and then began to experience an identity crisis. *The next five years of my life were the most complicated, but the most formative in terms of what I ended up doing and where I am sitting today.* The crisis started with a falling out with his colleagues at Volunteers in Asia. *I love these people and am in close touch with them still. To make a long story short, my peers felt that they were adopting in the workplace an Asian indirect way of communicating. I was trying to be politicized, assertive—in a sense an angry young Asian American who didn't want to be told to go to dental school. And so it came to a head, and I resigned. I said, "Hey you guys, I'm the Asian here. I'm trying to get this very resource-poor nonprofit organization off the ground, and you're hiding behind this pseudo-Asian mask. I'm trying to find myself, so the hell with you." I grew up with a lot of petty racism in this fairly redneck, semi-rural part of California. So to have gone to college and to have gotten rid of that through these service-oriented, Asian-oriented groups, and then to have felt betrayed by them—I felt I didn't know where I belonged.*

During his internship at CEIP, David had recognized his weaknesses in terms of theoretical and historical knowledge. Rather than returning to SAIS for a quick master's degree, he decided to apply to PhD programs at Stanford and Berkeley. *I went to graduate school to study Chinese politics and political science. But inside, this fire was burning in me. "Who am I, why am I here? I'm not Chinese either. Why am I studying Chinese politics? I care about the world and I care about American politics, and American poverty, and American injustice. But do I really care about who's who in the Chinese communist political hierarchy?"* David attended Stanford,

Berkeley, and Berkeley again. In each of those three years he dropped out. *I had these wonderful professors who would say, "You're going through this identity crisis as a refugee. Just be kind to yourself. If you can't write your papers, don't worry about it, just get out of here."* David finally took this advice after the third try.

In the meantime, he had been trying to find himself in other ways. He went to work at a family planning agency in San Francisco's Chinatown. *It was great work. I was working with boat people from Indochina. That work was very satisfying, but the hard-core people who grew up on the streets of Chinatown and had become social workers were also very young and angry, and said, "You know, man, you're this banana from the suburbs. Don't come to Chinatown and work out your identity crisis. We don't need you here, we don't want you here."* David resolved his identity crisis by getting involved in the Asian American theater community in San Francisco. *It was more inclusive in terms of people who were trying to figure it all out. It was a great experience artistically. And the people were quirky and not rigid in terms of either you're in or out. Everybody was in, as long as they had a commitment to exploration artistically.* At first David thought he wanted to become an actor, but eventually determined it was not what he was meant to be.

So after five years, David petitioned SAIS to dust off his application and acceptance. *I wrote a letter saying exactly what my journey had been. And they were supportive. So six years later I came back, certainly strengthened and clearer about who I was and who I wasn't. I didn't want to be an academic. I was interested in international relations. I wanted to be a practitioner and an activist. I wasn't quite sure how it would work out. The only guiding direction was that I was clear I was a refugee, and what that meant to me psychologically and professionally was that I wanted an international career. . . . But I also knew I wanted to put down roots in this country. That was important to me.* After graduating with a master's from SAIS, David was selected for the Presidential Management Internship Program, a competitive federal program designed to recruit the best and brightest master's and doctoral graduates for public service in the federal government,[1] where he completed two years at the State Department, working on refugee issues—on both settlement in the United States and the protection of refugees abroad.

Knowing he wanted a Washington-based career, David then decided to pursue a PhD at SAIS. *I wanted to enhance my options by having a PhD. I liked research and writing, even though I didn't want to become a professor. The role models of people who went in and out of government service and could be in think tanks—people who had PhDs—seemed to have a lot more options than other people. If one could write well and defend a position in writing, it gave you a voice—unlike a civil servant who couldn't write an op-ed piece, or an NGO worker who was limited by the funding ties of his patron. I always wanted to maximize my independence intellectually and career-wise. I think that having that degree helps you do different things, particularly in terms of people valuing your voice outside of bureaucracy.* David wrote his dissertation on Woodrow Wilson and the League of Nations and the historical, theoretical genesis of peacekeeping.

It was now 1992 and a friend was recruiting for the Clinton Administration. Confident there would be an interest in hiring minorities, several of David's Asian American friends urged him to apply. *I said, "I've been in Washington long enough to know there are three entrées for newcomers into a political administration. You work on the Hill, you work on the campaign, or you work in a think tank. And of the three the only one that applies to me is the last, and I was only a research intern."* They urged him to apply anyway. He sent his resume to the Asian American Coordinator, who forwarded it to the Foreign Policy Team, and directly to Margaret Carpenter, who happened to have been David's supervisor when he was an intern at CEIP fourteen years earlier. She called and indicated that his resume looked interesting, but said, "Don't call me, I'll call you." She eventually called six months later. By then she had her own political appointment, as the head of the Asia Near East Bureau for USAID. She offered David the opportunity to apply his peacekeeping expertise in advising USAID how to proceed in Cambodia as the United Nations was withdrawing. *Initially, it was weird because, first, there were career people who would say, "Why are you here?" Second, campaign people said, "Why are you here?" And the hard-core party people had an equal number of questions. But then you kind of lie low, and then people started leaving and I just did this exciting work.*

After a year working on Cambodia and learning the ins and outs of USAID, David wanted to do something broader, applying his knowledge of democratic theory. Brian Atwood, the USAID Administrator, came with an agenda to lead and strengthen the democratic institution-building agenda initiated in the previous administrations. David petitioned for and was approved to become the democracy advisor for the Asia and Near East Bureau. *Democratic governance was still relatively new, and many donors wouldn't even dare call it democracy. People with a theoretical background, who could bring theory into the realm of practice, were at an advantage over practitioners who may have had the field experience but didn't have theoretical experience. I was kind of the intellectual policy gadfly for field people coming in, who, to be fair to them, didn't have much experience crafting a democracy program.*

After three years working and traveling from Washington—*everywhere from Mongolia to Morocco*—David had become fascinated by the development world, but *given my sort of broader interest in international politics, I really wanted to marry the programmatic development world with the diplomatic world. I wanted to do democracy and human rights, but I wanted to use both tools simultaneously. It became clear through four years at AID that there are limits of developmental technical assistance without—to put it bluntly—political backing diplomatically, both multilaterally and bilaterally, in trying to assist countries in political reform. Unless you had a political/diplomatic agenda to go with your training programs, you weren't going to go anywhere, particularly in hostile political settings.* It was now the transition to Clinton's second term, so still in the political appointee system, David applied for a position in the State Department and was appointed as a junior speech writer for the Secretary of State. *I loved it. It gave me an introduction to the panorama of diplomatic issues. So I felt I went from the really micro world of a regional bureau and one sector to the full panorama of global policy.*

But David still had his agenda of wanting to work on democracy and human rights, and new positions were opening up in the appointee system, including one that was a perfect match to his interests. The Assistant Secretary for Human Rights, Democracy, and Labor at the time, John Shattuck, had held his position since the beginning of Clinton's first term. *He now knew the limits of diplomacy. And so he became interested in supplementing diplomacy with aid programs. He knew you just couldn't bully people or threaten to cut off aid, that you need positive proactive programs that would actually help train people, to give them the tools to enact political reform.* Assistant Secretary Shattuck had heard of David through the grapevine and knew he had applied for a position to be one of his deputies. *It was, again, having the perfect skills to fit that kind of job that didn't really exist before. But given the way the field was moving, they needed somebody, certainly with my skills, but also with my interests in merging the two sets of tools.*

True to his vision, David spent the next four years building bridges between the diplomatic world in the State Department and the development world of USAID. He also built bridges to the development community beyond USAID, attending Development Assistance Committee (DAC) meetings at the Organization for Economic Co-operation and Development (OECD) in Paris, often as one of few, if not the only, diplomats among a sea of development practitioners. He networked with other bilateral development agencies, counterpart foreign ministries, multilateral banks, and UN organizations. *It all began to make sense, that one could be both a human rights and democracy activist but make it fully integrated into the concept of human development and what development practitioners were doing. At the same time, I felt I could be a small part of a push within the development community, after the end of the Cold War, to embrace the taboo political development agenda. So it all came full circle.*

David stayed at the State Department until the very last day of Clinton's second administration. His day of reckoning had come. *My wife had been saying for years, "What are you going to do?" I said, "I'll figure it out." But I didn't have any place to go after.* David was interested in starting a think tank to further democracy promotion and human rights. He won a two-year grant from the Hewlett Foundation to start the Institute for Global Democracy. *I'm always the optimist. I told my wife, "I'll retire as the president and founder of this think tank. In twenty years I'll hand it over to somebody else." It didn't quite work out that way.* As a result of changing priorities after September 11, 2001, Hewlett ended its human rights and democracy programming. *So my board said, "It ain't gonna happen. You've made a valiant effort. Not all good ideas get funded. Don't go down with the ship. Find a job. We'll help you."*

By then it was the summer of 2002 and the UNDP had just issued its pathbreaking Human Development Report on democracy. *So I said, "Oh, that's perfect. I want to work on that. I want to work for UNDP. I want to work for Mark Malloch Brown."* Having met people from the UNDP's Washington office during his think tank effort, David approached them. *I asked, "Do you need someone to promote the democracy agenda for you in Washington?" And they said, "Let's talk about it." Again, I was in the right place at the right time, had the right skills, yet they had embedded democratic governance in the field and in New York.* Given the importance of Washington as a donor capital and democracy promoter, UNDP decided it would be good to have a democracy expert in their Washington office. They offered him an initial two-month trial contract, followed by a six-month contract "but no promises." David eventually negotiated a full-time direct-hire position with benefits.

So now I'm doing the same thing I was doing in the State Department Human Rights Bureau vis-à-vis AID but doing it with New York and multilateral players. It's my same community, but through a UN forum, which is very exciting. It's the same work, translating what the field does, pushing the field to do more, linking the field and New York headquarters with new thinking in the academy, in think tanks, in Washington institutions. It's not fieldwork. It's not headquarters writing memos kind of work. It's truly growing networks of cooperation, but using ideas to fuel those networks. I love it. I think, "This is using some sort of creativity and chutzpah to break down barriers, to truly work on the politics of human rights and democracy and development." I can't beat it, you know?

Note

1. The program has since been renamed the Presidential Management Fellows Program. See Appendix 5 for contact information.

CHAPTER **5**

Serving in Community

Public service is rarely a solitary endeavor. There may be times when you undertake some individual piece of analysis or reflection, but for the most part service to bring about change involves working with and through other people. As that overused slogan "Think globally, act locally" conveys, when you work with people directly it happens in the context of a distinct subset of individuals or social groups, which, for shorthand, is often referred to as a community.[1] Working in community goes to the heart of working for change. As Najma Siddiqi (Profile 3) puts it, *I don't think I have ever gone as a lone ranger. I don't think I can do that. If I'm interested in bringing about change in society, then I can't do it by myself.* More specifically, she reflects on the origins of her path, working with women. *I was interested in the situation of women, and how they were excluded from major policy decisions, personal decisions, societal decisions, and political roles. So how do you change that? You have to go back and see why that is happening. And you want to see how you can begin to bring about change there. You can't change it overnight. You can't, you know. You have to work with all kinds of people, you have to understand all kinds of interests, and you have to start working from there.*

Working for change requires working with others. In the previous chapter, we encouraged you to develop self-awareness, including reflection on what development means to you. Having done so, you may feel that now you've clarified your thinking and are ready to make your vision a reality through working with the community that your career choice at this particular moment puts you in contact with. You've got your skills, your idealism, your vision, and you're ready to get out there and make your chosen community a better place. So what's wrong with this picture?

As Najma Siddiqi's quote suggests, your understanding, goals, and vision are only one side of the equation. The people you want to work with have understandings, goals, and visions of their own, along with a great deal of knowledge about what works or doesn't work for them. So first of all, you need to gather information on what their world looks like, what constraints and limitations they face, what their incentives to engage with you for change might be. Clearly, you can't know everything about their world and worldview—perfect information exists only in the ideal world of economic models—but you can be attuned to learning about them. Second, you need to interact with people in ways that enable them to develop their own comprehension so that you can begin to develop a shared vision for change. This happens most effectively if they think of the change process as theirs, and participate in influencing and guiding how it happens, where it goes, and what the intended results are.

Reaching this happy situation rarely occurs through the one-way transmission of expertise, or pointing out to people what they "should" see or want. So working in community doesn't mean getting them to buy into your self-awareness. You may believe you're right, but as we've said before, genuine service is not just about you. We bet you're nodding your head as you read this, saying to yourself, "Well, of course, I knew that already." However, acting on the two-way street orientation of systems change, where you are open to being changed as well as helping to bring about improvement, is not easy; and you may find yourself in job situations that reward the transfer of expertise over dialogue and facilitation. The underlying premise of the facet of development management that deals with supporting international donor agency agendas frequently reinforces the one-way transmission of expertise and capacity from Northern specialist "haves" to Southern "have-nots."

In this chapter, we will explore how you serve in community from two different perspectives. First, we will discuss your relationship to the community whose situation you seek to change and whose capacities you want to build. In keeping with the two dimensions of community—common geography or shared characteristics—this community could be a rural village, an urban neighborhood, or a province; or it could be poor women needing health care for their babies, primary school children and their parents, agricultural extension workers in a ministry department, or civil society organizations mobilizing for political advocacy. Second, we will talk about the community or communities that encompass those who are serving. As we said in Chapter 3, what we mean here includes a range of groups such as your coworkers in the organization that employs you, the counterparts you work with in the country where you may be serving, your university classmates, or members of professional associations you may belong to. The distinction is actually somewhat artificial in that there can be overlaps between these two views of community. Much of the overlap derives from the two-way intersection between you and the community. If you are benefiting and being served as you serve others, who is the catalyst and who is the beneficiary or recipient? You receive as well as give in both types of community, leading to mutual transformation. Over the course of a career that involves you in a number of communities, the connections that emerge as you seek to live out your personal service vision, and are served in turn, can be deeply satisfying.

The Meaning of Providing Service

Practically all service-provision relationships contain an implicit, and often explicit, structure that distinguishes between the service provider, or the helper, and the recipient of the service—the helpee. Remember Ram Dass and Paul Gorman's view on helping from Chapter 2? The title of their chapter on the subject is called "The Helping Prison." When we play the role of helper we need an object for our efforts; this is the helpee. The role of helpee, recipient, or beneficiary—whichever label you choose—holds an element of passivity, of a gap needing to be filled in order to render the recipient capable, cured, developed, or empowered. As the helper, you are the primary actor, intervening on behalf of an "other," filling the gap, building capacity, and offering solutions. This relationship can be a prison in the sense that you become locked into your role, which, according to Dass and Gorman, limits your ability to be fully human. Whether or not you buy the argument that being a helper can endanger your humanity, the point to grasp is that the helper role, as frequently conceived and operationalized, establishes an innate hierarchical relationship that reinforces the one-way thinking we talked about above.

The degree of hierarchy is reinforced when there are strong asymmetries between the parties involved, for example, when the helper is highly educated and of a different social class or nationality from the helpee, and/or when those receiving the service are uneducated, poor, and marginalized. Paulo Freire, the influential Brazilian educator and social activist, argued that this inherent hierarchical imbalance renders service recipients passive, powerless, and silent. He stressed the importance of the poor transforming themselves into actors, rather than remaining the acted upon. The appropriate role of the helper/change agent is to ask questions and to encourage others to do so as well. Why are things as they are? Why should we take them as given? Through this process of critical consciousness raising (conscientization), the community enters an iterative cycle of analysis-action-reflection that forms the basis for liberation and empowerment, which releases the creative energies of people.[2]

This is a shared process, through which, according to Freire, we all become more fully humanized. He argued that this is our vocation as human beings: to avoid dehumanization and to recognize the humanity of others, connecting with them in ways that generate mutual growth and empowerment, and that reduce social, class, and economic asymmetries. Zen Buddhism offers a similar perspective, and refers to seeing the divine in others. As Sarah Newhall (Profile 1) puts it, *in a service orientation, what you're getting back from these relationships is as much about helping and strengthening you to have a quality life experience as anybody else.* During his Peace Corps experience, it made perfect sense to Jef Buehler (Profile 5) that he would benefit more than the community of Los Jobos. After all, there was only one of him giving, and there were many, many more community members giving back. Derick felt the same way during his Peace Corps years in Chad, in the early 1970s. He got a lot more out of the experience than the students learning English in his classroom.

Given the inherent power and expertise differential built into the helping vocabulary, in reflecting on her evolving vision of development management, one of our GW students refers to a process of accompaniment—*a horizontal relationship between those organizations and institutions with more power, resources, influence, and perhaps expertise (generally based in or associated with the North), with those local organizations who have a better understanding of the local context, but who may be struggling to develop their scope of influence and make a difference. This involves facilitating relationships, contributing to skills development, and promoting good development practice, but it does not involve imposition or paternalism.*

Doing With, Not Doing For

When you step into a community as a change agent, whether in the North or South, seeking to make things better in some way, you arrive with some advantages: resources, technical expertise, options, and decision-making power. Some of these advantages derive from what you personally bring; others flow from the organization that supports the work you're doing, whether by virtue of having hired you to do a job, given you a grant, or placed you as a volunteer. The community has resources and power too. The community members bring their knowledge and local understanding, their motivation and commitment, and their power to mobilize themselves to organize and act. They also have the power to withhold these things, and to resist you in either subtle or direct ways. They can nod and smile, and then when you leave, go back to doing things as before. By our yardstick, this outcome would signal failure, so we would rather see the people of the community use their power to create change themselves. How does that occur?

Much of our understanding of what change agents are and what they do comes from process consultation—the process facet of development management, drawing on organization development—and emerges from the analysis of experience at the local or grassroots level. In fact, the lessons for change agents and working in community, discussed below, apply equally to your work on your own team, within your organization, as you interact with partner implementers in the North and the South, and ultimately with those whose behavior you hope to influence. As discussed in Chapter 2, this is not a process based on a doctor-patient model, where the change agent comes in, diagnoses the situation, and prescribes the solution. You still need to contribute your knowledge and experience, but this occurs by doing work with others, not for them.

Process consultation is a way of intervening in an organization or a community where the external consultant assists organization/community members to review their problem-solving behaviors and procedures to identify sources of blockage, misalignment, dysfunction, and/or success, with a major emphasis on *how* things are done rather than on *what* is done. Once these issues are clarified, the consultant works with the members to decide how to modify the unproductive behaviors and procedures, and/or to build and expand on those that already work well. The consultant then helps them to make the transition to new, more effective ones. Throughout the change effort, the onus for deciding what to do and making the necessary changes lies with the organization or the community. The consultant facilitates the process and provides coaching along the way. Process consultants do not portray themselves as experts who arrive with the answers in hand, ready to apply them to the problem for the organization or the community. Rather, they come with a portfolio of analytic and management tools, a process for using them, and knowledge of other relevant experience, ready to work with people to ask questions, collect and analyze answers, and develop solutions jointly.

To succeed in working with communities using the principles of process consultation, "change agents must listen more than talk, learn more than teach, and facilitate more than lead."[3] Bhasin summarizes the reflections of experienced change agents in Asia, who identified the following common weaknesses and inadequacies of change agents:

- Being paternalistic in their approach;
- Doing everything themselves;

- Emphasizing short-term projects more than long-term efforts;
- Inadequately understanding the political forces at work;
- Failing to coordinate or cooperate with other change agents; and
- Doling out material goods, creating additional dependencies.

As agents of the development industry and implementers of the specific agendas of the organizations in which you serve, you cannot always avoid these behaviors. Some organizations offer more potential for operating in community than others, and you may factor this criterion into your career choices (see Chapter 8). Finding a position that allows you the space to engage in service by assisting communities to identify their problems and devise their own solutions can be a continuous challenge. However, be aware that it's not always the donor agencies or consulting firms that hire you that are the ones pushing you into a top-down, expert-driven way of working (in fact sometimes it's just the opposite). More often than you might assume, the communities and counterpart organizations you work with will expect you to be the expert, to identify the problem, and devise the solution. Effective facilitation and process consultation are often invisible to those you're working with, so the irony is that you may have been quite successful at getting community members to engage in their own problem-solving and empowerment process, and they turn to you and say, "And just what is it that *you* did?"

For example, in his work on USAID's Implementing Policy Change Project, Derick found that the best way to engage policy reformers in a change effort was not to start out by introducing a set of process tools, but by undertaking some sort of technical analytic task that established the change agent's expert reputation in the eyes of the reformers. After they saw that the outsiders contributed something of recognizable value, they then were open to seeing facilitation as a legitimate and useful way of working together. This illustrates another of the tensions among the four facets of development management. You may feel comfortable with a balance that accords primacy to process and empowerment, but those you want to work with may have a different view. Negotiating a mutually agreeable compromise that still achieves the desired socioeconomic development objectives is sometimes hard.

Humility, Trust, Respect, and Listening

But just because it's tough doesn't mean you can't get there. You can avoid the change-agent pitfalls listed above, and construct for yourself and your partners a working style that remains true to the notion we've been talking about of providing service in community. For starters, creating this style calls for humility, trust, respect, and listening. Our profiled practitioners have a lot to say about these qualities.

Humility can be a particularly hard one to learn. Aaron Williams (Profile 4) recounts his learning process. *You often have to fight the people you think you're trying to help. That's one of the first lessons I learned in the Peace Corps. You arrive there and you say, "I'm here to help." And these people you're trying to help are trying to figure out ways to create obstacles in your path to helping them. Why is that? "Don't you get it? I'm here to help!" It's a very sobering experience. And they're thinking, "Who asked you here in the first place? Why would we want you? You're not from here. You don't understand our customs. How can you help us anyway?" That was revolutionary. It really changed my whole mind-set. I've never forgotten those lessons no matter where I've worked, in terms of looking at a particular development program in its social context. Those are the times you really reach down into your own character and you find out what you're all about.*

Jennifer Butz (Profile 6) summarizes the need for humility by offering the following advice: *The most important thing is to wonder more and know less. It's amazing how often we tend to feel we know our own mysteries. But when we stop and wonder about them, it becomes a whole new world. When we go out of the United States and we're seeing new cultures and hearing new languages, it's amazing. My advice is to not just jump to the, "Oh, I know that because of this or that over there," but to just let it be for what it is. To try instead to piece the experiences together with, "I wonder why I saw that there and now I'm seeing it again here."*

David Yang has practiced this kind of humility throughout his career. As a Washington headquarters-based person in all the work he's done, he has had the luxury to collect information from a variety of experiences, to analyze it, and to look for patterns. *I have an intellectual and principled sense of what human development is and what human rights as a component of that mean. But as a non-field person, I'm the last person to tell somebody how to do it. And even if you're a field person with fifty years' experience, humility always has to be your abiding and operating ethic. You bring new experience to bear on a culture you may not have grown up in. You can bring comparative experience and knowledge and let them choose.*

Najma Siddiqi (Profile 3) provides a good illustration of humility in action. *I remember the first meetings we had to introduce NRSP* [National Rural Support Program] *in the communities. The first message I used to give to the communities was, "Don't trust me. For generations, you have been tricked by people who came in and said, 'We are good. The others are bad.' You have no way to know I am good unless you have tested me out. So keep your eyes open. Test us out. Listen to what we are saying. Apply it and see if it works. Then trust us. No blind trust, either way."* Whether it's made explicit or not, and as is true in every new relationship no matter the context, we test each other out. You have to prove yourself, to demonstrate that there is something meaningful to be gained by relating with you. This is true on the job, whether it's working with your colleagues within your organization, or with the communities you and your organization are reaching out to.

And trust works both ways. As a change agent, you have to trust that those you seek to influence or assist are capable of creating their own change. You may assist by facilitating that process, providing new information for them to think about and incorporate, but you have to also believe that the knowledge they possess is valid, and that they are capable of creating their own vision for change and of accomplishing it. Such trust begins with respect. You need to respect others for who they are, what they have experienced, how much they can do, and how they perceive the situation you are trying to address. Just because you are assuming a service role doesn't mean that others are helpless. Just because their experience and knowledge are different doesn't make them inferior. Sarah Newhall talks about the refugee community she worked with in Portland. *I've always had such awe that people whose lives had been thrown into total disarray could come with virtually nothing except their value systems and their grit and survival skills, and learn a new language, a new social system, acquire property, and try to raise a family in a hostile environment.*

Najma Siddiqi tells a story of when she worked with porter women in Nepal. The women had carried stones, one at a time, up a mountain slope for the construction of a hotel. Yet, once it was completed, they had never had the opportunity to enter it. Through the International Labour Organization and the Ministry of Panchayat and Local Development, Najma organized a local development planning exercise with the women. One of the objectives was to facilitate their empowerment—this would be the first time they came together for any leadership role. She decided to hold the workshop in the hotel. After agreeing to the plan, the hotel management realized there might be logistical challenges regarding the use of facilities that the women were unaccustomed to. Rather than cancel or relocate the workshop, Najma worked with the management to set up outdoor latrines. It seems a simple thing, but sometimes those of us who are more privileged can get hung up on aspects of others' habits and customs that we may find less than appealing, or even distasteful. But such practices need not impact on our perception of others' abilities. And in embracing their capabilities, you don't necessarily have to teach them your cultural preferences, either, since this presumes they are doing something wrong. In this example, the workshop organizers took to heart one of the first principles of process consultation: start where the client is, and do so with respect.

Sometimes, our change partners have a clear idea of what they want and where they want to go. Aaron Williams interacted with empowered clients as USAID Mission Director in South Africa. *We put together a philosophy and an approach whereby the South Africans were in the lead. It wasn't as if they were going to relinquish this stuff anyway, but it was important for us to recognize that, and to shape our policies and programs so that these reflected what they wanted to do. South Africa in those days was the most independent country anywhere on the earth. In most of the developing world, when a country is involved in a transition, the World Bank, the IMF [International Monetary Fund], and other regional banks come together with the bilateral donors and they prepare a CG [Consultative Group]. South Africa had never had a CG. They called the donors to Pretoria and said, "We want to review what you think you want to do in South Africa. And we'll decide whether we think it is appropriate for South Africa." No one else had the moxie, the vision, the leverage to do that. It became a very innovative and challenging way of doing development assistance.*

Respect also means that if the community decides to take a path other than your preferred option, you accept that and continue to support their efforts to realize their vision. This was something Jef Buehler experienced in Peace Corps. He confessed to being disappointed that the community opted not to follow through with a demonstration he had helped to initiate, but he shared in the celebration of their success in meeting their own objectives, their own way. The Main Street methodology, which he applies now in New Jersey, embodies the same kind of respect. *It's a very specific methodology of organizing people in a vertical fashion to improve the physical, social, economic, and political value of their downtown or commercial corridor and their whole community, but using their vision and their resources of both time and money to make it happen.* Here, again, values play an important role. As GW student Rachel Surkin acknowledges, *recognizing the existence of values as motivators for people's actions is critical to gaining an understanding for why people act as they do, and even for developing empathy for why people make choices that you may not agree with.*

To take it even further, respect means you will also defend the interests of the community, both within and beyond your own organization. This was the principle that drove Najma Siddiqi to defend the integrity of the NRSP so fiercely, when faced with external pressure to forfeit allocated money and to modify priorities. She saw the resources as belonging to the communities and believed the priorities for hiring and program content should be driven by their needs. So the transparency that she championed was not just for the benefit of potential auditors, or for government. The communities also knew, for example, the staff's daily living allowances.

Much about these principles—humility, trust, and respect—can be summarized in terms of listening. Here's how Sarah Newhall sees it: *If it's my own hometown, my own home community, or my own organization, I lead in one way. If I'm a guest in somebody else's home community then I lead in another way. When you're a guest you should listen and be polite and learn the best of the local knowledge, and then offer humble suggestions based on what that local knowledge is and help people organize. That's what I did in Cambodia. My strategy was common sense: find the best thought leaders in this community, listen to them, and do what they say. You can put all kinds of fancy trappings on that and all sorts of social science jargon, but basically the strategy is to find the Nelson Mandelas of the world and listen. Find the people who believe in social justice and understand and listen to what they say the community needs. And then try to help figure out common sense strategies for addressing those needs.*

Not every community has a Nelson Mandela, so we're often faced with choosing between the ideal and what is available. A starting place is to identify who the community views as their most competent leaders. And even in your own territory, listening is important. While humility, trust, and respect are essential when working with communities targeted for development, they are equally important in the relationships among those serving.

Communities among Those Serving

Recall Najma Siddiqi's recognition that to work for change, *you have to work with all kinds of people.* And *if I'm interested in bringing about change in society, then I can't do it by myself.* Among the many people you need to work with are those who, like you, see themselves in a serving role. In this sense, community refers to the professional community of development management or other technical area scholars and practitioners, including your coworkers, whether these are consultants, colleagues within your organization, or counterparts in collaborating organizations. Many of the lessons above apply to these communities. In fact, when you get to the end of this chapter, we encourage you to reread the section on "The Meaning of Providing Service" with this community in mind. Communities among those serving have added benefits in terms of other types of learning and moral support.

The learning benefits within these communities are endless. As Aaron Williams (Profile 4) advises, *seek ways to continue to build on your knowledge base. Reach out to people, ideas, and organizations, where you can continue to be fresh, and understand new and innovative thinking that can contribute to the body of knowledge that you're involved in and the work you're*

involved in. There are many different communities that you can participate in. Among others, Jennifer Butz (Profile 6) is a member of the
International Association of Facilitators. Membership affords her access
to new ideas and approaches via the Internet. So despite her somewhat
remote field locations, she can continue to keep a pulse on what is
happening in her profession. Derick is a founding member of the
Development Management Network (DMN), an informal professional
association of practitioners, academics, and students who focus on development management work. In fact, it is through the DMN that he
met Jennifer, his future wife. Since 1981, the DMN has organized workshops and seminars, usually in conjunction with the annual meeting of
the American Society for Public Administration. The workshops bring
members together to exchange ideas and problem-solve around emerging issues in the field, share innovations, and, always, to foster networking. Jennifer currently serves as the coordinator of the DMN,
managing an e-mail listserv and facilitating an annual DMN workshop.
Appendix 1 lists some professional associations you might consider joining. We will discuss professional associations a bit more in Chapter 8.

In reflecting on her service vision, GW student Tara Hill has also
discovered the importance of *continued collaboration with other fields that
emphasize the same values as the development management field. For example,
many service-learning professionals in the United States also highlight the
importance of process and empowerment. I think it could be extremely beneficial
if the two subfields sought a space where they could intentionally share their
learnings and experience.* Tara's reflections confirm that we can create our
own service communities, crossing traditional disciplinary or practice
boundaries as we see fit.[4]

Learning spaces can also be created within organizations. Najma
Siddiqi's current job is to create such venues for the Environmentally
and Socially Sustainable Development (ESSD) Network at the World
Bank. Previously, she created and coordinated learning spaces for the
Social Development Family within ESSD. *Every two or three weeks, we
would have a dialogue on different topics. We treated it as a place where people could come to test out their ideas. You've done a study; you want to discuss
it. You're designing a project; you want feedback on it. We started doing those
kinds of things. We also consciously started bringing together different teams.
What are they doing? Are they overlapping? For example, social analysis and
conflict prevention—do they link up? Where are the links? Can they work
together better?*

Creating these spaces and connections may also be at the core of
your effectiveness on the job. This was David Yang's agenda and service vision at the State Department. *I spent four years there, educating State
Department colleagues about supplementing diplomatic actions and diplomatic*

bullying with programs. At the same time, I was educating or bridging back to the programmatic world, helping my AID colleagues harness diplomatic resources, not only in their embassies, but among the higher echelons of the State Department. We really pioneered a sense of strategic planning and bureaucratic institutionalization, ways to merge those two sets of tools, bridging the diplomatic world and the development world. In his work in New Jersey, Jef Buehler (Profile 5) looks to the National Main Street Center, the hub for the network of state-level Main Street programs, for feedback on ideas and questions for problem solving.

Learning in community is frequently an explicit component of social change efforts, and as we discussed above, helps to blur the line between the roles of change agent and beneficiary. Sarah Newhall talks about this: *I think building coalitions, building networks, building strategic alliances is the smart way for political activists or social activists to operate, because you can make broader-level change than just being a voice in the wind. But all these things start from good ideas and courage. So first you have to see it. You might see it better because other people are helping you to see it. That's a reason for being part of a group. Or if you see it and you want to try to influence a group, then that's another reason to align with others.*

As these experiences attest, working in community is not just an occasional, formal effort. It can be strategic. Who that community consists of will depend on the work at hand, and can shift as new goals and tasks emerge. Referring to her work at the World Bank, Najma Siddiqi confirms, *it depends on what you are doing and how you want to do it. Governments became my community during the PRSP* [Poverty Reduction Strategy Paper] *process, also the delegations of trade unions and the parliamentarians. So I hooked up with* [a World Bank specialist] *on the parliamentarians. I hooked up with the Human Development Group for the trade unions. When we wanted to change the Bank's approach to the NGO sector, we had to work with* [World Bank President James] *Wolfensohn and the Board. They became our community. When I do the work with Community Enhancement Need Assessment, the community is the local partners and community groups that we work with.*

Of course, working in community with those serving is what you will do on the job, day to day. Embracing this community is just good management. As Aaron Williams (Profile 4) emphasizes, *be prepared to work with the brightest people you can find to work with. Always look for the smartest people in any given situation, because that's how you're going to energize your organization. That's how you're going to energize yourself in terms of your career. And it's going to make for a much better product. Everybody says that, but a lot of people, I think, are threatened by smart people. They're not so sure they want to give them a lot of room to get the credit or to be seen as being brighter than they are. This is a case where you really want to do that. Give them the opportunity to do their work. You hired them because they're smart and they understand what needs to be done in their area. You give them the latitude to do that. You don't micromanage.*

Jennifer Butz (Profile 6) fosters community and empowerment in the workplace among her staff. *I believe it's important at critical junctures that my staff be responsible for helping me make decisions. So fully informing individuals of the choices that face me as a manager and seeking their advice and guidance and strategic directions is something that I do. Every six months, I conduct a staff-wide strategic planning session so that we can check ourselves, because things do change and we need to make sure that what we decided six months ago is still the right thing.*

Sarah Newhall similarly recognizes and promotes learning from empowered board members and staff at Pact. *I'm working to try to have a state-of-the-art board at Pact, where we have governance issues on our board agenda every meeting. So the board looks at itself as a board, not just feels good that they have a great staff, we're doing great program work, and the bottom line seems to be okay. It's more important than that.* This attitude extends to staff mentoring. *I see in my leadership of this institution that we have an obligation to try to help grow the next generation of good development workers. I don't think that's just me. I think every employer does the same thing. Here, the leaders try to take a non-patronizing approach. You've got to try to build for the future.* It was not surprising to us that so many of those we profiled are very conscious in their approach and commitment to mentoring others.

In mentoring and building relationships with others, you expand your personal service network. They become resources for you—you have shared experiences and mutual understanding of how each thinks and what skills and knowledge each brings. So you can cultivate a broad network, all your own, to whom you can turn for professional support and advice. You never know where these individuals will end up. During his tenure at USAID, Aaron Williams benefited from such networks in a number of ways. *I've been very fortunate. I've been able to move people from country to country with me, from different departments with me, and keep them on my team.* At the same time, *I give them the ability to look for ways to develop their career, which might mean you might lose them. You know, somebody comes in and says, "You've got this very talented health officer working for you in Honduras. This person needs to be health officer in Egypt, our largest program in the world." Well, you can't stand in that person's way just because they're critical to what you're doing in Honduras. Number one, it doesn't make sense from an organizational standpoint. Number two, it's a great career move for that person and you need to be enthusiastic and supportive of that. Because at some point in time, especially in a career in service, you'll have a chance to work with that person again, probably. And you want to be the person who helped them move their way up the ladder. . . . I'm very proud of the fact that every one of the people on my senior staff has now gone on to be a mission director or deputy mission director.*

This quote illustrates how a personal network of people with shared work experience, vision, and commitment can offer not just support and advice, but job opportunities as well. Aaron Williams is talking about job moves within USAID's structure, but the international development industry, like any other specialized field, is a "small world," where people circulate over the course of their careers among donor agencies, consulting firms, NGOs, and think tanks. Those in hiring positions often turn first to their personal networks, where they have the confidence that candidates not only have the requisite technical skills, but also share their values and perspectives on development goals and working styles.

Let's return now to something Sarah Newhall said. She said that working for change requires *good ideas and courage*. Okay, so we've discussed the good ideas. What about courage? Communities among those serving are one of the best sources of moral support. We've already discussed (in Chapter 4) how difficult it is to know if and when you're successful, and how challenging your change agenda can be. We will further discuss sustaining your service motivation in Chapter 9. But an appreciation of the importance and benefits of communities of understanding is not complete without considering moral support. Where do you go for encouragement? To whom do you turn for a sympathetic ear? Who simultaneously knows you and your work the best, to know just the right thing to say or do—or when to say or do nothing—to help you get back on track?

For some people, their professional support network is also their moral support network. This is Najma Siddiqi's approach. *It's the same people. Because that's the point of alliances. You're supporting each other. You don't go elsewhere for moral support. You have to start trusting your allies for them to be allies. And you have to find ways to trust them, and they have to find ways to trust you.* Sharing your need for moral support and encouragement brings you closer to others and them to you. It creates space for mutual support. David Yang also finds moral support and inspiration through his professional network. *The people who come to this kind of work, particularly in the United Nations, are from literally every country. That kind of shared ethic is stunning and moving. There is a daily kind of wellspring of support and inspiration there. Not that bureaucracies don't breed competition for resources or ambition, but beyond that, those other things are so muted given that kind of shared mission.*

It's obvious that you will want to seek moral support in the fulfillment of your development vision and personal service vision. While family and friends are always an important source of support, as we discussed in Chapter 4, many of your family members and friends may not even understand what you do, let alone know how best to support you when you feel discouraged. That kind of support is likely to be more readily available through the communities of understanding you create and/or participate in with your professional colleagues. Finding kindred spirits there is not always straightforward. A lot will depend on your vision, its complexity, and how it deviates from existing approaches and communities. GW student Jason Berry has already begun to struggle with this. *I guess I will have to work harder than most others to find a supportive "community of understanding" that not only shares my* [environmental] *conservation goals, but also my conviction that participatory, sustainable development is the key to conservation.* Creating networks of support requires that you be proactive—you have to make an effort to identify people and discuss these ideas.

Your support network may comprise family and friends, members of professional associations, and colleagues in your professional networks and within your organization or in other less obvious places, as we'll discuss in Chapter 9. Especially if you're based overseas, you might rely on Internet discussion forums and listservs—of friends, interest groups, or like-minded professionals. Communities surrounding your hobbies and personal interests can also be a good source of support.

The Promise and Reward of Working in Community

A lifestyle and career of service is not possible outside of community. First, as our profiled practitioners attest, you can't be effective on your own. Alone, you lack sufficient understanding of the need, the obstacles, the incentives, and the techniques for creating change. Second, who would want to go it alone when the challenges are so great and you face so many disappointments along the way? And with whom would you share the joy of accomplishment?

An appreciation of the power of community emerges through reflection and experience. GW student Tara Hill shared a bit of her path. *I realized my freshman year in college, as a service project leader, that though I had at first wanted to "save the world" by myself, working towards change with others would be a much more effective way to learn about and achieve progress in our world. I think it was that realization which led me to work with others in an Americorps program and then as an Americorps program officer.* Similarly, GW student Jennifer Villemez declared, *I have little interest in founding my own organization. To the contrary, I believe that greater collaboration and partnership in the field of international development is essential for efforts to be successful. Development work requires such a range of issues to be addressed that it only seems natural for organizations with specific expertise to work together to achieve broader goals.*

Public service—however you define and enact it, whether as trying to "save the world," making life better for one village or family, or (for some of you) founding your own NGO—combines the noble, the ambitious, and the mundane. Your individual efforts matter, but the message of this chapter is that those efforts can rarely succeed in a vacuum. Public service is, by definition, a communal endeavor. Greater effectiveness and reward are found in working with and in community, regardless of the national borders, organizational boundaries, and definitions or expectations of service that may separate us. You have already read some of the lessons Najma Siddiqi identified from her experience working in community. Her story encompasses many and varied communities of understanding.

Notes

1. Community is usually defined geographically, as a group of people who live in the same area, or the area where they live. Community can also refer to a group of people who have some kind of common background, particular characteristics, or shared interest.

2. For more on Paulo Freire see recommended selected biographies to explore, Appendix 4. For further discussion of the role of the change agent, see Stan Burkey's chapter, "Agents of Change" (see recommended reading on community development and empowerment, Appendix 4).

3. From Kamla Bhasin's book, *Breaking Barriers: A South Asian Experience of Training for Participatory Development* (Bangkok: Food and Agriculture Organization, 1978), quoted in Burkey (see recommended reading on community development and empowerment, Appendix 4).

4. The International Association of Public Participation (IAP2) is an example of a learning and exchange network that brings together US and international professionals for the kind of sharing that Tara advocates. See http://www.iap2.org.

Profile 3. Najma Siddiqi:
Working for Change at Home and Abroad

Najma Siddiqi is a Pakistani woman who went to a Home Economics College and ended up working in senior management in the Environmentally and Socially Sustainable Development (ESSD) Vice President's Office at the World Bank. *I'm not a career person at all. And I have done really what I wanted to do. I reacted, I think, initially to the society I saw around me. I reacted to things that I saw around me and I wanted to change them. That's how it started.* Initially, it was about reacting to her inability to play soccer with the boys at her coed primary school. Later, it became much, much more. Whether in Pakistan, Denmark, Nepal, or now in a broad range of World Bank borrower countries, *wherever I'm coming from, it's both from inside and outside to change—to understand the complexities and then try to change what are the controlling factors and to bring about something which expands the ability of people to control their own lives and shape their own future.*

Najma's service orientation comes, in part, from her father. Her family migrated from India to Pakistan in 1947 when her father opted for service in Pakistan. *He was the only one from his family who came. He left everything behind. Probably that is one of the values that is inculcated in me: that you give to something that you believe in. He believed in the new country and he opted to serve there.* So he transitioned from the Indian Taxation Service to the Pakistan Taxation Service, and later became the Director of the Finance Services Academy in Pakistan.

Najma's earliest reactions concerned how girls were treated differently from boys. Happily, this was less of a concern in her immediate family, where she and her sister were the last of nine children and the only girls. So it is somewhat ironic that she ended up in the newly established, Ford Foundation-supported College of Home Economics. *I saw it as preparing women for their real career in life, which is to get married and be a good wife to the elite in the society—because it was an expensive college, only a few people could go there.* But pressure mounted from her father and from her sister, who was two years ahead of her and had joined this college herself. In the end Najma assented. *I tried my level best to fail. I managed to do quite badly in the second year, but I didn't quite fail. So I couldn't leave. But by then I also said, "Okay, why am I fighting this? Let's get on with life."* Najma gained a broad liberal arts education and was able to choose courses on child psychology and education. She eventually earned her master's degree in education administration from the College as well.

Najma (along with her sister) then accepted an offer to work as a research scholar at the National Institute of Public Administration

(NIPA). This did not endear her to her father, who had come to believe that his girls shouldn't join the workforce. And it didn't help that she cut off her hair to make life simpler for herself! With the support of her mother, Najma continued to work at the NIPA and led the work on a USAID contract concerning family planning practices. The work entailed focus group discussions at the community level with both men and women in five districts (of central Punjab). Having completed the project, Najma decided to pursue a second master's degree in clinical psychology at Government College. After several months of study, she wanted more direct experience and took a voluntary position at Fountain House, a halfway house for schizophrenic patients. *I think that is also part of my reaction to society: "Okay, the society does this to people. So let me work with these people." And somehow, having worked with those people, and having brought some to a certain level where they were ready to go back in their own locations, I realized that they couldn't make it. The society hadn't changed, so of course, you have to do something about society.* By then, her eldest brother, who was Secretary of Education, was dismissed from service when he refused to consider locating a girl's college preferentially rather than based on need. This confirmed to her that serving through government is not always what service ought to be.

Soon afterwards, Najma married a colleague from the psychology department, and joined him in Denmark for a six-month exchange program in Clinical Psychology and Psychiatry. There, she began working with migrant women and children. She started as a school psychologist for the commune (a local municipality in the Danish government system) where they lived. *Looking at the system I said, "Why are we labeling these guys? The problem is not with them. The problem is elsewhere." So I was there, I saw this, and I said, "Hey, I need to do something here."* Their professor encouraged her, suggesting that they do the work together in the context of pursuing a doctorate. He helped her secure funding, including a one-and-a-half-year Danish International Development Agency (DANIDA) fellowship, and sponsorship from a group of bankers. Najma returned to Pakistan for the birth of her son, and then came back to Denmark to work with the migrant community.

She reflected critically on the psychology profession, and how psychology is used as a political weapon. Psychologists can support authorities in the view that *"I know more about your mind than you do. Therefore, I am in a better position to control you." We used the tools that we have not to help people but to label them, and to marginalize them, or to include them, or to change them.* Her second focus area was on resources. Many resources were allocated in the name of migrants, but what happened to them? How were they being used? Pakistani migrants in Denmark were mostly from the middle peasant community, educated to some extent but with little or no Danish language skills. They worked largely in menial factory jobs. *They were basically blind to what was happening to them in that society.* Dreaming of going home, they were not preparing their children for life in either country. Women were at a particular disadvantage. Even though they were working as wage earners, just like their husbands, they were still expected to perform their traditional roles, and remain subservient to men. In some cases, they were expected to wait on their husbands' mistresses; in other instances, the husbands had them declared insane and shipped back to Pakistan so they could marry anew. Najma also explored the migrant women's use of contraceptives, especially abortion. *They didn't have the language; they didn't have the confidence; they didn't know what to do. They were not using contraception, the men didn't want them to, but they would use abortion. And then the society, without their knowing it, would sterilize them on the basis that they "breed like rats"—which is what one of the rightist party politicians in Denmark had said officially.*

Aside from the Social Ministry of Denmark, where she had been training health workers and teachers in how to work with the migrant community, Najma didn't make many friends through her work. The Pakistani Embassy was particularly unhappy, as was the local commune. *It became pretty nasty, to the extent of stones being thrown at our apartment, and by the local commune sort of trashing me and, then, threats to my son.* So after two years, Najma decided it was best for her and her family to return to Pakistan.

At the invitation of a family friend, she and her husband took jobs with the Overseas Pakistani Foundation (OPF), a semiautonomous entity under the Ministry of Labour, where the friend was working to establish a welfare program. It had been a difficult time in Pakistan, where former President Zulfikar Ali Bhutto had recently been hanged by the military regime. Najma, like many others, had participated in a related demonstration in Denmark, where, she later learned, a snapshot had been taken of her and her family. This was in addition to the displeasure of the Pakistani Embassy officials in Denmark, who were concerned that the work she initiated had made the immigrant communities more vocal, hence increasing problems for the Embassy. Within six months at the OPF, political accusations had been made against her. A series of investigations followed. She resigned when the matter was finally settled, but her resignation was not accepted, and she continued to work there for two years. *I joined because we could do a lot of stuff. But then we couldn't do what we really wanted to do. At some points, you were supposed to rubber stamp, at some points you were supposed to write what you were told to write, and at some points you were supposed to follow, toe the line. I don't want to do that.* Najma left the Ministry, but her husband stayed on. Soon afterwards, they parted.

The International Labour Organization (ILO), which had previously expressed an interest in Najma, hired her to direct a project promoting self-employment for female-headed households in southern Pakistan. *We, of course, did what we wanted to do. We focused on rural women and building their skills to earn a livelihood, improve their standards of living, but also to improve their own conditions of life, which goes beyond the standards of living.* During this time, Najma met and married her current husband, who also joined the project. Her choice of working in the South raised suspicions, because this was considered "Bhutto territory." The situation became politically intense, and her husband was picked up for questioning. Najma was advised by friends that it would be best that they leave the country as soon as they could. So she took her family with her to attend an ILO conference in Malaysia, and did not return for several years. After a few months in Kuala Lumpur, the ILO offered her a four-month position in Nepal, where they stayed for the next five years.

In Nepal, she became advisor to the Ministry of Panchayat and Local Development, working through the regional coordinating office in India, which also oversaw some projects in Bangladesh and Pakistan. During that time, the Aga Khan Rural Support Program (AKRSP) invited her to Pakistan to review their women's program, after which they asked her to to take a lead position in the program. After completing some work in Nepal she returned to Pakistan with the intention of remaining, but could not stay long for medical reasons. She returned to Nepal and took ILO consultancies for various projects. *You know, just picking up things at random and saying, "I can probably make a difference here."* But after some time, she *decided that I needed to be more in the middle of the action than I was. I was an advisor, although I was not the kind of advisor that you would expect, of course. I was putting my nose into everything. But I was ready for a change.*

Najma wrote a couple of proposals for what she thought she wanted to do next and sent them around to her friends and acquaintances. One of her early ILO contacts was now at the Institute for Social Studies (ISS) in The Hague. What she really wanted to do was a project, but the ISS offered her a four-year fellowship to pursue her ideas through a doctorate. By then, Najma and her husband had both been offered jobs with AKRSP, and her husband preferred that option. But Najma wanted something different, and headed to The Hague. The doctorate there required a public seminar, which normally takes about eighteen months to complete. Missing her son, Najma quickly completed her seminar and returned to Pakistan after only nine months. AKRSP had deferred her position, so she was able to start work there right away. The plan was to return to The Hague to write up the dissertation after one year, but Najma had immersed herself in her work, her mother's illness took a serious turn, and she never returned. *I had my commitments, personal and professional, I mean to my work. I couldn't take another break. So I stayed on.*

After two years at AKRSP, Najma felt the program was stagnating. She and her husband resigned and they moved to Islamabad, where their son was about to start high school. They did a number of consultancies, and Najma founded the Association for Development of Human Resources in response to numerous requests to train staff and community activists of other development programs. *When I resigned from AKRSP all of my colleagues from the different programs, who knew me, said, "Hey, this is a great chance to set up this thing." So we set it up.* Many of these organizations *didn't have the capacity, and the people with that kind of passion for working to help people meet their potential. So they sent their staff to us for training.*

But it wasn't long before Najma received a message from Shoaib Sultan Khan, the head of AKRSP. He was on the Board of the National Rural Support Program (NRSP) and had been asked by the political government at the time to expand the program in all parts of the country. The government wanted an NGO to organize people so they could absorb the services offered by the government's own Social Action Program. They were looking for a General Manager and Chief Executive of that program. Najma insisted on a transparent hiring process. *I said, "Okay, let's announce it, let's advertise. Prove to me that I'm the best person. I will apply. And if you guys think that it will work, I'll take it."* A panel of senior civil servants interviewed and hired her. But this, too, was not an easy path.

NRSP was registered as a private company. As such, it was autonomous from the government, but not subject to the NGO registration laws. Still, the Board of Directors was composed of many senior civil servants, as well as internationally recognized social mobilization experts, who all served in their capacity as private citizens (not representatives of their agencies). *It gave us some protection. It gave us the opportunity and the excuse to do what we wanted to do, and yet to work very closely with the government, which was a big thing.* A lot of money was involved. One billion rupees had been committed for the first year; and NRSP had received half of that amount. At approximately fifty rupees to the dollar, this was around $10 million.

There were five changes of government in the first year and a half of NRSP's expanded phase, and given the stakes, the situation became highly politicized. Not surprisingly, the remaining half of the committed funding was never received. *Since the money was first allocated by the Sharif Government, the* [Benazir] *Bhutto government felt that we were building a constituency for ourselves, and that we were eating away the money. I was approached for a fifty percent deal. And I said, "You must be joking." To be fair to them, they had actually thought that we had eaten up half the money anyway, so we should just give them the remaining half. And I said, "No, it's all sitting there. We are living off the income of the money." And that meant that they became even more interested.*

Najma began receiving pressure from a number of sources, including a senior civil servant who claimed to be a former student of her father's. *I said, "If you were my father's student, you should know where I come from. I come from a different set of values. You've got the wrong person. You have to install another person if you want to work the way you want to work."* In fact, Najma was quite serious in suggesting that she be replaced. The "offer" was reduced from fifty percent to ten percent, and other forms of pressure were exerted. The program was investigated by the Prime Minister's Inspection Commission, who after four months found nothing negative to report. But that wasn't all. *My finance manager was held at gunpoint; some of my staff were beaten up. I was threatened, my son was threatened. Some of my senior staff came to me and said, "We'll take a salary cut. We will take only a third of the salary."* And these are very small salaries. *"Let's return the money. Let's generate funds from elsewhere and get the government off our backs."* Beyond the money, she and the board were also pressured to make specific hiring decisions. *So one story was, "Give us the money" directly, and the other was, "Take our instructions."* This was very reminiscent of her brother's experience in the Ministry of Education, yet NRSP was supposed to be independent.

Najma recognized that the increasing pressure was making the work suffer. *I remember when I took the final decision. I was under a lot of pressure. My son didn't know the threats to either my life or his. He just knew that he was being controlled and protected. Finally, I told him. This was during his finals and his prom, and I told him he had to go with this person and come back in that car. I said, "I can't avoid that. I can't allow you to be on your own." And so he turned around and he said, "So why don't you quit?" And I thought, "That's such an interesting question. I never thought of that." So that started me thinking.* Another major concern was for her field staff. *Young men and women, living in these one-room places, out in the remote areas, totally unprotected.* If that wasn't enough, there were scandalous newspaper stories about family connections, "lavish" salaries, luxurious lifestyles, and even promoting "prostitution," with posters being placed on the walls of the NRSP Head Office. Since there was no truth in these stories, Najma chose not to confront them. The final straw was when the board decided to agree to some of the government's "suggestions." *And I said, "That's it." I wrote my resignation. I thought about it, and then I handed it in.*

Najma returned full-time to the Association for Development of Human Resources, until she received a phone call from a friend who was working at the World Bank. Her husband was already doing short-term consultancies for the World Bank. Now that they were both available, her friend had called to see if he could interest them in moving to Washington. Her husband took the opportunity, and Najma stayed in Pakistan for the next several months until her son finished high school. Then, she came to Washington with the intention of staying four months to get her son settled in an American university.

While in Washington, another friend from Aga Kahn Foundation, who now worked at the Bank, called her up to see if she was applying for the position in the Bank's NGO Unit. She hadn't even known about it, and it was the last day to apply. She was not quite convinced and reluctantly submitted her resume. *It was the whole interview process that really impressed me. I always used to say, "They played a trick on me, because they got the best people in the Bank lined up to interview, rather than the run of the mill. So I got tricked into it." Fantastic people. Obviously, I thought, "The Bank is a great place to be."* Najma became an NGO Specialist in the NGO Unit. At that time, the agenda was to influence senior management and task team leaders, encouraging them and showing them how to work effectively with NGOs. This, of course, required a strong emphasis on educating staff about what NGOs are, how they operate, and what they might have to offer to Bank Operations.

Najma's approach was to first learn about the Bank. *The way I operate is to look at what exists and then try to push the walls a little bit, rather than try to demolish something before knowing what it is. I like to understand the roots and work at the roots. And this sounds ominous: I work at eroding the roots rather than knocking down the structure. Because if you knock down the structure, and the roots are there, it will grow back.* She has now worked in the Bank, in various capacities, for eight years. Structures have evolved around her, with many reorganizations, and she has taken advantage of these changes to look for new opportunities to create change. *I came with the title "NGO Specialist." I have shed it. I've shed several titles over this time. I'm a person who is really assertively and consciously looking for different paths. Where can I make a move? I don't want to say difference, because you don't always make a difference. But which path can I take which can create the kind of situation for myself and for others that I want to create?* From early on, Najma took on the learning agenda of the various departments and groups with which she worked. This included the training of the World Bank's newly established group of NGO Liaison Officers in the Resident Missions (she organized the first global forum in 1997); training on participation and civic engagement in support of the Poverty Reduction Strategy Paper process initiated in 2000 (a process required for debt relief); piloting capacity needs assessments and civic engagement courses for government officials and citizens in client countries with the Community Empowerment and Social Inclusion Teams;

and acting as the Learning Coordinator for the Social Development Department, working to promote shared understanding and collaboration across units. Najma was recently appointed as the Knowledge Sharing and Learning Coordinator for the ESSD Network, based in the Vice President's Office.

In reflecting on her career at the Bank so far, Najma adds: *To give the Bank its due, I joined one year after Wolfensohn opened up the Bank. The Bank started looking for profiles like ours. It wasn't just the NGO Unit. That's when the Social Development Family came into place. There are so many of us now, in the Bank. Now we come from different perspectives. We come from anthropology backgrounds, or we come from sociology backgrounds, or political science. . . . But the profile of the Bank has changed—not as much as it should, but it has changed over the past five or six years, and that credit goes to Wolfensohn. He has created spaces. There is a lot of space in the Bank. If you know what you want to do, you can get around to doing it. You know it's a huge bureaucracy, so you can find pockets—pockets of excellence, pockets of stagnation, pockets of resources, pockets of poverty. You can find everything. It's a matter of building the right alliances and finding your way to do what you want to do. Really. That's how I feel about it. And that's how I can continue to do work for change. And I mean work—it's hard work to get satisfaction. I want to make that point.*

CHAPTER 6

Skills and Skill Building

You have your vision, and you know you need to work with others in community. What skills and knowledge should you acquire and how?[1] Skills and knowledge relate to the tools and process facets of development management. They encompass both technical knowledge and skills—specific to a particular sector such as health, education, the environment, or governance—as well as process knowledge, such as how to work with others (emotional intelligence), participatory processes, and process consultation. As with all steps along the service-choice spiral, acquiring skills and knowledge is not a one-time event, but a lifelong process. And it relates to all of the other components of the service-choice spiral.

As we discussed in Chapter 4, in considering the skills and knowledge necessary to your service vision, you have to begin with understanding where you are now. What preferences, skills, and knowledge do you currently have? From there you can begin to identify the gaps and determine a course of action for acquiring those skills and knowledge necessary to effectively pursue your service vision. For some of you, this may rest primarily on your preferences for where you think you want to go with your career. Others of you may be mid career and may be contemplating a career transition. Some of your current knowledge and skills will be transferable, so you'll need to explore how and what other knowledge and skills you will need.

Looking at these gaps between what you know now and what you need to know is a continuous process. In the short run, applying your existing knowledge and skills is likely to feel good because you know it's something you do well. But in the longer run, will you be satisfied? And will you continue to be effective? Most of us aspire to continuously learn and grow. So, even if you're satisfied with applying your current knowledge and skill set for now, you may discover that 1) it's not sufficient for doing the best you can in reaching your service objectives, and 2) it becomes boring after awhile. What may be important to know and to learn is something your communities of understanding can help you to identify (as you can help other members of these communities). Again, they provide feedback, like a mirror, to tell you what you may be doing right and what you may need to improve upon. Your closest colleagues and allies may also recognize when your service work has lost its luster because you aren't sufficiently challenged anymore. Your service communities can be an excellent forum for exploring together why something may not be working as well as it could, and what you can do to make improvements.

You may also want to acquire certain skills and knowledge, based on your own preferences and belief that they are necessary to your service vision. For example, if you know you want to relieve physical suffering, but you don't necessarily want to work in a clinic or hospital ministering to individual patients, you may choose to pursue a graduate degree in public health. If you recognize the ideas and technology that can help in relieving people's suffering but are frustrated because the systems of delivery don't seem to be working, you might decide to pursue a master's degree in public administration. Once you're on the job, you may discover there are other areas of skills and knowledge that you need to do your job well. For example, if you're in public health, you may realize that you need a deeper understanding of how policy processes shape the agendas for what you can do. If your degree is in public administration and you find yourself working in poverty alleviation, perhaps on microenterprise, you might decide you need a deeper understanding of economics and finance.

In this chapter, we discuss general skills and knowledge necessary to effective international public service. We also touch on more specific technical areas you may want to pursue. And, we get to the "how" question: how can you acquire the necessary skills and knowledge? On that, we provide a brief overview of formal training programs, focusing on academic degree programs, and internships. Contact information for selected degree programs and internships can be found in Appendices 2 and 3[2]. It's essential to understand that neither this discussion nor the accompanying appendices are exhaustive. There are many, many other specific skills sets and related degree and internship programs besides those we discuss here. Our purpose throughout the book is to provide you with some initial options to consider as you begin to reflect on your own vision and path. As our profiled practitioners make clear, each path is unique and the greatest rewards come to those who are proactive in seizing opportunities and creatively pursuing new and existing options, corresponding to their own service vision.

What Skills?

As we emphasized in Chapter 4, your values are an important motivator and sustainer of your service work. One challenge, though, is to balance your humanitarian impulses with getting the job done. The latter refers both to working within the confines of an industry that may not always be consistent with your values and vision, and applying technical skills to your work. The necessary skills and knowledge include: 1) a general understanding of the lay-of-the-land in terms of how things work; 2) technical skills and tools, some of which are process and management oriented; and 3) people skills, sometimes referred to as emotional intelligence, which are the glue that brings the other skills and knowledge areas together, making them most effective. The range of skills and knowledge can be intimidating. No one is expected to master all of them at the start of a career or solely through one training/education effort. Many of these represent a lifetime of skills and knowledge acquisition, a process you have already started, and many will be acquired on the job. The following discussion can assist you in being more strategic and proactive in your skills and knowledge development.

General Knowledge and Skills

Generally, a successful career in international public service requires knowledge of geography, and the histories and cultures of regions outside of your own. For some, this may mean becoming an expert in a particular region or country. For others, a general foundation of understanding will suffice and then you can invest in more in-depth knowledge as opportunities emerge to specialize. The way the industry works, you may not be able to predict where you will end up and for how long, so unless you become a specialist—and even if you do—you'll need to acquire country-specific knowledge along the way. Situations are constantly changing and you will need to continuously learn about the contexts in which you work, including how transnational issues affect them. For example, who would have predicted in the 1960s and 1970s that we would be providing development assistance to the former Soviet Union and Eastern Europe in the 1990s?

And this isn't just about reading through the CIA (Central Intelligence Agency) Factbook for a country. Beyond the dry facts, you have to have some inkling of the culture. As a modest start—and an entertaining supplement to the hard-core facts—we recommend you see movies and read novels from the country you will work in. These will never give you a complete picture, nor a sufficient understanding, but they can certainly sensitize you to some cultural features and cultivate your appreciation for them. More helpful, accept every invitation to dine in people's homes, and offer your counterparts the same opportunities. Inviting someone into your home not only provides a unique view into local culture, it is also symbolically important in nurturing relationships and understanding.

Related to the history and culture of a particular region or country, we are often asked, "Do I really have to learn a foreign language? And which ones are most important?" The common language of the industry—and increasingly the industrialized world—is English. And that's fine if you want to stay Washington-based or you only want to work with the most professionally educated counterparts. To give yourself the widest options, however, speaking a second (or a third) language is crucial. And this doesn't mean that you become fluent in every language you're exposed to. But developing some linguistic skills so you can begin to decipher at least some of the written or spoken word and transfer those skills to other languages and contexts is very helpful.

Much also depends on which language you choose. Let's face it, if you are an Anglo-Saxon American, you can take all the Spanish classes you can find and still not compete with the many, many highly qualified Latin Americans and native speakers in the international development industry. Don't misinterpret. We're not suggesting you stop studying Spanish (or French). You will still have many more opportunities with good skills in these languages than without. On the other hand, we've all heard about the increased demand for Arabic and Chinese speakers. So competitiveness based on language skills varies according to the demands of a particular moment in history and may be specific to the countries where your service interests lead you.

In our conversations with employers, we hear that if all other things are equal, the candidate who speaks the language will get the job. As Sarah Newhall put it, *it's always seen as an additional asset rather than a bottom line. If we could get more language skills around here, it moves people up. If two candidates are otherwise equal, we'll take the one with foreign languages.* But all other things are not often equal, so even without the language you can have a good shot at the job. This is most likely for jobs where your technical expertise outweighs the importance of language, where the position is one that will entail working in multiple countries and languages, or where the language is somewhat obscure and few people with the required expertise would be expected to speak it.

Language skills are much more important than their immediate functional benefits. Anyone who has worked with a translator—and we've worked with many (for example, Russian, Chinese, Mongolian, Uzbek, Hindi, Malagasy, Arabic, and Bulgarian)—can tell you how frustrating it is to spend intensive time with people, maybe even over the course of several years, and not be able to speak casually with them or build a direct and less formal relationship. Especially in a cross-cultural context, much learning occurs outside the workplace. The social hour after work can be invaluable to understanding what your colleagues are really thinking and what drives them (and, therefore, how to best mobilize them). But the social part of that hour requires communication in a common language. Sarah Newhall also emphasizes the symbolic importance of learning another language. *I think foreign language skills are an invaluable skill. It makes you more a citizen of the world. Pragmatically, if you asked, do you need to know a second language* [other than English] *in this world? The answer is no. Does it enrich one's experience? Yes. And anything you can do to demonstrate that you're putting yourself in another person's shoes is good. So whenever you're doing your work and people see that you're struggling with their language, it's an indicator that you're trying to come closer. It's the connectivity thing. It puts a smile on people's face around the world.*

Jennifer Butz (Profile 6) has nurtured relationships based on respect and trust with her Albanian staff, in part through her use of language. She doesn't speak Albanian fluently, but she speaks and understands it well enough to enrich her staff training, among other things. In her training and periodic strategic planning workshops, she delivers her message in English, but takes questions in Albanian. This not only ensures comfort with each person's communication abilities, it also helps to confirm shared understanding and symbolizes a mutual effort and equality from a cultural standpoint, even if she is still the boss.

Anywhere you land—figuratively and literally—you have to know how things work. Who are the major players? What is the process of decision making? How are programs designed and implemented? As Aaron Williams (Profile 4) states, *there's no substitute for understanding your business. In the case of AID, you need to know contracting. You need to understand project design, the way you put a project together. If logframe* [the Logical Framework] *is the tool being used, know how to use that logframe better than anybody else. You need to know why evaluation is important. You need to understand how you bring in all the players in any particular sector, so you have a broad picture of what the development problem is, the issue you're trying to focus on. I always felt I had a pretty good command of all the elements that were important, whether it was contracting, or project design or evaluation or analysis of certain technical sectors. I reached out to people who had expertise in areas I did not have: health, education, whatever it happened to be.*

This last point confirms an often overlooked element of knowing the lay-of-the-land—knowing what you know is only one piece of the puzzle; you also have to know what you don't know. So while you can't be expected to become an expert in every facet of your chosen service area, you have to have enough proficiency to speak some of the technical language, know how everything fits together, and know what you don't know. Jef Buehler (Profile 5) provides a list of the various areas of expertise required for the Main Street Program, including economic development, macroeconomics and microeconomics, housing finance, historic preservation, political science, community organizing, community development, cross-cultural communication, architecture, public law, streetscape designing, special events management, marketing, public relations, and volunteer recruitment and management. Having a multidisciplinary background, as opposed to a sole area of expertise, can help you to be more flexible in dealing with the challenges that may emerge in the context of your work. It also helps for what one of our colleagues calls "scenario thinking," or seeing the big picture and how it all fits together, now and for the future.

You also need to know how important players think, as well as how to benefit from their knowledge. These may include some people whom you wouldn't necessarily consider important. For example, Aaron Williams emphasizes the need *to reach out to a very important group of people in any organization, especially government, and that's the lawyers. You have to know how the lawyers think. Most people tend to avoid and try not to be closely aligned with them. I found them to be my greatest allies. Especially because these are very creative people who are interested in trying to do innovative thinking and providing the analysis and the legal framework to pursue your ideas. Especially when you are trying to pioneer an innovation—and that's what change is about, right?—those whom you may see as your greatest obstacles can become key advocates and problem solvers.* Jennifer discovered this in her research on innovative partnerships within the World Bank. *I found that the most successful partnerships were the ones where the manager sought legal and administrative advice and support from the outset. With this assistance, they designed programs and legal agreements that no one could poke holes in, leaving their path to implementation unobstructed.* So knowing the lay of the land includes knowing who holds what power and how to access it. Our focus group confirmed the centrality of building a grasp of the political environment in which you're trying to make change.

General knowledge also includes knowing the vocabulary of the industry, your particular sector of expertise, and your organization and its network. For example, in USAID the current lingo for programming and project management includes the R4 and the results framework. R4 refers to Results Review and Resource Request, which builds on an analysis of progress as mapped in a program's Results Framework.[3] The Results Framework is based on the Logical Framework, which specifies goals and targets within a predetermined time frame. Results Frameworks specify how Missions and Washington bureaus intend to achieve their SOs and IRs (strategic objectives and intermediate results). Based on these, USAID develops projects where the work to be done is described in SOWs (scopes of work) or TORs (terms of reference). Whew! And if that weren't enough, the terminology changes with new administrations and reform efforts. In the past USAID used to talk about PIDs (project identification documents) and PPs (project papers) instead of Results Frameworks. Other international development terminology includes the World Bank's PRSPs (Poverty Reduction Strategy Papers) and the UN's MDGs (Millennium Development Goals). Don't let it intimidate you. The many acronyms often have to be learned on the job. One tactic is to write down each one as you hear it and then take the list to a colleague for definitions. This way, you don't disrupt meetings or feel embarrassed asking about something everyone else knows. Derick did this when he joined USAID.

Beyond terminology and the particularities of your employer, you also need an understanding of how the industry as a whole operates. Where does the funding come from? How is it awarded? What types of contracting arrangements are used? Regardless of where you choose to work (the subject of Chapter 7), you need to have a working knowledge of the different sectors—public (governmental and intergovernmental), private commercial (e.g., for-profit consulting firms, multinational corporations), and nonprofit or NGO. What role does each of these play in your particular service area? What advantages does each of them offer? How do they work together? This is an area where Aaron Williams excels, having worked in all three sectors. His career clearly demonstrates the advantages of knowing the ins and outs of the other sectors, being in a position to broker relations among them, and at the same time increasing his own opportunities to do new and interesting things in his career as he shifts from one sector to another.

There are also several general skill areas that are as important to international public service as they are to any career today. These include communication skills, including public speaking and especially writing skills; public relations skills; computer skills, specifically proficiency in the most common software programs (e.g., Microsoft Word, Excel, and Powerpoint); and time management skills.

We encourage you to take every opportunity to practice and develop your writing and public speaking skills. Try to publish, even if it is only letters to the editor of a newspaper, or a contribution to a professional association's newsletter. Speak at conferences, or volunteer to give brown-bag lunch presentations in the organization where you work. The more you do it, the easier it becomes. You can do a lot to develop these skills through formal training, but your communications skills will still need to be tailored on the job. If you're lucky, you'll have a coach or mentor to help you along, as Jennifer Butz (Profile 6) did. *I had this boss at the Asia Foundation. I think I probably had to buy him a box of red Bic pencils annually, because they bled all over my writing. But he really honed my writing skills. Later, at the Harwood Group, my boss told me I was a recovering academic. His approach was to be very quick and street smart, but to convey subtle insights. So I completely changed my writing style, and it's now somewhere in between. That was good, because it started me thinking about audience and perception, and how to shape my material—the craftsmanship side of presentations. One of the things practitioners don't do well is tell their stories, because they're so busy doing. That's fine and noble, except it won't get you funding.*

Obviously, these general knowledge and skill areas are not enough. You also need to have a more readily recognizable ability to add value through technical skills, as discussed in Chapter 5. And the two are not mutually exclusive. Your more general knowledge of the lay-of-the-land can be enhanced through the application of those technical skills and tools, including diagnostic tools such as stakeholder analysis, and SWOT analysis (analysis of internal strengths and weaknesses and external opportunities and threats) for starters.

Technical Skills

Technical skills are often referred to as "hard" skills. They are typically easily recognizable and often linked to sets of diagnostic, analytic, and evaluative tools. We have found that some of our students who are motivated by normative concerns for combating poverty and promoting empowerment bring with them an aversion to learning the hard technical skill sets. International public service requires a basic understanding of economics, budgeting, financial management, planning and evaluation, policy analysis, and performance measurement and management, as well as process tools such as facilitation, negotiation, and conflict resolution. For example, the young professionals in our focus group stressed the importance of knowledge of economics and budgeting in their current jobs, if only to be able to understand the bigger picture and to interact meaningfully and collaboratively with your colleagues. In addition, knowledge and skills specific to technical sectors, such as health, family planning, education, agriculture, food security, humanitarian assistance, and so on are called for. Development organizations often require a sophisticated understanding of, if not specific skills in, fundraising (including proposal writing), development education, and advocacy. Increasingly, no matter what your particular job is, you need to have skills in evaluation, including quantitative methods and survey

Table 6.1   A Sample of Skills and Competencies Called for in International Public Service Employment Announcements

Skill/Competency Categories	Number of Mentions	As Percentage of Total Job Listings*
Technical and Sectoral Expertise and Experience	420	77.1
Management and Leadership	226	41.5
Project and Program Planning and Implementation	312	57.2
Financial Management and Budgeting	119	21.8
Language Proficiency Required or Recommended	142	26.1
Monitoring and Evaluation	75	13.8
Fundraising	87	16.0

*Total number of employment announcements = 545

design. And basic management skills are always necessary. As Aaron Williams notes, you will need to learn the specific tools required by your field and your employer.

Just to give you an idea, we looked at a sample of job announcements from *Monday Developments*, the newsletter of InterAction, the association of US international development NGOs.[4] We coded 545 positions from 13 issues to identify whether the announcement called for technical and/or sectoral expertise/experience (including public administration and governance), management and/or leadership skills, project or program planning competencies, financial management and budgeting skills, language proficiency, monitoring and evaluation expertise, knowledge of economics, and fundraising ability/experience. These categories are not mutually exclusive, so the sum total for the skills areas is greater than the number of positions.

No matter how technical you see your role or position to be, you will still need basic proficiency in all of the more general skill areas. While management is sometimes referred to as having a generalist emphasis, it, too, encompasses specific technical knowledge, skills, and tools that should not be taken for granted. Some of you may choose to specialize and make a career out of these administrative and management skills, but you will still need a basic understanding of the technical area of your program(s) and organization.

Determining which path is best for you can be a long process, as illustrated by GW student Olivia Tecosky's experience. *I came back to school to become an expert in a particular area so that I would be more "useful" in development. I chose international health as my concentration because much of what I am interested in is in some way related to health and the destructive synergy between poverty and ill health. What I am discovering is that while learning very particular skills in public health, I will not gain deep expertise in* [the medical] *field by learning the foundations and basic tenets on which it relies. The other component of my course of study is development, where I also find it difficult to describe myself as an expert or in any way approaching expertise. Rather, the field itself is instructing me to approach contexts with an eye towards learning more about those contexts and learning from them, thereby expanding my own knowledge and allowing me to work within the context to effect positive change. Within the first couple of weeks of classes in development, and with the realization that I am moving in the opposite direction from my former aspirations towards expertise, I had a bit of a crisis and thought: why don't I just go to medical school? It didn't take long for me to remember the motivation for my interest in development, and realize that another set of school bills would not in fact help me get closer to expertise in development.*

Olivia's reflection underscores that the skills you need are dependent on your personal service vision, and that just because you want to work in a technical area, such as health, doesn't mean you have to become a technical service deliverer, such as a doctor, to do so. On the other hand, technical expertise can be relative to the context at hand. You may not be formally trained in a technical area, but don't discount the expertise you may have acquired on the job. If no one knows about conservation and you happen to have worked in a conservation organization, you are probably the relevant expert. And, in any case, you are likely to bring other comparative expertise to the technical sector at hand.

Perhaps some of you may not initially recognize the value of process and discovery inherent in international development. Perhaps you feel you are not an expert or properly trained if you don't have identifiable "hard" skills. We hope that our discussion has helped you to broaden your conception of technical skills and other knowledge necessary for international public service, most importantly, what it means to become an effective development manager. The discussion would be incomplete, without addressing a more subtle area of skills, those concerning people, including you.

People Skills

Regardless of which path you choose, you will always need skills related to working with people. Ironically, these people skills are often referred to as "soft" skills, when in fact, they are the most difficult to learn. Research demonstrates that these skills, sometimes referred to as emotional intelligence (EI), are essential, perhaps not to acquiring your first job, but definitely for advancing to increasing levels of responsibility and influence.[5] The component of EI that most readily comes to mind is relationship management, consisting of influence, communication, leadership, conflict management, networking, collaboration, and team skills. Working for change, especially since it entails working in community, requires the ability to mutually inspire and lead. Sarah Newhall's experience at Pact is illustrative. *Nobody is locked into a straightforward job description. Or you have a job description, it doesn't really define one's day. So the people who fail here, fail because they don't have interpersonal communication skills. It's almost never lack of intelligence that gets people into trouble. It's other kinds of interpersonal dysfunction. They can't listen. They can't communicate.* As we note in Chapter 5, an essential skill to working in community is listening.

Sarah goes on to say, *the absolute bottom-line skill is the ability to work in teams. Because people can't do the lone ranger thing anymore, the problems are too complex. Everything we do here at Pact takes teams.* Najma Siddiqi observes, *you have to work with all kinds of people, you have to understand all kinds of interests, and you have to start working from there.* Based on our own experience, and confirmed by everyone we talked to in our research for this book—employers and seasoned practitioners, advisors, and teachers—team skills are the most important for you to learn, regardless of where you choose to work. Depending on what degree program you choose to pursue, a course in teams and/or organizational behavior may not be required. We urge you to take one anyway.

Another component of EI is self-awareness, or knowing what you are feeling and why, recognizing the links between your feelings and how you behave and how feelings influence your performance, and being guided by your values and goals. This is the topic of Chapter 4. Since your feelings drive your behavior, influencing your relationships with others, it's important to recognize them and understand how they translate into behaviors that may or may not be constructive.

You're probably thinking, "Yeah, yeah, I know all of this stuff." You'd be surprised, though. In Jennifer's organizational behavior class, students assess their own emotional intelligence and are often confronted with the fact that they don't recognize their feelings and what is driving them at a particular moment. And it is frequently their teammates who let them know how their feelings are influencing their behavior and team performance. You are likely to be resistant to developing your emotional intelligence because 1) it's highly personal; 2) it's very difficult—it involves unlearning old habits of thought, feeling, and action; and 3) you are not the best judge of your capacity here—it's painful but necessary to learn from others. Self-awareness also includes knowing what you want to accomplish, where you are willing to compromise, what your strengths are, and having reasonable expectations. If you haven't guessed already, a significant portion of this book is geared towards encouraging you to develop your emotional intelligence, most notably Chapters 4 and 5.

You also need to develop self-management. Self-management incorporates self-control, trustworthiness, conscientiousness, adaptability, innovativeness, and self-motivation. Not surprisingly, several of our profiled practitioners stressed the importance of psychology. As Jennifer Butz put it, *there's a constant need for psychology, both to figure things out, as well as to stay sane, rational, and centered.* This implies the need for stress management skills, including maintaining a balanced life and avoiding burnout, a subject of Chapter 9. As one of our brainstorming groups concluded, a necessary ability is to produce success with minimal tension. And here, again, Jennifer's students are often surprised by their self-assessment results. Jennifer, herself, has been struck by how many people struggle with some of these elements, especially self-motivation. This reinforces the importance of communities of understanding and values and vision, which can help us to develop discipline, make sacrifices, and stay motivated more generally.

The final EI component is social awareness. Social awareness entails: empathy, taking an active interest in others' concerns and listening skills, as above; a service orientation, anticipating others' needs and responding accordingly; supporting and developing others through feedback, recognition, and coaching; taking advantage of diversity, embracing it as opposed to perceiving it as being threatening; and organizational awareness, understanding power and politics (as discussed above). When it comes right down to it, these elements contribute to good people management skills (in addition to technical management skills as noted above). They also encourage us to think more deeply about what good management means. If management is about getting work done through other people, as it is commonly defined, then all four components of EI are important.

As part of his service vision, over the years, Aaron Williams has developed a set of guidelines for his management and leadership, which he tries to embody and encourage in others. When he left the International Youth Foundation, his staff put these on paper and had them laminated with a picture of him, titling it "Williams' Rules":

1. Be nice to people, you never know when you will have to work for them.
2. Hire the smartest people you can find.
3. Give them far more responsibility than they can handle.
4. Don't get mad when they make mistakes.
5. Always acknowledge good work.
6. Don't meddle.
7. If the situation requires, create a new rule.

Acquiring Skills and Knowledge

The dynamic nature of careers in international public service implies a need for a broad range of skills and a high degree of flexibility to respond to changing job responsibilities, organizational contexts, emerging development challenges, and your own evolving service vision. General skills; technical skills, tools, and knowledge; and strong management skills, including emotional intelligence, are all necessary to an effective and rewarding career in international public service. No matter what you choose to do, you will need some competency in each of these areas. How you choose to balance these skills and which type of skill area you would like to emphasize are key to determining what kind of formal preparation you will seek. For example, you may choose to pursue a degree in area studies; a technical sector, such as health, education, the environment, economics or governance; or a management or public policy degree.

These are not easy choices. Remember Olivia Tecosky? Here's what else she had to say about choosing an appropriate degree program: *Do I want to focus on the analytic? On the more operational? How much will I be able to actively plan and choose what I work on, and how much will be determined by the job opportunities available at the time when I'm looking? Is this degree preparing me to do any of this, or all of it? How much additional training will I need, and if I really want to become a technician, should I go back and get my doctorate? Welcome to my neurosis.* We hope that you won't feel neurotic as you explore your options, and to help you along, we will discuss some possibilities to get you started.

Most professionals in international public service, and especially those responsible for hiring, concur that the minimum requirements for an entry level position in the field are a graduate degree and at least one year of overseas professional experience. There are many ways to accomplish these and you will always hear of some exceptions. But to cover all of your bases, you should strategize for how you will meet these requirements. And while we made no conscious effort to choose people who illustrated these components, it so happens that all of our profiled practitioners do. All of them have master's degrees (e.g., public administration, business administration, and international policy studies/international relations); Najma Siddiqi has two (education and clinical psychology); and David Yang went on for his PhD. As for early international experience, Aaron Williams and Jef Buehler did the Peace Corps; David Yang did similar work with Volunteers in Asia; Sarah Newhall took a sabbatical to work in Thailand; and Jennifer Butz lived and worked in China for a year during her graduate studies. (As a Pakistani national, Najma Siddiqi did not face the same need to satisfy the overseas requirement.) Some graduate programs require prior experience, such as several of those at Johns Hopkins' School of Advanced International Service in Washington, D.C. There are opportunities to pursue these two requirements simultaneously through the Peace Corps Masters International Programs. As you will see, this is the path Jef Buehler (Profile 5) took.

Before we discuss graduate degree programs and pre-service internships, it's important to note that much of what you need to know for a rewarding career in international public service and the expertise you will acquire will come through experience on the job, not necessarily formal training. This is true for everyone, but may be especially important for those of you who are mid career and seeking to transition to the international arena. It may not always be necessary to go back to school to make such transitions, especially if you are a technical sector specialist. But you will need to make some investment to prepare for international work. You may recall that Sarah Newhall has no formal academic training in international development. Rather, she took a sabbatical in Thailand and was fortunate enough to find Mechai Viravaidya, who was willing to mentor her.

Graduate Degree Options

Exploring internationally oriented degree programs is not easy. While accrediting bodies, such as the National Association of Schools of Public Affairs and Administration and the American Association of Colleges and Schools of Business, promote the internationalization of university curricula, unfortunately, the most widely used guide for selecting among the best universities and programs, *U.S. News & World Report*, does not rank programs according to their international components (international business is an exception). In any case, anyone familiar with these rankings knows that it's an imperfect system. Sometimes programs ride on their past reputations and it is only when you arrive that you discover, for example, that the star faculty member who generated the reputation in a particular area has retired or moved on. Your best strategy is to talk to as many people as you can, including those who are doing the kind of work you aspire to, and ask them for recommendations. At a minimum, check the Web sites of various programs and explore where alumni have gotten jobs. And when you've developed a short list, visit the universities to talk to current students, alumni, and professors before you make your decision.

We've already introduced three possibilities for degree programs: area studies (e.g., Latin American, African, Asian, Middle Eastern, and European Studies), technical sectors (e.g., health, education, environment, agriculture, economics), and generalist degrees, some of which also have technical components (international affairs, public administration, public policy, and business administration). While all three skills areas discussed above are essential to success, not all degree programs require them. So no matter what kind of degree you choose to pursue, you will need to seek out the skills-based courses that are not addressed, either as electives, or as an additional investment beyond your credit requirements. For example, at least one course in development economics is essential, and most universities require at least one other economics class as a prerequisite.

Derick and Jennifer are both experts in democratic governance and interorganizational relationships. While Derick accumulated expertise in agriculture, health, and the environment on the job, neither of us pursued technical sector degrees outside of public administration and public policy. As a practitioner, Derick illustrates the opportunities to acquire technical knowledge through experience. He will never conduct soil sample analyses, train forestry agents in conservation techniques, or dispense HIV/AIDS drugs, but he knows the vocabulary of the agricultural, environmental, and health sectors and how they work.

You may be asking yourself, since most graduates will emerge with some exposure to all of these skills and knowledge, "Does it really matter which umbrella I choose for my studies?" The obvious answer is that different types of specialization open different doors. So we recommend that you identify the type of job you aspire to, locate some people who are doing that kind of work, and ask them what kind of degree would be best suited to getting to where they are. The less obvious answer, but nevertheless very important consideration, is that different degree programs provide different kinds of professional socialization. Every field incorporates implicit values, which inform priorities and approaches. And different programs/universities provide additional socialization overlays, as do the various communities of understanding noted in Chapter 5.

For example, Jennifer often advises students interested in a management degree, who are debating between an MPA and an MBA. There are many factors to consider here, many of which will be particular to the specific school, faculty, and program. There are also some general questions that apply. For example, international public service requires a good working knowledge of governments, political systems, and how they operate. Does the MBA program in question offer such courses or leave room for related electives? Socialization is a huge issue here. Would you rather be surrounded by a majority of students who are primarily focused on a bottom line of profit, or those who may be more likely to share your service values?

The stereotype of MBAs as competitive money-mongers is a caricature; and in fact, in recent years, there have been some very exciting developments in business schools. The Aspen Institute and World Resources Institute, in their annual report "Beyond Grey Pinstripes: Preparing MBAs for Social and Environmental Stewardship," rank business schools according to their incorporation of social and environmental responsibility into curricula and extracurricular activities.[6] For example, George Washington University's School of Business has been ranked "on the cutting edge" in this regard in each of the last four years. A business student movement called Net Impact has sought to promote the role of business in contributing to social and environmental concerns. It has chapters at over 90 business schools.[7] Some of you may have a specific interest in more technical areas of an MBA, such as micro-finance and micro-enterprise. You will need to investigate if a university has related courses. They may be offered through an MBA program, such as at GW, but they can also be found in economics departments and development studies programs.

There may be other strategic reasons for pursuing an MBA, as Aaron Williams attests. *I thought an MBA would be a good degree because I suspected—although no one was talking about it in those days—that it would be a good bridge to both the public and private sectors, and I thought it would be very useful to get some very good business experience as part of my career development.* These links are well recognized today. Our GW Business School colleague, Hildy Teegen, specializes in corporate-nonprofit partnerships for environmental sustainability in developing countries. Her efforts are only a small piece of a much larger corporate social responsibility movement in business and education.[8]

We are not unbiased in encouraging people to pursue international public service through degrees in public administration and public policy. First, it's our own professional identification. Second, we find that many people are not familiar with these degree programs and the kind of opportunities they afford. And, third, we believe these degrees have much to offer in terms of effective public service, flexibility, and reward. A master's of public administration or public policy can enable you to acquire necessary analytic and management skills, expertise in governance—including the hot topics of anticorruption and accountability, and policy processes—including agenda setting, constituency building, and managing policy reform. But whatever you choose has to feel right to you. This was Sarah Newhall's experience with respect to the MPA. *Bingo! I'd never heard of such a thing before then. And it was exactly right for me.*

There are also programs that are highly specialized in international development studies (for example, the programs at Columbia University and Brandeis University), development management (e.g., American

University), international NGO management (e.g., School for International Training), and conflict resolution (e.g., George Mason University, University of Notre Dame) (see Appendix 2). If you know for certain these are the careers you want to pursue, then these are good choices to consider. However, given the many transitions you are likely to make in your career—including from overseas to domestic work as your personal and family life evolves—you might also consider the trade-offs for choosing a degree program that would give you broader options and flexibility.

If you choose not to pursue a management-oriented degree, you still need to acquire related skills and tools. This is a common shortcoming of international affairs programs (though certainly not all), area studies and, to some extent, the social sciences. We believe that the master's level is where you should focus on gaining practical skills targeted to employment, unless you know in advance that you will pursue a PhD or a research-oriented career. It's great to learn about a place, its history, politics, and culture. But you also have to think about what you will *do* with this understanding. We find that many of our international affairs students who take our classes go on to find very good jobs and lead successful careers. One of our concerns, though, is that as a result of your graduate study you should be prepared to find a job and excel beyond that first job. So, again, we encourage you to investigate what types of jobs alumni from these programs have found, and what services are available for job placement and career counseling. Some programs and disciplines have an anti-development establishment orientation. We feel that academic training should encourage critical thinking, but you should be aware that employment options for entry-level staff whose main credential is an ability to criticize donors are limited to a few advocacy NGOs and think tanks, and these positions require solid analytic skills. This kind of work may be what you're looking for, but if it isn't, you would do well to investigate before choosing your degree program.

Area studies or social sciences (such as anthropology) can lead to some interesting opportunities. A couple of World Bank projects are illustrative here. One, in Mali, is called Banking on Culture. In an effort to promote and sustain interest and appreciation in traditional culture and at the same time promote micro-enterprise, villagers can loan their cultural artifacts to a village museum and cultural center for collateral for a micro-credit loan. With the loan comes micro-enterprise training in support of artisan crafts production and marketing. In Sierra Leone, an anthropologist was hired to assess the roots of conflict at the local level. He found that much of the conflict was provoked or at least aggravated by generational conflicts among men over marriage rights. Without an understanding of the marginalization of young men, which leads to their recruitment by militia groups, the conflict is not likely to be resolved. Similar social assessments are now being undertaken in other conflict countries.

PhD or Not?

A question we are frequently asked is, do I need a PhD to have a successful career in international public service? A doctorate can certainly open a lot of doors, some of them different from those accessible with a master's degree. Clearly, for an academic career it is a prerequisite. However, there are jobs beyond academe where a PhD can be an asset, such as conducting the type of social assessments mentioned above. It can earn you increased credibility, possibly helping you to start your career at a higher level with a larger salary, and it can mean you may advance more quickly. But none of that is guaranteed. Attitudes towards PhD's vary. Some organizations, like the World Bank, place a lot of importance on holding a PhD. Other organizations stress the need to prove that your PhD is relevant, as they would with any potential employee's credentials. Still other organizations and individuals can be overtly anti-intellectual, assuming your PhD means that you will bring a theoretical orientation to your work that is irrelevant, impractical, or completely uninformed by how the real world works. This is the stereotypical ivory tower assumption.

If you choose to pursue a PhD, you should know why you are doing it. David Yang was clear about his reasons, as you may recall. *Even though I didn't want to go into academics, I wanted to get a PhD, knowing I would have a Washington career. I wanted to enhance my options. I liked research and writing, even though I didn't want to become a professor. I saw the role models of people who went in and out of government service and could be in think tanks as having a lot more options than other people. If one could write well and defend a position in writing, either as an NGO advocate or think tank occupant, that gave you more options not only career-wise, but also politically. It gave you a voice, rather than a civil servant who couldn't write an op-ed piece, or an NGO worker who was limited by the funding ties of your patron. The PhD gave you more academic license, more intellectual license, to state your views rather than to just work inside an institution. I always wanted to maximize my independence intellectually and career-wise. And I think that having that degree helps you do different things, particularly in terms of people valuing your voice outside of bureaucracy.*

You may also find that once you're on the job a PhD is not necessary for what you want to do. Najma Siddiqi started a PhD program twice, but she didn't complete either program. In the first instance, her activism overcame her; in the second, she needed to make other choices for her family and eventually the PhD became less of a priority. Jennifer Butz (Profile 6) has periodically contemplated pursuing a PhD. Like David and Najma, she knows she doesn't want to be an academic. But her commitment to continued growth and learning, along with wondering what new doors might open for her, inspire her to occasionally ponder the idea.

Derick's career path has focused on applied research and policy analysis, as well as hands-on technical assistance. The positions he has occupied over the years, which have bridged the academic and international development worlds, would not have been possible for him without a doctoral degree.

Of course, for those of you who may be interested in a full-time academic career, such as Jennifer's, it can be very rewarding. And it does not require an either-or decision regarding involvement in the world of action. Most universities allow their faculty to consult the equivalent of one day a week alongside their teaching and research. If you're on a nine-month contract, you can pursue international consulting during the summer months (though these assignments can be difficult to coordinate with clients). This means that as a professor, you have the opportunity to teach, conduct research—exercising the freedom of speech and impartiality that David Yang values so much—and keep a foot in the practical world. Jennifer and Derick find that the three are closely related. Our consulting/practice work informs our teaching and leads to new and interesting research opportunities. This type of career requires a doctoral degree.

Internships/Preparatory Experience

You can pursue internship opportunities either independent from or in the context of graduate programs. The Peace Corps Masters International programs combine pre-service graduate studies with Peace Corps service, while the Fellows programs support graduate studies for Returned Peace Corps Volunteers (RPCVs). Both types of programs can include domestic service learning components. For example, the MI program at Rutgers University-Camden prepares students for Peace Corps placements in NGO and small business development and municipal management. When Jennifer became the director of that program in 1996, she formalized the local service that Jef Buehler and his fellow students initiated into a nine-month service learning requirement. The most common Peace Corps Fellows programs are in education, where RPCVs who taught overseas earn their master's in education while teaching disadvantaged populations in the United States. For example, George Washington University places students in a nearby school district.

Peace Corps experience is not automatically perceived as relevant. The burden is on you to prove to a potential employer that your experience was professional and that you gained knowledge and experience that relates to the job opportunity at hand. This is why the Peace Corps MI programs can be helpful. While each one is organized independently, with its own requirements and procedures, most of them encourage or require the application of the knowledge and skills you acquired during your graduate studies, which may culminate in a master's thesis or project design paper. This capstone exercise can prove to a potential employer that you have gained and already applied key tools and analytic frameworks. The Rutgers University-Camden MI program requires a Directed Study based on the student's Peace Corps experience. The project paper includes a review of best practices, and the application of a set of diagnostic tools, including needs assessment, stakeholder and SWOT (strengths, weaknesses, opportunities, and threats) analysis, Logical Framework, and evaluation. Many Peace Corps volunteers find that if they want additional professional overseas experience following the completion of their service, it can be easier to find those opportunities when they are still in country.

Some degree programs incorporate internship or practicum components. For example, Brandeis University's Master's in Sustainable International Development, Columbia University's Program in Economic and Political Development/Development Management Track, and the master's programs at the School for International Training organize opportunities for students as part of their requirements and/or course credits. Some models are explicitly designed to encourage your own initiative as part of the learning experience. For example, George Washington University's International Development Studies Program requires a capstone project where students identify their own client; the GW Elliott School of International Affairs provides students small grants to support travel. In some instances, you might be able to get involved with overseas projects implemented by the university or your professors.

Other students may choose to take time off during their graduate studies to pursue independent internship opportunities. Since most master's degrees require two years of full-time study, many students opt to use the summer in between to gain additional experience. Other students may defer their studies for a year, as Jennifer Butz did.

Several formal internship opportunities are available. Appendix 3 lists a sampling of opportunities and resources. Many of these are volunteer based and may not emphasize professional skill building, so, as with the Peace Corps, you need to ensure that you will get the experience and exposure you need. Some internship programs are specifically geared to that, such as AIESEC, which is the world's largest student organization, operating on over 800 college campuses worldwide, in 83 countries. It facilitates international exchanges of students and recent graduates interested in economics and management, in paid traineeships or as volunteers for nonprofit organizations. Many employers maintain formal voluntary internship programs, such as USAID, World Bank, United Nations, regional development banks, and various NGOs (the Carter Center, Save the Children, Care, Interaction, etc.). The career development office at your university should have a library of resources for finding these opportunities. Some of these are more structured for training and advancement than others; and many, though not all of them, are unpaid.

Taking an unpaid internship, even when it requires out-of-pocket expenses, can be an important investment in your career. For example, UN internships are very competitive even though they are unpaid. Several of our students have taken such internships. One of them was offered the chance to do some fieldwork in Egypt. She seized the opportunity even though she had to pay all of her own expenses. Having this experience no doubt helped her in her application and selection process for her Presidential Management Fellow position in the Inspector General's Office of the State Department.

Finding internships with overseas organizations can be more challenging. There are several organized programs that require a fee in addition to your expenses. We caution you that these opportunities do not always provide relevant professional experience. Many formal internship programs can also be limiting in terms of what you are expected to be capable of doing. Aside from these international fee-based internship programs, some local NGOs implement formal internship programs, like BRAC in Bangladesh. We encourage our students to identify and negotiate internships directly, through personal and professional networks and Internet databases such as Idealist.org. Through Idealist, several of our students have identified local NGOs and created internship positions for themselves, negotiating by e-mail. Typically, they pay their own expenses, but the host organization finds them a host family to live with. This arrangement also gives you better insight into the culture. You'll want to confirm that the organization is the "real thing" before you commit too much, perhaps by asking for references from previous interns. These directly negotiated opportunities often lead to the best match between what you and the organization need and what you have to offer. Whether you pursue an existing internship program or negotiate one on your own, it's important that you set expectations—yours and your host's—appropriately. This is essentially what Sarah Newhall did for her sabbatical, though given her stage in her career she needed to negotiate sufficient financial coverage to break even.

For those who are entrepreneurial and/or research oriented, small grants programs are also available. Most of you have heard of the Fulbright Fellowship programs. These programs request proposals for research projects, often with priority countries and issues pre-specified. The United States Institute of Peace offers similar opportunities to postgraduates and academics. Lesser known programs include the National Security Education Program, which supports graduate students pursuing experience in languages, cultures, and regions that are critical to US national security but are less frequently studied by US graduate students. The emphasis is on cultural understanding, not security per se. For example, GW student Kipp Efinger took time off from his studies to implement a project in Azerbaijan funded by NSEP. With this funding he will deepen his Azeri language skills and conduct research on employment options for internally displaced people. Echoing Green, a global social-venture fund, provides two-year fellowships to support social-change efforts.

Skills Options: No One Right Answer

As we've noted in this chapter, the options for acquiring skills and knowledge are many. What you study, and where you choose to intern will depend on your initial ideas about where you want to work. We've encouraged you to talk to people in the kinds of jobs you're interested in to ask them about their skills background. Our focus group concurred on the value of informational interviews, so don't be shy, seek these people out. If you're not completely sure which service direction you wish to pursue, however, don't stress over it. As our profiled practitioners demonstrate, there is not a single "correct" route to the skill sets you'll find valuable. As the service-choice spiral indicates, you don't have to—and indeed you can't possibly—acquire all the skills and knowledge you'll need in a single degree program or internship. You'll be expanding your toolkit and your experience base throughout your career, as Aaron Williams has done.

Notes

1. In addition to drawing on input for this chapter from our profiled practitioners, GW students, and focus group, we benefited from two brainstorming sessions at workshops with the Development Management Network.

2. Since we are not experts in area studies or the technical sectors (e.g., health, education, environment), our sample of degree programs focuses only on management- and policy-oriented programs, generalist degrees (international affairs or relations), and specialized programs focused on international development.

3. See the USAID Policies and Procedures at http://www.usaid.gov/policy/ads. To investigate USAID programming and R4s for each agency and mission, see: http://www.dec.org/partners/r4/.

4. In addition to US NGOs, international agencies, such as USAID, UN Development Programme (UNDP), and Food and Agriculture Organization (FAO), private consulting firms, universities, and developing-country organizations regularly advertise employment openings in *Monday Developments*. University career development offices commonly subscribe to *Monday Developments*, so the newsletter represents a good sample of the types of jobs students might seek. We analyzed thirteen issues between January and September 2003.

5. For more on emotional intelligence, see Daniel Goleman's books, particularly *Working with Emotional Intelligence* (New York: Bantam Books, 2000); and Hendrie Weisinger's book *Emotional Intelligence at Work* (San Francisco: Jossey-Bass, 1998). You can also explore the Web site of the Consortium for Research on Emotional Intelligence in Organizations: http://www.eiconsortium.org.

6. School profiles and rankings are available at http://www.beyondgrey pinstripes.org/results/index.cfm.

7. For further information, see http://www.net-impact.org/.

8. See the Corporate Social Responsibility Forum: http://www.csrforum .com/.

Profile 4. Aaron Williams:
A Southside Chicagoan Embraces the World

How does an African American from the Southside of Chicago end up working with Nelson Mandela to improve the quality of life in a newly free nation? It certainly wasn't what Aaron Williams had envisioned when he began his career teaching high school in Chicago, but he did know he wanted something different. *There was something else out there that I needed to know about and it was a real yearning on my part. I didn't know what it was.* After hearing John F. Kennedy's speeches about the Peace Corps, Aaron did some research. As part of that effort, he spoke with a fellow graduate of Chicago State University who had served with the Peace Corps in Jamaica. *I was just absolutely fascinated about what she told me she did. And I said, "Hey, this is a person just like me—went to this college, was a teacher, went to the Peace Corps." I said, "I'm gonna do that. I'm going to try Peace Corps and see if it can broaden my horizons."* While there was a surge of people joining the Peace Corps in the late sixties, this wasn't the case in Aaron's circles. He remembers only two people supporting his decision: his mother, Blanche Green, who later visited him in every post he served; and his best friend, Harry Simmons, who, while not understanding Aaron's decision entirely, thought it was interesting. *No one had ever left Chicago from my family unless they went to the Army. So, why should I do this?*

But he did do it, and ended up serving in the Dominican Republic for three years. *I would have to tell you that from the first day I went into the Peace Corps training, I was certain that this was something I wanted to do. The Peace Corps changed my life forever. As they say in the Peace Corps recruitment, it's the toughest job you'll ever love. And it's extraordinary. It changed the way I look at the world. And it created the basis for my career as it has developed until today. It introduced me to the world of another culture. I learned how to speak and work in a foreign language. I really tested myself in ways that I never thought I would be tested.* Aaron began by teaching rural schoolteachers seeking a high school diploma, moved to work on curriculum development with the Ministry of Education, and ended up teaching a new teacher training course at the first private university in the Dominican Republic (Universidad Madre y Maestra). About halfway through his service, Aaron met his wife Rosa, a Dominican, who was studying medicine and was a high school science teacher. They spent their first year of marriage in the Dominican Republic.

At the end of his Peace Corps service, Aaron *decided that the world was a much bigger place, and I wanted to be a part of that bigger world.* Initially, Aaron worked for the Peace Corps in the United States as a Coordinator of Minority Recruitment. He visited universities across the country, speaking about Peace Corps and his experience. Through the contacts he made, he was offered a fellowship to pursue his MBA—something he would not have thought of before Peace Corps. *I suspected that an MBA would be a good bridge to both public and private sectors and I thought it would be very useful to get some good business experience as part of my career development.*

Upon completing his MBA in international business and marketing at the University of Wisconsin, Madison, Aaron was offered numerous jobs with large multinational companies, including Exxon, Procter and Gamble, General Foods, and Johnson & Johnson. He decided to work for International Multifoods, a diversified industrial foods company, because it offered him the opportunity to work closely with someone he perceived would be a good mentor. *Ted Rugland was from that famous class of 1949 Harvard Business School, where something like ninety percent went on to become CEOs of Fortune 500 companies. He said something no one else did. He said, "I'm going to give you a chance to look at this company at the highest possible level, working with me. But if you fail, I'm going to throw you out, whether it's thirty days or sixty days, you're out."* Aaron became his right-hand man, working on sales forecasts, potential mergers, and even the downsizing of the company. True to his promise, Rugland introduced him to all aspects of the company.

After two years, Aaron decided he wanted to shift to the world of consumer brands marketing, and he moved to work for General Mills. There, too, he worked with solid mentors, including *one of the smartest guys I ever worked for, Steve Sanger (CEO of General Mills), and I gained a lot of insights from him.* At General Mills, Aaron was introduced to the pressures of the bottom line, where each day he was faced with a sales report for which he was accountable. New MBAs were joining the ranks every year, so it was a competitive environment, with pressure from below as well as above. *At the same time, it was an era where there were very few minorities in management in any of these professions, and I often found myself being the first this and the first that, and was driven to excel in all aspects of my work.*

But Aaron still longed to work in the international arena, and at that time—the mid- to late 1970s—rather than send Americans overseas, American companies hired talented people from their countries of operation who had been educated in the United States. *So I said, "I'm sitting here with all these language skills, all these cross-cultural skills. I want to be able to use them."* Aaron's Peace Corps mentor, Henry Reynolds, now at USAID, called to ask him if he would be willing to do some work in Honduras. Aaron took a leave of absence to help design an agribusiness project as a consultant for the USAID mission to Honduras. *And I really liked it. It was good to be back in Latin America, to be working again in Spanish. Rosa thought it was a great idea to return to Latin America and escape the Minnesota cold. And our lifestyle was very busy. We were very much caught up in our careers. This was our opportunity to make some changes and add some balance to our lives, and at the same time for me to do something that I was terribly excited about.*

So Aaron joined the Foreign Service in 1978, beginning a 22-year career in USAID. Aaron arrived at a fortuitous time: this was the beginning of USAID's search for public-private partnerships. *They didn't even call it that. It was "working with business," or "private sector development." And not many people in AID knew how to do that. A lot of the AID people were ex-Peace Corps volunteers who were into the social development side and had degrees in anthropology, sociology, and development economics. They had little or no business experience. And I knew how companies operated and how business executives thought.* Aaron used this experience from the outset. In Honduras, banana companies were the only actor equipped with the technical staff, refrigerated shipping, and the know-how of the US market necessary for implementing a successful nontraditional agribusiness project. The banana companies were interested in diversifying their product line away from bananas, but they were hated at the time. There had been a series of scandals, and neither the Honduran Government nor the US Embassy was eager to work with them. *So I figured out a way to bring those three parties together. It was a perfect time to be there, and I got superb guidance and encouragement from my first boss in USAID, Tony Cauterucci, one of USAID's legendary executives.*

Building from this experience, Aaron became a leader in USAID on private enterprise development and public-private partnerships. He pursued this agenda in overseas missions, such as in Haiti and Costa Rica; he created some of the first private sector development offices and became the Director of the Private Sector Office in the Latin America and the Caribbean (LAC) Bureau of USAID; and he worked centrally with the Private Enterprise Bureau. He then moved into senior management positions, as the Mission Director for Barbados, the Deputy Assistant Administrator for LAC (number two position), Assistant Administrator for LAC (head of that bureau), and the head of the Executive Secretariat for the Agency under then Administrator, Brian Atwood. Again, as at other times in his career, he worked for another extraordinary leader while he was LAC bureau deputy: Ambassador James Michel, who was one of the pioneers in developing democracy and governance initiatives in Latin America.

Aaron ended his USAID career as Mission Director to South Africa. *South Africa in those days had a very large US Embassy presence, similar to Paris or Rome or London. Fifteen different agencies on the country team, all vying to show how they're furthering United States' support of President Nelson Mandela and his Cabinet. Those are conditions where you could have had a lot of inter-agency rivalries and battles, but none of that occurred because Ambassador James Joseph set the tone and provided integrity and leadership that resulted in effective teamwork. We worked in areas that were very important to the future of South Africa and we put together a philosophy and an approach whereby the South Africans were in the lead.* As Mission Director, Aaron's accomplishments included leading the development of programs that trained over 30,000 South Africans in democracy and human rights, managing education assistance that resulted in the training of 35,000 South African teachers in the administration and use of a new national curriculum, providing leadership in USAID's housing assistance that made available for the first time housing-mortgage credit for thousands of poor households, and leading the design and management of several national programs that provided micro-enterprise and small business loans to thousands of disadvantaged entrepreneurs.

Aaron was offered an ambassadorship and had already been vetted through the White House, when he decided for family reasons to take early retirement from USAID and return to the United States. His mother had just been diagnosed with cancer; his youngest son, Steven, would be starting his senior year in high school; and his oldest son, Michael, was now in his second year away at college. *At that time I had an extraordinary offer that just kind of appeared as I was going through this emotional crisis of, what was I going to do? I was thinking, "Okay, I'll just move back to Washington and get another senior position in AID." And then this opportunity came to continue to do things I've always been doing, which was building public-private partnerships.*

Aaron became the Executive Vice President for the International Youth Foundation (IYF), an international nonprofit that supports youth development programs worldwide. *IYF's mission is to improve the lives of young people wherever they live, learn, work, or play. What better thing to do than that? They wanted me to develop corporate partnerships for them, and to work with AID and the World Bank. It just seemed right up my alley. I had always been planning on going into the nonprofit world because I'd worked for business; I'd worked in government; so now I wanted to complete my professional circle, and focus on the third sector. It just all came together.* At IYF, Aaron focused on developing partnerships with companies like Nokia, American Express, Cisco Systems, Merrill Lynch, Intel, and Lucent Technologies, all of which are *companies that believe in corporate social responsibility and thought they could make a difference in investing their resources in good social programs—really cutting-edge corporate social responsibility programs. It gave me access and the opportunity to do things in a totally different environment.*

After four years at IYF, again for personal reasons, Aaron decided to make a change. He was traveling seventy percent of the time. *I just didn't want to spend that much time away from my wife and my home. I decided I needed to do something about the travel, but I wanted to do something that's consistent with my career, that would give me the opportunity to continue to work in international development.* In 2003, Aaron became the Vice President for International Business Development for RTI International (Research Triangle Institute).

CHAPTER 7

Where Will You Work?
Organizational Options
for Service

The combination of creating self-awareness (Chapter 4), finding shared meaning and support in service communities (Chapter 5), and building skills and knowledge (Chapter 6) leads to choices about where to work. One of your communities of understanding is necessarily the organization for whose mission and agenda you choose to work. Since working in and through community is a two-way street, one aspect of public service for socioeconomic development and change is an ongoing redefinition and transformation of your workplace organization and its agenda. Most people prefer to work for organizations and agendas consistent with their own values. This is one of the reasons for the popularity of NGOs as employers; they are seen as values-driven organizations that pay attention to what their staff think should be done, which can be very appealing (this is an idealized view of NGOs, and is not always the case). Other people may choose to work for organizations with an explicit intention to influence and change them from within, such as international donor agencies. You may think that because donor agencies are large bureaucracies, changing them from the inside isn't possible. But you'd be surprised at what can be done. Later in this chapter, you'll hear more from Aaron Williams and Najma Siddiqi on this topic. In either case, whether or not it's an organization you feel comfortable and compatible with, you are likely both to transform and be transformed by your workplace—public service and shared meaning are created in dialogue.

In this chapter, we talk about some of these service employment choices and options. The possibilities are vast, so our discussion is necessarily selective and partial. In Appendix 3 we provide some sources on where to go to find out more information and details on selected potential employers. We begin by looking at North-South issues relating to careers and jobs, and overview some of the major categories of organizations in the international development landscape.

We next turn to choices of where to work for change: from the inside or the outside. Given the range of choices, the designation of inside versus outside is somewhat relative and dependent upon your particular perspective. The easiest line to draw is the one we just mentioned above, an organizational boundary. However, there are others as well, such as political or economic systems, where we can make distinctions between "mainstream" and "fringe" that represent opposite poles where inside and outside can be situated.[1]

Finally, we talk about frontline service delivery versus supporting and facilitating roles. In many instances, this translates into job choices between field versus headquarters positions. It also can relate to the practitioner-academic divide.

North/South

A major choice is whether to pursue public service overseas, in transitioning or developing countries (the global South) or to engage in service at home. This book is focused on careers that concentrate on the South, but as we pointed out in Chapter 1, issues and needs related to socioeconomic development, social change, and empowerment cannot be neatly separated according to a country's overall degree of economic advancement. As is widely recognized, there are many Southern communities in the global North. Responding to the needs of these communities is what drives Jef Buehler to work for grassroots urban development in New Jersey. The commonality of service needs across the North and South also means that the skills and experience you accumulate can be transferable, as Sarah Newhall's career path demonstrates. She took what she'd learned from working in Portland, Oregon, and, in a mid-career switch, applied it in Thailand and Cambodia, and then in Pact's programs worldwide when she came to Washington, D.C. *It was very empowering, because I could see very clearly that the skills of planning, organizing, implementing, and evaluating were transferable into any environment. It's as important to be culturally sensitive in both environments* [US and development countries].

Sarah's experience also demonstrates that North or South is not a decision you make once and for all. At different points in your career, for different reasons, you may choose to switch your emphasis from one to the other. *I don't think domestic work is going to be able to be domestic in the same way anymore because of the interconnectivity of things on the economic front and on the education front. No matter what domestic job you pick you cannot do it without a global consciousness. And if you're in global development, it's just as important to try to influence the provincial American outlook to become global. So I think the more people who are moving back and forth, the more sense we'll have in both spheres.* And the essence of service is the same. As Jennifer Butz (Profile 6) puts it: *I don't think much changes. One still brings a core set of values, and one still brings compassion and a commitment.*

Making the North-South choice is not always easy; and you'll need to bring to bear the thinking you've done as part of building your self-awareness. One of our GW students reflects on this decision: *Many of us are attracted to this field because of a strong interest in living and working abroad, yet at the same time I am in general opposed to having expats* [expatriates] *manage local people when we should be dedicating our time to developing the capacity of local people to promote change themselves. So, where will I fit in? On one hand my hope is to make myself obsolete. On the other hand I want to be personally and professionally fulfilled, and pushing paper in the* [Washington] *D.C. office of an international NGO just won't do it. One option that I have considered is eventually applying my experience in international development to issues of community development domestically, working with immigrant populations in urban areas . . . . I have always felt strongly that many of the tools we use internationally could be applied domestically, and vice versa. I also have a certain commitment to making change at home.*

Overview of Different Actors/Organizations

The major sources of employment for international public service are government agencies, multilateral international agencies, for-profit consulting firms, nonprofit organizations and NGOs, and universities. An evolving job market is the international business world, where the corporate social responsibility movement and the increase in public-private partnerships have created new employment opportunities. We can't offer you a comprehensive list of all your potential job possibilities. There are simply too many out there to cover in a single book. What follows is a selective overview of the employment landscape, which along with the sources in Appendix 3, gives you a place to start your own personal exploration of where you'd like to pursue public service.

Government Agencies

The two main US federal government entities with international responsibilities are the State Department, which handles foreign policy, diplomatic relations, US business promotion, and consular affairs, and USAID, which has operational responsibility for managing assistance for socioeconomic development, humanitarian relief, and post-conflict and disaster aid.[2] The US Department of Agriculture, through the Office of International Cooperation and Development, is another federal agency with a long history of international activity. A trend begun about ten to fifteen years ago has been an expansion in the international portfolios of agencies that traditionally have had a largely domestic policy and program focus. Agencies such as the Departments of Commerce, Education, Health and Human Services, Housing and Urban Development, Labor, and Transportation; the Internal Revenue Service; and the Environmental Protection Agency all have active programs overseas, for which they need staff.

Today's federal job market is an expanding one. Departments and agencies are acutely aware that the cumulative result of the hiring freezes and reductions in force begun in the 1980s has been a serious depletion of their human resources. Many agencies are facing a mid-level and senior management crisis over the next decade as the baby-boom generation starts to retire in significant numbers, leaving widening staff gaps throughout the government. Federal recruitment efforts have moved into high gear, including for internationally oriented positions, across a range of agencies. Many avenues exist to pursue employment with the federal government. Except in the foreign service, federal employees are civil servants under the General Schedule (GS), which classifies positions according to level of responsibility, skill requirements, experience, and salary range.

The Presidential Management Fellows (PMFs) Program is one option for entry into public service in federal agencies for those pursuing graduate degrees. PMFs currently serve in more than fifty federal agencies. The PMF program offers extensive training opportunities, membership in an elite network of current fellows and alumni, and accelerated advancement in the GS system (fellows enter at GS-9, and are eligible for promotion to GS-11 after the first year, and GS-12 upon completion of the two-year program). Placements with federal agencies include at least one rotation to another position, with the aim of broadening fellows' understanding of the federal government and its programs. Another avenue is the Student Educational Employment Program. It includes an opportunity to begin to work for federal government while completing a degree program. After graduation, students' positions are converted to the GS system.

State Department

Employment for Foreign Service (FS) positions depends upon passing the Foreign Service Exam, which has a written and oral component. Foreign Service Officers serve in embassies and consulates around the world.[3] Career tracks include: management, consular, economic, political, and public diplomacy. The State Department also employs civil service staff (GS positions) in its Washington, D.C. headquarters. These positions cover a range of opportunities, from administrative and information technology support to technical and analytical jobs. Among State Department policy priorities are transnational issues such as environment and climate change, science and technology; the global struggle against diseases, such as HIV/AIDS, tuberculosis, and malaria; international law enforcement cooperation and drug trafficking; arms proliferation and terrorism; and international efforts to combat trafficking in persons.

USAID

Employees in USAID fall into several staff categories. Direct Hire positions constitute the core of the Agency's staff; they consist of FS and GS slots. People in FS slots rotate out of Washington to USAID Missions overseas on a regular basis, spending 75 percent of their time in the field over the course of their careers; those in GS positions are based in Washington. The number of permanent FS and GS positions assigned to USAID is fixed at a level below the staffing needed to cope with the agency's workload, due to continuing political pressure across all government agencies to downsize. In response, USAID has developed several hiring mechanisms that allow the agency to temporarily augment its workforce.[4]

One of these is interagency personnel agreements whereby USAID transfers funds to other federal agencies to hire staff who are then assigned to USAID. These fall into two categories: RSSAs (resources support services agreements) or PASAs (participating agency service agreements). RSSAs serve in Washington, D.C. and PASAs in overseas Missions. The benefit for USAID is flexibility and speed of implementation. Such staff can exercise all the duties and responsibilities of FS or GS staff, but they do not have the status of permanent federal civil service employees. For example, Derick had a USDA RSSA position for the two and a half years that he worked at USAID's Office of Rural and Institutional Development in the early 1980s.

A second mechanism is the Personal Services Contractor (PSC). This is a fixed-term contract position (usually one to five years) in which USAID advertises for an individual to fulfill a specific scope of work, and candidates are selected from a competitive pool of applicants. PSCs serve both in Washington and abroad. Particularly in small overseas Missions where there are only a few Direct Hires, much of the Mission's workload is carried out by PSCs and local hires in-country (Foreign Service Nationals, or FSNs). You can find PSC positions listed on the FedBizOpps Web page under USAID.

USAID also imports expertise through several programs that bring in technical specialists for fixed-term contracts, typically one or two years in length with some renewal provisions. The Agency has eight different Fellows Programs. These include, for example, the Democracy Fellows Program, the American Association for the Advancement of Science (AAAS) Diplomacy Fellows Program, and the Health and Child Survival Fellows Program. These programs can be useful avenues to "test the waters" of work-life in USAID and to gain valuable practical experience. In many cases, though there are no guarantees, if you perform well and are interested in staying, USAID will seek to retain you through another form of contract employment or a Direct Hire position.

Other entry points into USAID are through the Agency's two entry-level Foreign Service Programs: the New Entry Professionals (NEP), which targets mid-level applicants, and the International Development Intern (IDI) Program, which is designed for junior-level people. Both programs require US citizenship and expect candidates to live and work overseas for at least 75 percent of their career. The positions seek specific technical and/or administrative skills. Applications for these programs are made on the Internet in response to advertised positions only.[5] USAID also uses the PMF program to recruit new professionals. Appendix 3 lists Web site information for USAID.[6]

Other US Government Agencies
We urge you to investigate and consider the many options available for international public service through the US government beyond the State Department and USAID. Some of you may find entry into these agencies through corresponding technical expertise. Others of you may seek to serve through a more generalist orientation, perhaps entering an agency through the PMF program. We noted several agencies with international programs above. Appendix 3 includes contact information for some. Specific programs that might be of interest include International Trade Administration, Department of Commerce, where, for example, one of Jennifer's former students has worked on the accession of African countries to the World Trade Organization; the Food for Peace Program, an

interagency program; and the Federal Highway Administration, Office of International Programs.

Multilateral International Agencies

In many large bureaucracies, positions are commonly filled from within or through introductions by those already working in them. While many of these organizations maintain public Web sites with job announcements, not all positions may be posted there (at least in a timely way), and you may find yourself competing with an inside track. You can better access those insider tracks by starting as an intern or a short- or long-term consultant and creating a network for yourself within these organizations.

The World Bank has traditionally been the domain of economists, though over the past ten years, and increasingly under Wolfensohn's presidency, social scientists (including political scientists, anthropologists, and sociologists), management specialists, and NGO/civil society experts have been brought in. Najma Siddiqi was hired in this latter category, for example. So at present the World Bank recruits for a much broader range of technical specialties than it once did. Employment is extremely competitive, drawing upon a worldwide pool of highly qualified applicants from both North and South. Permanent positions are difficult to obtain (the Bank, like USAID, is under pressure to cut costs), and many of them are not advertised externally. The Bank also augments its permanent staff with fixed-term consultant positions, which have a ceiling on the number of days per year that can be used. The Bank's Young Professionals (YP) Program recruits for high potential talent that is groomed for management positions; applicants must be no older than thirty-two. Many of the Bank's current senior management entered as YPs, and the program is seen as one of the building blocks of the organization's technocratic meritocracy. A new program is the Junior Professional Associates (JPA), which brings in people twenty-eight years old or younger on two-year, non-renewable contracts. While not an entry portal into World Bank employment like the YP Program, the JPA can give you a taste of work in the Bank, provide you with membership in a formal network of JPA alumni, and in some cases lead to a later position at the Bank (JPAs are excluded from World Bank employment for two years following their JP term).[7]

The United Nations family of agencies covers a wide range of international development arenas. These include general socioeconomic development (UNDP, United Nations Development Programme), health (WHO, World Health Organization), family planning (UNFPA, United Nations Fund for Population Activities), children and youth (UNICEF, United Nations Children's Fund), education and science (UNESCO,

United Nations Education, Scientific and Cultural Organization), humanitarian assistance and refugees (UNHCR, United Nations High Commissioner for Refugees), labor and employment (ILO, International Labour Organization), and agricultural development (FAO, Food and Agriculture Organization).[8]

Each agency has its own personnel office that handles human resources management, including hiring. Terms of employment are governed by the UN's international civil service regulations. Most of the UN agencies have young and junior professional programs, as well as some internships and volunteer positions. It can be difficult, though not impossible, for external job seekers to penetrate the UN system. As with the World Bank, the UN agencies recruit from a worldwide candidate pool. Positions are highly competitive, and US citizens are sometimes at a disadvantage when contending against equally qualified applicants from the South. In individual agencies, internal candidates often have an advantage in bidding on vacant positions; thus openings that are advertised externally are often already filled.[9]

For-profit Consulting Firms

Accompanying the downsizing across the US federal government has been the growth of contracting out. Thus, what USAID used to do internally in its heyday years in the 1960s and '70s when its staff worldwide was about 15,000, is now carried out via contracts and grants by an assortment of private consulting firms, NGOs, and universities. Today, USAID has fewer than 2,000 full-time direct-hire positions. Here we talk about the for-profit firms, what sometimes you hear referred to as "beltway bandits," the beltway being the ring road around Washington, D.C. The range of firms in the development industry is broad, stretching from small businesses that specialize in a narrow technical area to larger firms that seek to be multi-sectoral "full-service" providers. Examples of small firms include: Social Impact, specializing in monitoring and evaluation; Pragma, concentrating on enterprise development and financial markets; and QED Group, LLC, focusing on a range of development topics. There are also medium-size firms, such as International Resources Group, which specializes in the environment and energy sectors, and Management Systems International (MSI), which has a large democracy and governance portfolio. A sample of larger firms with an extensive array of services includes Abt Associates Inc., Associates in Rural Development (ARD), Bearing Point, Chemonics, Development Alternatives Incorporated (DAI), and Management Sciences for Health (MSH). These are just a few of the many firms that do international work through USAID, World Bank, and other donor contracts.

Federal procurement policies and the structure of contracting vehicles play a huge role in shaping the employment possibilities in for-profit firms (and in nonprofits that pursue grants and contracts too). Procurement policies encourage the growth of niche businesses, with some contracts set aside for small businesses, and women- or minority-owned enterprises. Larger contracts often call for a certain percentage of the work to be allocated to small or disadvantaged businesses, so large firms have incentives to include them in their proposals when they assemble a consortium of firms for a particular bid.

An important trend in USAID contracting has been the increase in what are called Indefinite Quantity Contracts (IQCs).[10] These are contracts where the actual work done through the contract depends upon demand from Missions around the world and/or Washington-based bureaus for the particular set of services offered, so the bidder cannot know in advance what the ultimate value of the contract will be, although USAID sets a ceiling value at the time the contract is let (usually a high amount). For example, USAID's Office of Democracy and Governance manages twenty-three IQCs for civil society strengthening, judicial reform, anticorruption, democracy building, and so on. Each IQC has been completed and for each one there are multiple award holders; that is, more than one firm (or consortium of firms) has won the same IQC. Work under the contract takes place through Task Orders (TOs); these are descriptions of tasks, along with specification of what kinds of personnel and/or equipment are needed to carry out the tasks, and a timeline. The IQC holders then bid against each other on these TOs, and the USAID Mission or Washington-based office that initiated the TO decides who wins and gets to do the work. Winning an IQC has been cynically referred to as earning the right to go on fishing expeditions. Once a firm wins an IQC, it still needs to market itself and the availability of this mechanism, and to bid competitively on each TO.

Because the IQC doesn't have any funding in it until a TO comes along, firms tend to keep their full-time staff levels small and build up a flexible stable of part-time specialist consultants they can draw upon as needed to staff the TOs as they come in over the life of the contract. Taken to an extreme, this business model leads to a firm that consists of "one guy, a telephone, and a rolodex," or what is disparagingly called in the development industry a "body shop." While USAID purports to prefer firms that nurture in-house technical capacity, the cost structure of many of the Agency's contracting vehicles makes it difficult to maintain full-time technical staff and encourages the use of short-term consultants on TOs rather than staff.[11]

Why should you, the prospective job-seeker with an international development consulting firm, care about all this? First, because it's part of understanding how the international development industry functions. As Aaron Williams says, *know your business. I think that's very important. . . . And it can't just be superficial.* Second, because understanding something of how these contracts operate, and of the hiring incentives they create, will help you to figure out what the job market in the contractor world is really about.

First of all, when you approach a consulting firm looking for a full-time job (unless you're responding to an advertisement for an open position with an existing project), the conversation is likely to be friendly but somewhat hypothetical, as in, "you're the kind of person we're looking for, you have good skills, thanks for the CV [curriculum vitae or resume], and we'll get back to you if anything comes up." So don't hold your breath waiting to be called. Most likely, your CV will be added to an extensive database to be called up if and only if you have the precise expertise sought for a particular TO or Request for Proposal (RFP). Your name and CV may even be included in a project proposal, but, again, don't hold your breath. The job will come only if the firm in question wins the bid. You'll also be competing with internal staffing priorities, such as finding ways to keep full-time staff billable (see below).

Second, full-time entry-level positions that are not project dependent tend to be administrative, with a focus on contract management and/or proposal development (a combination of technical research and writing, recruitment, and budgeting). These are essential skills to learn, so don't be shy in taking a job like this early in your career. And you may find you enjoy it and decide to become more of a specialist. These are areas where, with good skills, you should face fewer challenges in finding jobs. Third, if you are hired for a technical position that is not specific to a particular contract, you will be expected—after a grace period of anywhere from two weeks to six months—to "sell" yourself within the firm so that the majority of your time is covered on projects. This is what is called being billable, and the key to job happiness in a consulting firm depends upon billability.

Nonprofit Organizations and NGOs

This category of employers includes a wide range of organizations. A significant subset is what USAID calls private voluntary organizations (PVOs) or NGOs. These organizations reflect a mission-driven, values-based orientation, and combine their own resources, and sometimes individual contributions, with donor funds to carry out their mission. Many of these organizations have a long history of working with USAID in both humanitarian and development assistance.[12] USAID's

Office of Private and Voluntary Cooperation is the primary interface between the Agency and its PVO/NGO partners, including facilitating their inclusion into Agency policymaking.[13] Well-known examples include Africare, Care, Mercy Corps, Pact, Save the Children, World Learning, and World Wildlife Fund. Some are faith-based organizations with varying degrees of religious emphasis, such as Adventist Development, Catholic Relief Services, Relief Agency (ADRA), and World Vision. In the past these organizations received USAID grants that accorded them significant leeway in what they did with the funds and how they implemented their programs. These grants, or cooperative agreements, include requirements for matching funding and local partners.

A trend, begun in the 1990s, has been a relative decline in the availability of discretionary grant funding in favor of performance-based financing, leading the NGO community to complain on occasion that USAID treats them the same as for-profit contractors. Today, NGOs compete with each other and with for-profit firms for contract and grant funding (cooperative agreements) to implement development projects. They have devised operating procedures and hiring practices very similar to those at for-profit firms, so many of the points discussed in the previous section apply to nonprofits as well.

One way of distinguishing among NGOs is the extent to which they rely on other sources of funding besides donor contracts and grants. A nonprofit such as the Academy for Educational Development operates solely on the basis of donor funding, and thus in terms of its organizational culture and operating procedures it is very nearly identical to a profit-making firm. NGOs like Care and World Wildlife Fund receive contracts and grants but derive portions of their funding from individual donors, which provides them with the independence to pursue their own policy and program agendas. Some NGOs that are substantially dependent on USAID funding still retain many of the characteristics typically associated with nonprofit organizations, such as a strong values-based mission. Pact is one such organization.

Another category of nonprofits contains organizations that focus on research and policy studies, sometimes including technical assistance, such as RTI International (Research Triangle Institute, where Derick works), the Urban Institute, the World Resources Institute, the Center for Strategic and International Studies, or the Brookings Institution. Many of these organizations do both US domestic-focused and international research and analysis. Still others are policy advocacy organizations, such as Bread for the World, the Bank Information Center, Freedom House, or GenderAction. Additional internationally focused NGOs pursue specialized international development interests but unrelated to the development industry, for example, Ashoka, which supports social entrepreneurship.

The nonprofit umbrella extends to cover foundations as well. Several of these have important international programs, hire technical specialists in a variety of disciplines, and/or offer fellows programs to support research. Examples include: the Ford Foundation, the Kettering Foundation, the Rockefeller Foundation, the Rockefeller Brothers Fund, the Bill and Melinda Gates Foundation, and the John D. and Catherine T. MacArthur Foundation. There are two foundations that are quasi-governmental agencies and receive funding from the US Congress: the Inter-American Foundation and the African Development Foundation. Other nonprofit entities that have congressionally mandated support are the National Democratic Institute and the International Republican Institute. Both of these organizations are active in international democracy promotion around the world, and have a record of hiring young professionals for overseas positions. The US Institute of Peace, another entity with government funding, offers research and training positions related to conflict resolution, peace studies, and human rights.

As our quick overview reveals, the international development missions and the job possibilities among this wide array of organizations are numerous and varied. You can find organizations that emphasize policy and advocacy work, research and analysis, or grassroots community development and service delivery. The larger nonprofits have a corporate and bureaucratic feel to them; the smallest ones can be like working in a family environment, with all the pluses and minuses that go with that. And in between you can find all sorts of combinations. Before making any assumptions based on the NGO label, you should investigate each organization. Make sure you understand what you are dealing with, and discover whether it is the right organization for your current career objectives. Appendix 3 offers some sources on where to look.

Universities

State land-grant universities have been long-time partners with USAID and USDA in development activities largely focused on agricultural and rural development, and have traditionally been a powerful lobby group for international assistance. In 1975, Congress passed the International Development and Food Assistance Act. One of its provisions, known as Title XII, is to expand the participation of land-grant universities to work with the US government to "increase world food production and provide support to the application of science to solving developing countries' food and nutrition problems." The law has been amended several times, most recently in 2000—the Famine Prevention and Freedom from Hunger Act, which broadened the focus of university collaboration to include food security, sustainable resource use and conservation, and expanded trade.

Under Title XII, universities, both individually and in a variety of consortiums, have been engaged in research, training, and technical assistance through cooperative agreements, grants, and Collaborative Research Support Programs, fielding teams of faculty, graduate students, and technical specialists around the world. Universities such as Michigan State (whose current president, Peter McPherson, is a former USAID Administrator), Washington State, Purdue, and University of California Davis are all active internationally. Their programs offer employment opportunities in international agriculture, natural resources management and environment, food and nutrition policy, social anthropology, and economics. For graduate students in these sectors, there can be opportunities to combine dissertation research with overseas work experience.

Beyond agriculture and natural resources work under Title XII, some universities have established centers, or in some cases commercial entities, to pursue international development work. A well-known example is the University of Wisconsin's Land Tenure Center, established in 1962, but there are many others. In 1983, for example, USAID, USDA, and the University of Maryland created the International Development Management Center (IDMC) at the College Park campus. Derick worked at IDMC for ten years, serving as Associate Director for Research for six years, until the Center was closed in 1993. Another University of Maryland, College Park center (still in operation) is the Center for International Development and Conflict Management, which has an active program of research, training, and technical assistance. Also at the University of Maryland is the IRIS Center (Institutional Reform and the Informal Sector), attached to the economics department, which pursues contracts and grants related to economic policy, democratization and legal reform, and institutional economics.

These kinds of centers offer both long- and short-term employment opportunities in international development. In the health sector, for example, the Johns Hopkins University School of Public Health set up a nonprofit affiliate in 1973, JHPIEGO, to undertake research, training, and consulting contracts in international family planning and reproductive health, maternal and child health, and HIV/AIDS. JHPIEGO implements numerous USAID and foundation-funded contracts, and recruits regularly for Baltimore headquarters and overseas positions. The private sector may also partner with universities for implementing development programs. For example, in the mid-1990s, Rutgers University-Camden implemented an education technology program in South Africa funded by a multinational corporation.

Another set of university partners in international public service and development can be found among HBCUs (historically black colleges and universities). These schools have been a source of training and technical assistance for USAID projects in a variety of sectors, such as agriculture and health. USAID policy includes strengthening HBCUs, and thus other organizations are often partnered with them to provide capacity building assistance to an HBCU along with technical assistance in developing countries. For example, in the mid to late 1990s, USAID funded JHPIEGO to work with Morehouse University's School of Medicine to develop a core team of physicians and nurses to provide clinical training overseas. Together, JHPIEGO and Morehouse conducted training workshops in Uganda, Zimbabwe, and the United States (Georgia and California) for health care providers. More recently, the private firm Electronic Data Systems Corporation partnered with Prairie View A&M University's engineering school in 2003 on a USAID-funded project to provide information technology and training to Ghana's Kwame Nkrumah University of Science and Technology.

Because of their mission to serve disadvantaged populations in the United States and their location in often economically depressed locations, both rural and urban, HBCUs frequently have a strong public service orientation and a sense of solidarity with developing countries, particularly in Africa. Given their participation in USAID-funded projects and partnerships, as well as in state, local, and federally funded service outreach, HBCUs represent another potential source of employment opportunities in public service, both international and domestic.[14]

Inside/Outside Systems

Clearly, there are many options for where to work in international public service. At different stages in your career, perhaps in different contexts, you may decide to work for change from inside the organization or system you have chosen, or from the outside. You may seek, for example, to work for large bureaucracies, such as the World Bank, USAID, or the Department of Commerce, with the intention of promoting new understandings and change from within. Or you may choose instead to participate in an advocacy NGO, such as Bread for the World or the Bank Information Center, to improve the workings of these institutions through pressure from the outside. You may opt for direct service provision, say working on local democracy promotion in Eastern Europe as a staff member at the NGO, World Learning; helping rural villagers in Madagascar manage their natural resources through a contract with the private firm, International Resources Group; or assisting Senegalese women to establish a community health insurance organization as part of a health project implemented by Abt Associates Inc.

Making the choice has to do with where you are on the service-choice spiral. Specifically, how do you see yourself at a particular point in time, in terms of your skills, your goals, and your values/self-awareness? And how do you see the organizations you're considering working for? Sarah Newhall sees herself as someone who chooses to work from the inside: *I'm more likely to have always viewed myself as the guerilla inside the bureaucracy, than from outside the bureaucracy looking in. I worked for Portland city government, I worked for the Ecumenical Ministries of Oregon, which is a large social service network. I worked for the last decade inside Pact, which is a [nongovernmental] institution. I work for policy change within all of these systems. . . . I view myself as a change agent within large and small systems and I also take to the streets whenever I feel like it. I'm a believer in peaceful, nonviolent protest movements that also put pressure from the outside.*

David Yang expands on Sarah Newhall's thoughts, and stresses knowing what you want and like to do as an important consideration in choosing where to work. *Whether I'm trying to start a think tank or work for another NGO, or work in the US government, or in a multilateral institution. . . . I know the things I do well, but more importantly, I know the things I like to do, and the things I resent doing. So to me, it's less important working on the inside or the outside. I see the value of both and I see the opportunities and pitfalls of both. It's not much fun working for a bureaucracy unless you think you can really do something, push an agenda. So for me, it's a matter of knowing my skills and limitations, knowing what I want to achieve in terms of an institutional reform agenda, and looking for opportunities on the outside or inside of those institutions to push that agenda.* David Yang's career demonstrates the importance of working in a variety of settings as part of the process of finding out (and building) your work-life strengths and discovering your preferences.

The World Bank is often characterized as the quintessential international development "bad guy"—rigid, arrogant, and impervious to change. Najma Siddiqi, however, has a different view. *I'm working for change in all kinds of situations. I mean, of course, I am in the Bank, right? So everyone can say, "What change are you working for?" But when I joined the Bank, the idea was, "Okay, this is an institution I disagree with completely. How can I change a little piece of it? Obviously, I can't change everything. But let's see what I can change from inside. How can I expand spaces for people who believe in things that I believe in and want to bring about change in the world?"*

Aaron Williams also talks about pushing the envelope from within the organization where you're working, which means knowing that organization well. *For my entire career, I've been in some type of organization which required organizational norms to a certain extent. But I'd like to think— this might be foolhardy on my part—that I've always been a revolutionary within these organizations. I interviewed for a job one time and a person told me, "You know, we never talked to anybody from AID before because AID is a big bureaucracy, things are very slow there. We're an innovative organization that moves very quickly." And so I looked that person in the eye and said, "You know, that just goes to show how little you know about AID." I said, "One of the things I've always enjoyed about AID is that AID allows an individual to be an entrepreneur within the system, if you're determined and persistent to pursue your ideas." Now that takes a lot of courage and determination. Frankly in a bureaucracy like AID if you have a good idea, and you can make a difference in a very short period of time, people will give you a lot of room. I found that all the time. I never found myself blocked by the bureaucracy at any level in getting through new ideas.*

That's why I said, I've always viewed myself as being kind of a rebel, a revolutionary in doing innovative things wherever I've worked. I never wanted to have somebody tell me, "Well we've never done that before." That's when I say great. Now we're going to do something. And that's at IYF [International Youth Foundation], *it'll be at RTI* [Research Triangle Institute], *it was at AID. I just believe in that. And I think that one of the reasons is that I had this really good grounding and experience base in the private sector where innovation is important and you're always looking for the good ideas. It's deadly to say in a business environment, "Well we've never done that before. We never thought we could put sugar on Cheerios. We can't tamper with that. We can't have chocolate flavor in Wheaties." Well, in those environments, everything is on the table. That's how companies grow. And I've tried to bring that perspective to government and the nonprofit world.*

Front Line vs. Facilitating

Another aspect of the choice of where to look for employment opportunities involves your preference for working on the "front lines," that is, participating directly in service delivery or technical assistance; or serving in a facilitating capacity, which can be management backstopping of some sort, general headquarters administration, technical research or policy work with donors and other international development decision makers, or training and teaching to prepare others for international development and public service work. One of the main distinctions here is whether or not you are working directly with those to be affected by development policies, programs, and projects. You may be more skilled in organizational processes, or you may prefer working through direct human interaction. Similarly, you may prefer facilitating others who are more skilled at working on the front lines of direct service delivery, or you may choose to be on the front lines yourself. Perhaps you represent some combination of these skills and preferences.

For example, Jennifer enjoys working with students and prefers this type of human interaction to direct service delivery to disadvantaged populations. *This was something I learned working as an assistant shelter manager for the American Red Cross after an earthquake. Seeing and working to alleviate the suffering in the shelter on a daily basis was overwhelming. The final straw was when I discovered a three-year-old girl who was suffering from child abuse. Since we were about to close the shelter, there was nothing I could do but refer the family to the appropriate welfare programs with an added note in the file requesting the program administrators to investigate. It was difficult to be in the position of trusting these anonymous bureaucracies to take care of this child. I decided then that I wanted somehow to be involved in or to influence those bureaucracies and the policies and staff that populate them. Social work training includes preparation for handling burnout and the stress associated with daily exposure to others' suffering. I would have benefited from some of this training.* We encourage you to pursue such training if you choose to work on the front lines.

In international public service, working directly for program beneficiaries—or affected populations—most often means choosing to work overseas (though not all who work overseas are on the frontlines). Jennifer Butz (Profile 6) places herself squarely in the camp of those who want to pursue a career overseas in the field. *We* [overseas project staff] *are the field presence of the international organizations that we work with. We tend to be really good at handling ambiguity, since we never know if things are going to continue or not. We tend to be the people who want to be right where the actual programs get played out. We're not particularly interested in administration or a lot of the institutional details, although as you move up the food chain and become higher ranking in the programs oftentimes that's what you do more of. But the gratification is the direct interface, in the cultures, with the communities, or with your chosen field.*

David Yang, on the other hand, made an explicit choice for an international career based in the United States. *I was a refugee and what that meant to me psychologically and professionally was that I wanted an international career. But I knew also I wanted to put down roots in this country. That was important to me. Because even though I probably grew up much less itinerant than many people in Washington, certainly diplomatic people, psychologically being a refugee, you never felt you were American, that you belonged. So I always had this plan that I would be a Washington kind of person, who would travel and be involved in international groups. Even though I knew the level of "commitment" or intensity of the work might be attenuated given that I would be based in Washington, I always knew it would be my compromise, and as a first-generation refugee, that that commitment to my children who were yet to be born was as important—in terms of the entire gestalt of my life and my service—as going off to a Third World country, either as a* [diplomat] *or a development worker. Certainly at times professionally it's thrown up road blocks, but I've been lucky enough to have never regretted it.*

Both the field and the Washington-based work are essential for sustainable development. One of our focus group participants who works for an advocacy organization summed it up this way: *None of the policy work that we do would mean anything without the project and the grassroots stuff going on. Why are we playing this game in Washington and pushing for greater accountability at international financial institutions if it's not backed up by some kind of project work on the ground? It's very real for us. We get calls from people who have just been drowned out of their homes. For us it's very much on the ground and people's lives. And I take that with me when I go to the Board room and when I meet with* [the Department of] *Treasury. I take that experience and what is happening to people around the world because of decisions that are made in D.C. and that's what drives me on a day-to-day basis. When I feel like I'm totally disconnected, like who cares about the governing structure of the World Bank?, I think of everyone in Chad and Cameroon who is suffering from corruption and economic disparity, yet there's a huge amount of wealth in those countries. I think about, Why aren't their voices represented here?*

Like David Yang, you may not be interested in pursuing a career based overseas. However, to be effective throughout your career, you need to have some field experience to inform how you think about your work at headquarters and to understand your interactions with those in the field. All of our profiled practitioners had such experience early in their international public service careers, regardless of what they are doing now. It's also very important to visit the field periodically, even if it is not the location of your day-to-day work. Seeing those you are serving and the impacts your work has on the ground is essential to sustaining your motivation and passion for service, as illustrated by our focus group member. Working at headquarters can breed a bureaucratic mentality and/or cynicism. So you need to see the field on occasion to refresh.

Similarly, if you are based in the field, you need to connect with headquarters on occasion. You should cultivate a network of people from headquarters who can keep you abreast of what is happening there, changing priorities, politics, and so on; and who also know and understand you, your work, and the challenges you face so they can best support you. So, for example, when a mission from headquarters comes to town to observe or assess the work, don't roll your eyes or run for cover. Take the opportunity to tell your story and build a relationship with them that you can sustain by phone and e-mail.

Many Options, Many Choices

As the service-choice spiral indicates, your decision about where to work for change will be made not once, but many times over the life of your career. The dynamic nature of careers in international public service will push you toward a high degree of flexibility to respond to changing job responsibilities, organizational contexts, and emerging service delivery and socioeconomic development challenges. You will likely have not one but many employers, and more than one career. As your values and competencies evolve over time, your job preferences and choices are likely to change.

From this chapter, there are several key "take-away" messages. The first is the wide array of job and career choices that relate to international development and public service. We've tried to provide an overview of the categories of organizations out there where you might work, but we can only scratch the surface regarding specifics. The Internet sources we list in Appendix 3 should help you to go deeper on your search.

The second message is a more subtle one, which can be framed as an admonition: don't stereotype organizations and the people in them. Doing so both limits your options and constrains your ability to truly understand how change takes place and how to support making development happen. As some of our quotes indicate, the assumption that donor organizations are uniformly rigid and ossified structures full of robot-like bureaucrats, where nothing new or innovative is possible, is inaccurate and misleading. Don't presume that for-profit firms and those who work for them care only for making a buck, feathering their nests, or taking illegitimate advantage of their funders. While there may indeed be some firms that fit this stereotype, the majority are staffed with dedicated and hardworking people who want their work to make a difference in the world. The phrase "beltway bandit" denigrates the intentions and the spirit in which many private sector employees labor. It may be a popular phrase, especially among politicians, but the reality today is that much of what we know of as good, compassionate public service would not happen without the service visions of those who staff these organizations. Finally, don't take it for granted that NGOs occupy the moral high ground in terms of values, idealism, and commitment. Some are exemplary, yet many fall far short; that doesn't make them necessarily "bad," just subject to the same amalgamation of positive and negative motivations that drive all types of human endeavor.

A third message relates to a question that challenges all of us at some point or points along our career path: which employment option is right for me? The only answer is that it depends. You can't make a "right" choice in the abstract because what's right for you will be a function of where you are on your path and what options are available to you at a given moment. The histories of those we've profiled and our own career paths show that all of us have worked in a variety of organizations at one time or another, and we've all learned something valuable along the way. Thus, in one sense, the only choice that is "wrong" is one we don't learn from so that we're less able to make the next choice that confronts us. We delve more deeply into this topic in the next chapter. In the meantime, Jef Buehler's story demonstrates how keeping an open mind can enable you to work for change from seemingly unexpected places, in his case from the New Jersey State Government.

Notes

1. Clearly, there are significant value dimensions to the relative determination of inside and outside. For example, the environmental NGO, Greenpeace, is viewed by some as an organization that pushes the envelope of legality in pursuing its mission. Depending upon your values, you may feel that Greenpeace acts appropriately and deserves your support, or you may reject its tactics as unsuitable and counterproductive.

2. See USAID's White Paper, "Foreign Aid: Meeting the Challenges of the Twenty-First Century" (Washington, D.C.: USAID, Bureau for Policy and Program Coordination, January 2004), available at http://www.usaid.gov/policy/pdabz3221.pdf.

3. For an in-depth discussion of jobs in US embassies, see *Inside a U.S. Embassy: How the Foreign Service Works for America*, edited by Shawn Dorman (Washington, D.C.: American Foreign Service Association, 2003). See http://www.afsa.org/inside for details.

4. To cope with the surge in demands on the agency imposed by Iraq, Afghanistan, and other emergencies, USAID is rethinking its personnel system. Some of the hiring mechanisms described here may be converted to "FS limited non-career appointments." See the description of USAID's Business Transformation Executive Committee at http://www.usaid.gov/policy/par04/.

5. As of this writing, the NEP program's starting salaries fall between $37,254 and $67,517. The more junior IDI program begins salaries at $33,304.

6. Both the United Kingdom and Canada have foreign assistance agencies that serve the analogous function to USAID. In the United Kingdom, the Department for International Development (DFID) fulfills this role, and in Canada, it is the Canadian International Development Agency (CIDA). Some information on employment possibilities with these agencies can be found in Appendix 3.

7. The Bank also has a program specific to individuals of sub-Saharan African descent: the Junior Professionals Program for Afro-Descendants, which has a higher age limit than the JPA (thirty-five or younger).

8. In addition to these entities and its classic peacekeeping mandate, the United Nations deals with a variety of international issues that are not directly

related to socioeconomic development, for example, atomic energy and its regulation (IAEA, International Atomic Energy Agency) and weather (WMO, World Meteorological Organization).

9. Other multilateral organizations worth exploring include the regional banks, the Inter-American Development Bank (based in Washington, D.C.), the Asia Development Bank (based in Manila), and the African Development Bank (in Abidjan), as well as the Organization of American States (also in Washington, and primarily staffed by Latin Americans).

10. The rise in IQCs derives from USAID downsizing, which leaves fewer staff in Missions to design, let, and manage project procurements, and from the government-wide trend toward performance-driven mechanisms. The IQC rationale is that contractors, since they compete first for the right to bid on task orders and then on the individual task orders themselves, are subject to the influence of market forces (the market being the USAID Missions seeking services), and thus will be more responsive to their client. IQCs for which there is little or no demand risk nonrenewal, the market equivalent of "going out of business."

11. In a nutshell, most IQC contracts call for bidders to propose a "multiplier rate" for personnel costs (this is called a time and materials, or T&M, contract). This multiplier is intended to include fringe benefits, overhead costs, and fee. The maximum that the firm can charge for someone's time on a particular task is that person's daily rate (salary divided by the number of workdays in a year), times the multiplier, times the number of days allocated to the task. Competition encourages firms to bid low multiplier rates, but this means that a firm staffing a TO, and using only its in-house personnel, will lose money: the cost to the firm will exceed what it can bill the IQC contract. The only way to break even or make a profit is to include consultants in the staff mix because the firm pays them only a daily rate times the number of days worked, but is allowed to bill the contract for the multiplied rate. This spread allows the firm to recoup the losses on using its in-house staff to work on the TO.

12. A list of PVOs working with USAID can be found at http://www.usaid.gov/about/resources.

13. The Advisory Committee on Voluntary Foreign Aid (ACVFA) provides input and advice to USAID on issues relating to development policy and programming, as well as the role of NGOs. ACVFA holds several meetings every year in Washington, D.C., which are open to the public. Attending these meetings can be a good opportunity for networking with US. international development NGOs as well as keeping informed on development issues and policies.

14. Other categories of institutions include what the US Government terms Hispanic Serving Institutions (HSIs), Tribal Colleges and Universities (TCUs), and an umbrella term, Minority Serving Institutions (MSIs).

Profile 5. Jef Buehler:
Service Is Where You Are

Despite his international ambitions, when Jef Buehler first arrived in Camden, New Jersey, to start his graduate studies in preparation for the Peace Corps, he said to himself, *why do I even have to go to the Third World? I'm in the Third World! So let's start doing community service here.* And so his commitment to a life of service, wherever he lived, began. Jef didn't abandon his international plans—he served with the Peace Corps. But his service career so far has come full circle. Jef is now the Director of Main Street New Jersey, working for the state government to help communities revitalize their downtowns.

Jef is a first-generation American. His mother and grandmother are refugees from World War II Latvia. This family heritage, combined with the bullying he was subjected to as a child, gave Jef a deep respect for, understanding of, and commitment to the underdog. *I had heard stories from my grandmother who escaped with my mom, about all that they went through, with the war, and under Stalin, and the Hitler time. And I was always fascinated by that. It appealed to the underdog kind of sense that I had. And also because it was my family, it was very personal.* Jef remembers becoming interested in national politics at age twelve, when he worked on Carter's 1980 campaign. He was fascinated by Jimmy Carter *because he had a message that was about peace, about working together, and about human rights—both internally and internationally.*

With these personal and political service motives forming, Jef chose Juniata College for his undergraduate studies because it offered a program in Peace and Conflict Studies. He began as a computer science major, in part because he was adept at computing, and also to please his refugee mother in terms of job prospects. He also pursued a minor in Peace and Conflict. But within less than a year, Jef abandoned computer science and declared his major in international politics with a focus on Peace and Conflict Studies. Jef's political views and yearning to learn more convinced him that he needed to experience more of the world. *I felt like there's more out there and we need to understand it. I wanted to see more what the truth was. Because you could read about the truth in a book, but you couldn't really understand it until you lived somewhere else and really experienced it.*

Jef wasn't particularly driven to pursue a graduate degree, but he decided he would consider it if he could find a pragmatic program that would enable him to discover more about the world. He was accepted at Rutgers University-Camden to pursue a master's of public administration offered in cooperation with the Peace Corps. This was the first of Peace Corps' Masters International (MI) programs and, at this time, it was only in its second year. *The program was very much in formation. Seeing the abject destitution in Camden, I decided to agitate for some community service activities within our group of twelve master's students, and most of my colleagues were very supportive.*

Jef learned that Camden schools either didn't have arts programs or were in the process of severely cutting them back. So he initiated RAP, the Rutgers Arts Program. He organized some of his fellow MI students and used his contacts with the undergraduate theater program to design and implement three arts events that year for Camden City school children. *We brought a couple of busloads of kids from the local schools down to each of these things. For Halloween, we did one on Edgar Allan Poe. We had Halloween candy and face painting. So it was fun, but it was also educational.* These experiences inspired other service activities on the part of MI students, resulting in the group winning a University Service Award, the first of its kind. But Camden also raised a lot of questions for Jef. *"Why am I even going international? There's so much need here, and it's clearly not being addressed."* Camden had already become infamous for its corruption—from 1978 to 2000 three of its five mayors were indicted on corruption charges. *So in that sense it was good preparation for the Third World, because there's a lot of corruption and wasted resources there, and the few rule over the many.*

Jef completed his coursework and headed off to Peace Corps service in the Dominican Republic. After his training, he sought the most remote site he could find. *I had a real thirst to get really deep into the culture, and to stay away from the Americanized resorts and the barbed-wire and the SUVs of the time. So they sent me out to literally as far away as possible from civilization.* Jef was placed in Los Jobos, twelve miles from the Haitian border. *It was in the middle of the desert, about as far from Caribbean water as you could get in that country.* It was a deforested twenty-five-square-mile area with no electricity, and it was the beginning of a sixteen-month drought. He was assigned to be a community education promoter, acting as a liaison between the local school, its principal, and the PTA. However, after his first meeting with the principal, who was also the principal for several other schools in the region, it didn't take him long to realize that Los Jobos was not a high-priority community and it was likely he would never see the principal again. And, in fact, he didn't. So Jef was left to create his own job. *Once I realized that the whole community education promotion thing was out the window, I decided just to live in the community and get a feel for what was going on. I worked in the fields. I used a machete. I learned as much as I could to live like they did, and to experience life like they did. By doing so over time, I realized, boy, these people are incredibly disempowered.*

Jef worked in agroforestry, supported the farmers, discussing what he learned in his training about crop choice, helped out in the school teaching Spanish literacy, and pitched in where he could, including harvesting and making fence posts. But he kept thinking about this idea of disempowerment and the fact that he would only be there for a short while. He recognized that there was a core group in Los Jobos who had a sense of themselves and their community's value. *These were people who were scraping by just to subsist, so it's hard to have high self-esteem when you're just trying to survive. But some of the people did. They were dirt poor, but they had incredibly high motivation and self-esteem. And they wanted change.* Jef designed a series of empowerment workshops. *The idea was to help them democratize themselves, and to explore their assets as a community.* Jef was fortunate to benefit from the Peace Corps library in Santo Domingo, where for thirty years volunteers had been adding and exchanging books, many of which concerned community development and community organizing. There, he discovered Paulo Freire and his model of conscientization.[1]

With the drought, the local river the community used for irrigation was at an all-time low. Water distribution occurred through political processes behind the scenes. It would determine whose crops would grow to be harvested, and, ultimately, which villages and towns would survive. So the Los Jobos community came together to consider its options. In the past, community members had tried to draw on their own personal contacts, though that had rarely worked. So Jef asked them, *"What can we do differently this time? Let's look at our assets. What have we got here? We have a lot of people here. What are our options?"* Everyone agreed they wanted to avoid violence, so Jef suggested a nonviolent protest of the water authority, thirty minutes away by pickup truck. A brainstorming session ensued, with the women suggesting they could prepare food for everyone. Someone else said they knew a group that could provide a school bus to get as many people there as possible. The community put a plan together. Jef was advised to leave the area during the time of the scheduled protest, and was surprised on his return to discover that it had not taken place. The community leadership had decided that it was in the community's best interest to seek other means of resolving the situation. Instead, they'd sent a delegation of people to Santo Domingo, representing each of the political parties, to talk with their respective party officials, and the water distribution issue was resolved. *So, we didn't actually have to do the action. But I perceive that we had success, because we raised the consciousness of the community and enough people within it to realize that they could do something, that they had the power to better their lives.*

When Jef returned to Camden to write his thesis he began doing community organizing work there. *After being in the DR* [Dominican Republic], *it was the logical extension. I went to the DR, and I learned some community organizing. I now understood the Latin culture a lot better, and the language too. So it was full circle.* Jef became a Housing Scholar with the New Jersey Department of Community Affairs. The program subsidized his salary as he worked for a local nonprofit organization, the St. Joseph's Carpenter Society, which encouraged Jef to see if his DR experience might be applicable in East Camden. *These people were being terrorized by drug dealers. If they called the police, their cars were fire-bombed by the drug dealers. I saw some of the wrecks. They were totally scared. They lived literally behind bars. They all barred in their porches. And I walked around and asked them, "What are your needs? Can we talk?" And people were scared to talk with me.* Since St. Joseph's was a housing organization, the idea was to connect this work with a home-ownership program, especially since many people in the community were renters without stable housing. St. Joseph's established a home-ownership program for the area, funded by a grant from Campbell's Soup.

For the next three years, Jef worked at various posts with the Department of Community Affairs, gaining experience, particularly with respect to housing issues. In that process he met the Director of the Main Street New Jersey program. *She seemed very different, less bureaucratic than the rest of the people I'd seen in state government.* Jef became more familiar with the Main Street program as his work complemented some of theirs. *I thought, "Wow, this is so cool. This is about community empowerment; it's what I like to do."* When the director needed a new assistant, she asked Jef if he would consider applying for the job. *I said, "In a heartbeat!" Not even knowing what I was getting into.* Jef has been with Main Street New Jersey ever since and is now the State Coordinator of the program.

Main Street is a community revitalization program focused on downtown areas that was started by the National Trust for Historic Preservation around 1980. It helps people develop a vision for their community, and facilitates goal setting, work planning, and resource identification and acquisition. *I came to Main Street as a community developer and a community organizer; not as a historical preservationist, which is the basis of the program; not as an economic development person, which I knew nothing about when I started doing this. It's about moving people. It's about getting people to focus on—get this—their assets in their communities—the exact model that I used for the DR. For me, it's practically spiritual, because when people own their downtown, then they have some say in at least their corner of the world. And in the world today, that is almost priceless, if you can have some say in the fate of your corner of it, and thereby make the world a more peaceful place, one community at a time.*

Note

1. See recommended reading on community development and empowerment in Appendix 4.

CHAPTER 8

Career Evolution

Even if you have a better idea of your vision of development and your personal service vision and have some inkling of where you want to work, reality may also be nagging at you saying, "These are my ideals. How will it really work?" In a perfect world, you could jump right in to pursuing your vision in the organization of your choice. Realistically, the field of international public service, like many professions, can be a difficult one to break into and move through. You can't always start out with what you want, where you want. You also have to consider what you *can* do and where. This doesn't mean you take the first opportunity and let yourself be derailed from your initial vision. We encourage you to look strategically at your career, and each step along its path, in a bigger picture and a longer time frame. Being strategic doesn't mean you can figure everything out ahead of time. It means acting on the information you have in hand, but being mindful of a larger goal, not just the immediate choice you're faced with.

You have your ideal vision, or hopefully some basic core components of it, but what can you do and learn along the way that will help you to be most effective in achieving it in the longer run? In Chapter 6 we discussed a broad array of skills. No one starts out possessing them all and, as we noted, many of these will necessarily be gained on the job. So as you consider your options, you should always keep in mind, "What do I need to learn next?"

We've explored each of the service-choice spiral components. In this chapter, we'll look at how you move along the spiral and progress in your career. We'll pay particular attention to the most challenging transitions in an international public service career. Some of these depend on the choices you make with respect to where to work, for example, transitioning from domestic to international work, or from the headquarters to the field. Others are more general features of the international public service career path, for example, getting the first job, moving beyond the first job, and, specifically, transitioning from administrative support to more technical work. We start with some general issues regarding career development.

Moving along the Spiral

As we've discussed, finding your place in international public service begins with self-awareness. It then builds on humility as you continuously contribute to and benefit from communities of understanding through dialogue, as you apply your knowledge and skills. This process culminates in transforming the organizations and broader systems in which you choose to work. The spiral is not a one-time sequence. As you accumulate work experience and develop personally and professionally, you will attain new levels of self-awareness. Maybe you'll become more aware of the importance of different values, or you'll discover new and different preferences. Or maybe you'll find that your original service vision is not your heart's calling or that you may have comparative advantages in other areas.

This continuously developing self-awareness will lead to progression and growth along the service-choice spiral, not necessarily in the original order. You will likely discover that to be effective in your service vision, you need to acquire additional skills and knowledge. Changes in your self-awareness may lead you to modify your vision for development or your personal service vision. Hopefully, it will encourage you to pursue new skills and knowledge strategically. Perhaps you will come to know yourself better by working in community, as your colleagues and those affected by your work hold a mirror to you, letting you know what you do well, and what you may need to improve. In discussing your challenges with these communities, you may learn new and better approaches to fulfilling your service vision. This might include working for a different organization, or a shift from working for change from the inside to the outside of systems.

In this sense, the service-choice spiral is about continuously expanding your personal growth and professional development, both in depth and breadth, as you advance on your career path. As we will explore in Chapter 9, through successive repetitions of the spiral, your individual career path will, ideally, balance your personal interests and career aspirations with the larger goal of international public service. Following is a general discussion of tips and advice for career advancement.

Plan? What Plan?

Since movement along the spiral is iterative, with growth in one area leading to adjustments and growth in others, we hope it's clear to you that careers are not completely planned in advance. The notion of a path is apparent largely in retrospect. As the philosopher, Soren Kierkegaard said, "life is lived forward, yet understood backward." We encouraged you in Chapter 4 to begin to reflect on your vision for what development means, and even to begin to articulate what you think your personal service vision will be. But the emphasis is on "begin." These are continuous processes that will lead you to make adaptations and changes along the way. Every career consists of movement, including ups and downs. Think for a moment about what that looks like: up, down, and forward; up, down, and forward. If you were to map it graphically it would look like a heartbeat. It is in the movement, the changes, and the growth that we experience life. Imagine if you had a clear roadmap from the start and if you stuck religiously to it. Would you ignore new opportunities that you couldn't have predicted? Of course not. What if you didn't meet your goals? Would that mean failure? No, it would just mean you do something different, in a different time frame, perhaps something that's a better fit for you. No one can be all knowing. So it's impossible to develop "the" plan for your career and stick to it rigidly. Just as international development cannot be managed according to some sort of blueprint, neither can your job and life choices.

In mentoring young people through Pact and in her personal life, Sarah Newhall worries a lot about this emphasis on having a plan. *There's a very clear logic in terms of what issues I was pursuing throughout my career, as opposed to a strategy to become this or that by a certain time in my life. Sometimes when I'm interviewing candidates for jobs—I think it's a mistake—but they have a roadmap and they're always judging themselves against their roadmap, which is a recipe for misery. And so they either feel like they're behind or ahead, based on that roadmap. And it's messing up their mind.* Sarah never planned to transition to a career in international public service. She just felt ready to do something different as a sabbatical. The core of her vision and values has not changed; only the way it is expressed.

Our other profiled practitioners offer similar examples. David Yang and Jennifer Butz could not have predicted that they would be pioneers in a new technical area of international development programming, democratic governance. Najma Siddiqi certainly did not set out with a master's degree in clinical psychology to do international and community development work. When she started at the Home Economics College, she could not have envisioned that she would end up working in a Vice President's Office at the World Bank. As he was growing up in South Chicago or even later as an international business executive, Aaron Williams could not have thought that he would one day work with Nelson Mandela as USAID Mission Director to South Africa.

Our point is that a plan is important to clarifying your values and the core of your vision, but it should not be fixed in concrete. Having a plan, or at least the fundamentals of self-awareness discussed in Chapter 4 (including preferences and skills), is still very important. It can help you to be more strategic in the choices and investments you make along the way. We encourage you to use your self-awareness to move consciously and strategically along the service-choice spiral to ensure that you have an effective, meaningful, and satisfying career.

Imagination, Courage, and Confidence

So where do you start? Sarah Newhall recommends that you *keep working to develop your imagination and your vision. This is as important as other skills that you can have, because if you can't imagine doing something you really can't do it. So developing one's imagination is a piece of advice that I give to people who come through here when they want to know, "well, now what should I do?" I say, "Develop an active imagination. Discover what your passion is. Spend a lot of energy trying to figure out why you get up in the morning." I tie that back to a humanities orientation, to the questions about the meaningful life—which is different from technical skill sets. It's more about what ideas and values you have socially, emotionally, and spiritually that are going to guide you through all sorts of unexpected surprises in your life. So if you welcome surprise and are open to it, really, anything can happen. And you don't lose your way. So it doesn't really matter what you do, it matters who you are. End of story.*

Beyond imagination, this also means believing in yourself, having the imagination to visualize yourself doing what you want to do: in short, confidence. It takes confidence not only to envision a path and begin to walk it, but also to follow your gut and take the necessary risks along the way. With active listening, observing, and imagination, you are more likely to recognize serendipity, those unforeseen moments and opportunities when everything just fits. This was David Yang's experience in thinking about a political appointment to work on democracy promotion. Jef Buehler had a similar experience when he returned to Camden and began community organizing there. Najma Siddiqi uses these skills to recognize when she is stagnating and should be investing her energy elsewhere. Confidence is also necessary to seize opportunities and create openings where they didn't previously exist. Aaron Williams did this when he began promoting more cooperation with the private sector, both at USAID and in NGOs.

Imagine the assertiveness and confidence required when David Yang phoned the United Nations and essentially convinced them they needed a Washington-based person to promote their democracy agenda.

Imagine the confidence required not only to leave your friends and family for a two-year sabbatical but to abandon your professional home and networks, where you are known and respected, to work in a foreign country doing something you've never done before, as Sarah Newhall did in Cambodia. Imagine the wholehearted commitment required to persevere in your service vision despite scandalous accusations and pressure from others to compromise your values, as Najma Siddiqi did. And you will see, Jennifer Butz's moxie to assume the Asia Foundation would be better with than without her and then to wait until they realized it too, or at least found an opening for her. It also takes courage to build bridges between those perceived to be the "good guys" and the "bad guys," as Aaron Williams did at IYF in fostering partnerships between nonprofits and multinational corporations. And if you don't know you can stretch in these confident and courageous ways, the Peace Corps is a great way to learn, as Jef Buehler experienced. Despite formal plans and placements, many volunteers end up creating their most meaningful contribution and work independent of these structures. Najma Siddiqi's advice sums this up nicely: *Trust yourself. I normally don't offer advice, because everyone is their own person and they know what to do—but that's why I'm saying trust yourself. Trust your instincts.*

Points of Reference

Trusting yourself is easier said than done. One helpful tactic that can serve you throughout your career is to create reference points for yourself. These may evolve as you gain more experience. Here's what we mean: think of a time when you were challenged beyond your previous, maybe wildest, imagination and you succeeded. What was the hardest thing you ever did and succeeded at?

When Jennifer had barely started at the World Bank, her manager decided to send her to China to work on a project she wasn't familiar with. *I asked my manager what she wanted me to do, and she only responded, "I'm not exactly sure yet. We'll figure it out when you get there. In the meantime, read up." On the eve of leaving, I learned that my manager was pulled away on a family emergency and would not be joining me. The only message I got from her was, "I'm sure you'll figure out how to best use your talents." Yikes! I had never been to China, I didn't speak the language, and on top of everything else, I was charged with bringing four boxes of heavy training materials with me. I was fortunate to meet up with someone in the Beijing airport who just happened to be working on the project and was a native Chinese speaker. He helped me with the boxes, and navigated the process of changing money, finding a taxi, and getting to the hotel. I discovered the next morning that I had no professional interpreter assigned to me. A bilingual colleague helped me to understand what was going on. Based on that understanding, I began to design materials for the training teams that were being formed. In the end, my manager was very pleased with my work and we were able to travel there together on the next trip. So here's the lesson that I have subsequently relied on: if I could handle that China assignment and 1) survive, and 2) succeed on some level (any level), then I can probably handle what's in front of me now.*

We're not saying you can do *anything*, but chances are the challenge you face in this moment is not as daunting as the memory of your biggest challenge ever. So give some thought to your reference points and update them with new experiences. It can really help you to keep your doubts and fears in check when you face new situations. Note, too, that Jennifer's success depended on other people helping her. When you face something new, you often feel like you're all alone. Most often, people are willing and ready to lend a hand.

Proving Yourself

Jennifer's experience in China happened, in part, because she had already had the opportunity to prove herself. So confidence is essential, but you also need to be aware that in each new context, you are an unknown quantity. Before people trust you with responsibility, you have to prove that you can handle it. Aaron Williams offers two important pieces of advice on this that are relevant to leadership in addition to the initial proving ground. First, *be prepared to do the grunt work. I've always felt whenever I assigned anybody to do something, "I've done that myself. It's not like I'm telling you to do something I don't know, how long it's going to take, how hard it is. I've done it." You know, I've sat down and done the logframe. I've gone in there and negotiated the project agreement with the minister who didn't want to hear it. I've been through all that stuff. So, therefore, I'm not asking you to do something I haven't been willing to do myself. That's number one. A leader needs to have that credibility. I don't want to work for somebody and think, "They have no idea of what it's going to take to get this job done."* Doing the grunt work can do more than enhance the respect others have for you. And it's not just about proving your capabilities and generating goodwill and a "can do" attitude, though these are important. It also prepares you for later leadership positions and to be more effective in the moment, because you will be in the position of knowing how it all works, how all the pieces fit together, and what it takes to make success happen.

Aaron's second piece of advice is to *try to take on the tough assignments—be a volunteer. In situations where there was a tough issue or a tough assignment that people were reluctant to take on, I wanted to be the first one to say I'll do it. And there are two reasons for that. Number one, because there's a chance to do some very exciting work. And that's what we're supposed to be all about, theoretically, taking risks, doing exciting things. And number two, if you're the pioneer, there's no one to tell you that this isn't the way to do it. How do they know? You're the first one doing it. And you set the tone, you set the marker, you set the framework, you create the model for future replication. I've always found that to be very good. That's what I liked about the private sector work at AID. Very few people were doing that. I was among a handful of people who were in the forefront of doing that. And we set the tone. We were listened to. We became the gurus on private sector development in AID. So be a risk taker. Volunteer for things.*

Aaron's advice for managing talented people coming into the system is not surprising, either. *You give them more responsibility than they think they can handle. You load them up. You give them opportunity to balance that so they learn how to prioritize. They learn how to manage effectively within teams, because they have to think about, "Who else can help me do this?" And it turns out to be the best possible training you can give somebody. I really believe that. At first it looks as if it's abusive, frankly, and they might even view it that way. But it always pays off.* You will be fortunate when you find similarly visionary bosses who will give you these opportunities to learn who you are and what you're capable of, building your confidence.

Mentoring and Apprenticing

While it may seem an untraditional approach, what Aaron Williams is suggesting is a form of mentoring. Aaron's story is a good illustration of how mentoring can come in unexpected packages, and is sometimes very subtle. Many of us have a view of mentoring that includes hands-on, step-by-step coaching. That's great when you can get it. We view this model as more akin to the traditional apprenticeship, where you are in a privileged position to work with a master who oversees your work and gives you every possible feedback. In an apprenticeship, you are expected to imitate the actions of the master and learn as you go. Aaron Williams took the job at International Multifoods because Ted Rugland promised to take him on as an apprentice. Sarah Newhall's work with Mechai Viravaidya was such an experience. Others make a distinction between mentoring for the job and mentoring for career development. The best mentors are those who take a personal interest not just in how well you do your job or the contribution you make to the organization, but also in how you develop personally and professionally beyond your current position.

Mentoring covers a much broader range of relationships than apprenticing. In some respects, Jennifer was mentored by her World Bank manager who, like Aaron Williams, was willing to take risks and allow her to prove herself. Sarah Newhall had similar experiences: *Lou Mitchell was a very powerful mentor and supporter of me and "mid-wifed" me kicking and screaming into this job* [Pact CEO] *because he believed in me. I've been exceedingly lucky in the bosses that I've had, so they've often contributed to my career advancement. They've seen in me something that they thought was worth promoting. So rather than being in a competitive relationship with bosses, which can often happen—you know, the upstart subordinate— they've paved ways for me and saw that.* David Yang also benefited from others seeing his potential, including his first boss as a political appointee. Especially at the beginning of his career, Aaron Williams placed a higher priority on his ability to learn from good leaders and managers than he did on salary, benefits, or location.

Making these investments and, more generally, seeking bosses you can learn from doesn't necessarily mean you will be actively mentored. It might mean learning one skill area rather than the whole of a job. Jennifer Butz was fortunate to have coaching for her writing skills, for example. Sometimes it just means that you will have an opportunity to learn by example—observing your boss (and others) on the job and adopting the style and approaches that are effective and a good fit for your developmental needs. This applies to "anti-role models" as well, as one of our focus group participants noted. You learn what works, as well as what doesn't.

Aaron Williams was mentored and also learned by example during his work at USAID. For example, James Michel, former Ambassador to Guatemala, was the USAID Latin America Bureau Chief when Aaron Williams became Deputy Director. Aaron learned from him, incorporating some of Ambassador Michel's management style into his own, and eventually assumed his position. *Everyone had a fair hearing. No one felt that they didn't have a chance to present their views on any given issue, and he listened very carefully. And listening is a very important part of being a good leader.* Later, in South Africa, Aaron benefited from the leadership style of Ambassador James Joseph, who set a climate for teamwork. *South Africa in those days was like Paris or Rome or London, that size of an embassy. Fifteen different agencies on the country team, all vying to show how they're furthering the United States' support of Nelson Mandela and his Cabinet. Those are conditions where you could have had a lot of interagency rivalries and battles, but none of that occurred because the Ambassador set the tone and provided leadership, so that we all worked together as a team.*

Often young professionals mistakenly assume that being mentored is a passive role. In fact, it is a lot of work, and it can be scary at times, since good mentors push you to your limits. This was Jennifer Butz' experience: *I was extremely lucky at the Asia Foundation to have three very excellent bosses, each with very different skill sets, and me in three very different roles.*

They pushed me very, very hard, and I was always sort of like that cat on the bar, just hanging in there. But I never fell. And even on my one very spectac-ular "whoops" my boss stepped in and said, "No, Jennifer covered this with us, I was on board, I supported this, and if anyone's going to take the heat, it's me." So, that gave me courage to be a pretty bold thinker programmatically. This experience illustrates that mentoring is a two-way relationship. A good mentor will watch out for you. She or he will push you to your limits and take responsibility for any missteps.

Sadly, mentoring is rare. And those who are willing to mentor are necessarily selective. That's why we encourage you to follow the above advice about doing the grunt work, volunteering for the hard assignments, taking risks, and strategically seeking opportunities to build your skills and knowledge where you feel they are needed. Most often, those who follow this advice will gain the attention and respect of potential mentors. You know the saying, "The squeaky wheel gets the grease"? We're not sug-gesting that you become a pain to those you work with, demanding too much of their time and attention. But if you ask questions and express an interest in learning from others, most often they will be willing to accom-modate. This is also an important pathway to proving yourself. Your boss will become more familiar with you and your work and will more readily see what you are capable of. Some of you may find a mentor by simply identifying someone and asking her/him to play that role for you.

Learning from Mentors, Role Models, Heroes, and Others

The mentoring relationship is not for everyone. Sometimes we aren't fortunate to find someone willing to engage with us in that role. And it requires that you be willing to be mentored, which, in turn, requires humility, patience, and trust. We asked our profiled practitioners about mentors, role models, and heroes. While some of them noted specific examples and experiences of being mentored (as mentioned above), oth-ers observed that while they had learned a great deal from others, they had never been actively mentored. For example, Najma Siddiqi shared: *I don't know what mentoring is. I respect a lot of people that I came across, some professors, some practitioners, some philosophers, including my family. But I don't think I'm a good mentee. That may be true actually. But I like aspects of people and their work. And I'm probably much too reactionary in a sense that I can't say, "This person is good" and "That person is bad." I can't do that. And for mentorship probably you need to.* When asked if he had mentors, Jef Buehler responded, *probably not. Not in the sense of some lifelong mentor guy, who would know you for a long period of time, or something like that.*

We encourage you to reflect on the distinction we've made between apprenticeship, which is a more formal interpretation of mentoring, and other more subtle variants of mentoring. This can help you to recognize opportunities you might otherwise miss. These subtler forms are closely related to networking, discussed below. You learn whom to go to for different types of advice. As one of our focus group participants put it, *I have an informal network that I rely on that I go to for various needs. You build this little "Board of Directors" for yourself. At the beginning of your career those mentors are critical and you keep those people but as you go forward in your career you get more and more.*

As this quote suggests, there is a much broader range of learning possible than just formal apprenticeship and mentoring on the job. You can learn from many examples beyond your bosses. Our profiled practitioners frequently mentioned the influence and support of their family members. As indicated by the opening of her profile, one of Sarah Newhall's role models is Gloria Steinem. Jennifer Butz was influenced by Harriet Tubman. *I just thought hers is just such an amazing story of personal deliverance. You know, she did* [the Underground Railroad] *because it was right; it was about dignity. And she didn't wait for someone to do that for her. She really did that for herself.* Aaron Williams noted the influence of a high school teacher: *Mr. Calwell, my geometry teacher in high school. I was one of his star geometry pupils. I loved geometry. And he said, "You know, you can do anything you want to do in this world. You have the kind of mind that can take you to different heights. You just have to focus." And I said, "This is just geometry, Mr. Calwell." He said, "Aaron, I'm telling you, look beyond that, all right?" He said it in a very calm, reassuring way, as if to say, "Didn't you know that?"*

Not surprisingly, our profiled practitioners mentioned several of the same people among their heroes. Admired social activists include Gandhi, Martin Luther King, Jr., and Saul Alinsky. Religious figures such as Jesus and Buddha were mentioned. And public servants such as John F. Kennedy, Jimmy Carter, Woodrow Wilson, Eleanor Roosevelt, Nelson Mandela, and Kofi Annan were noted. Amartya Sen was also cited for his vision of what development means. Heroes and inspirations can come in unexpected packaging. Currently, Jennifer Butz is taking inspiration from Anastas, a seventy-year-old Albanian psychiatrist, who survived persecution under the Hoxha dictatorship, and Enxhi, an eleven-year-old Albanian girl, who was born after the regime fell. She calls them her "little buddhas," because they can teach her so much about what it means to live in Albania, to have survived the past, and to aspire to a future.

At the same time, our profiled practitioners cautioned that viewing people as heroes can be dangerous. They are still people, after all, and they can let you down. Aaron Williams focuses on people whose accomplishments he respects. And from that perspective, he included Bill

Clinton on his list. In this sense, Najma Siddiqi also noted several practitioners. *I have so many disagreements with Shoaib Sultan Khan* [the head
of the Aga Khan Rural Support Program, and board member of the
National Rural Support Program, Pakistan] *and yet there are parts of his
skills that I would love to have and I don't: the diplomatic side, building
alliances, different ways of doing that. I disagree with him on a whole lot of
other things. Akhtar Hameed Khan* [founder of the Orangi Pilot Project
in Pakistan and the Comilla Rural Academy in Bangladesh] *is a philosopher, practitioner, thinker, analyst—fantastic. And you can learn so much from
him. You can sit with him, and he will just talk, and you absorb. That's something that's just unbelievable. Where I totally disagree with him is in his
approach to teaching: "I will tell you what you don't know."*

In one case, Najma was more comfortable classifying a practitioner
as a hero: Maulana Edhi, of the Edhi Foundation in Pakistan. *He is a
person who used to stand with a begging bowl on street corners; he still does,
whenever there's an emergency. He's the only person who goes into conflict
areas to pick up dead bodies, and wash them and give them a burial. He's the
only person who, in the 1980s, had baby cribs outside his office, with a sign
saying "Put your illegitimate children here. Don't kill them." He has homes
for the destitute and the disabled. He gives them skills so that they can earn a
living. All these people then become converted to volunteering at his institutions. There are now Edhi Centers all over in Pakistan. They have their little
clinics along the motorway. They have their donation centers everywhere. They
are trusted. And he doesn't run it himself. He started a franchise. "I'm not
going to be in control." He's the only one who actually refused USAID money
that was offered. He has influenced so many people, and that's what so
impresses me.*

Heroes are important. They can inspire you. They can teach you.
Their examples can help you survive the rough patches along your path.
But any role model, whether boss, mentor, or hero, is still human. Putting
them on a pedestal is not fair to them or to you. Most of them don't ask to
become your hero, and they are still human after all. And if you expect
too much, you may come to perceive these examples as inaccessible, leading you to doubt your own abilities. High expectations followed by disil-
lusionment can also cloud your ability to take the powerful lessons that
are there. If we judged Gandhi only as a father (he has been criticized for
falling short), we would be overlooking Gandhi as an inspirational leader
of nonviolent social movements. Mother Theresa was famously difficult
in her no-nonsense approach, often offending others. Her compassion
did not always permeate her interpersonal interactions, yet what compassion she had!

We encourage you to seek out others from whom you can learn—
whether you call them heroes or not. And, like Jennifer Butz, go

beyond the obvious to the seemingly everyday people you encounter. There are many Maulana Edhis in the world. Try to find them in each country where you work—for example, Mechai Viravaidya and Sulak Sivaraksa in Thailand, Nelson Mandela and Desmond Tutu in South Africa, and A. T. Ariyaratne in Sri Lanka. Biographies can be a great source of inspiration and learning about others' vision. These biographies don't have to be of famous figures to speak to you about public service. David Leonard's portrait of four African civil servants provides interesting insights into their lives and the forces that shaped their public service careers.[1] Among the most beneficial aspects of learning about other people's lives is reading about their challenges and how they navigated through them.

Learning from others—historical and religious figures, practitioners, bosses, teachers, family members, etc.—is a lifelong pursuit. It encompasses every service community you engage in. And it offers endless opportunity to learn about yourself, as well as to learn from and with others. It can help you to acquire the pragmatic skills and approaches necessary to success, as well as to inspire your vision for what can be. It can also help to remind you that no one is immune from disillusion and cynicism, and, importantly, it can offer you examples of how to move through these challenges (we talk about career burnout in the next chapter). To expand your own list of role models and heroes, we provide some recommended reading in Appendix 4.

The Importance of Networking

As the experience of our profiled practitioners attests, who you know can often lead to what you do. Aaron Williams was initially inspired by a graduate from his high school who joined the Peace Corps. Knowing that someone he could identify with had pursued this path gave him the confidence to follow suit. He now estimates that ninety percent of his friends are Peace Corps related in some way. *Either we served together, or I met them through Peace Corps linkages, or they were in AID and were part of the Peace Corps before, which is not unusual. It's a pretty high caliber of people you meet in the Peace Corps. I happened to be with a group that was really extraordinary in terms of what they've done in their careers in public service: senators, newspaper columnists, heads of major NGOs, all involved in some degree of public service, lots of corporate executives.* Even with those you did not serve with, conversations about the Peace Corps with others who have served can be a bonding experience.

Sarah Newhall learned about the Pact job in Cambodia from a friend. Jennifer Butz, as you will see, was encouraged by a graduate school friend to pursue a job at the World Bank. Najma Siddiqi came to many of her jobs through personal and professional contacts. In Derick's case, one of the USAID staff he'd contacted in the course of doing research for his dissertation called him three years later to offer him a job in USAID, which is how he moved to Washington, D.C. David Yang's is perhaps the most telling example about how you never know when someone may cross your path again. He never could have imagined that his internship director at the Carnegie Endowment for International Peace would hire him as a USAID political appointee fifteen years later.

These examples already point to important networks that we all have: family and friends, fellow alumni from high school to graduate school, colleagues and friends from Peace Corps or other service networks, professors, and those we meet along our career paths. Our focus group emphasized the importance of peer networks, both for professional and moral support, and also because they have connections with the organizations in which you may be looking for work. They can provide important information and/or introductions to help you in your career. Another of our colleagues stresses that whenever you leave a job, you should tie up loose ends and leave a good reputation behind: *Don't burn bridges, even if you have had a terrible working experience.* In networking with people, you should focus on building relationships, not necessarily getting your immediate objective met—for example, finding a job. Think about what the other person might be interested in talking about. The emphasis should be on building a long-term network of relationships.

You should consider joining formal professional networks. Even professional associations that may seem relatively academic offer opportunities for networking and developing your skills and knowledge. Some that might be relevant to you include the American Society for Public Administration and its Section on International and Comparative Administration, the Association for Research on Nonprofit Organizations and Voluntary Action, the International Studies Association, the Association of International Business, and associations specific to area studies and technical sectors. Other professional networks are more practitioner oriented, such as chapters of the Society for International Development, or informal networks like the Development Management Network, which Derick co-founded over twenty years ago.

Still others are specifically designed to promote networking among and for young professionals, such as the UN Young Professionals for International Cooperation. The World Bank's Junior Professionals Program has an alumni association as an integral part of the program. Your university alumni groups may also be a good source. These can be more or less formal. We've met young professionals who have organized their own "development/career salons," where they get together to discuss new ideas in the field, as well as to support each other in the challenges of job search and career development. They invite speakers—all informally—to discuss these topics. Returned Peace Corps volunteers have created nonprofits for most countries of service (e.g., Friends of Madagascar, Friends of Nicaragua). Joining these organizations can introduce you to multiple generations of RPCVs and can also provide opportunities for you to acquire additional professional experience. Sports leagues are a good way to meet people informally across professional ranks (e.g., soccer, softball, running clubs).

Regardless of which organized networks you join, as with everything in life, you get what you give. You will only benefit from these opportunities if you are active in them and invest time, energy, and sometimes money. Here, again, we encourage you to volunteer and be noticed. Since most of these associations are run by volunteers, there are ample opportunities to do grunt work and assume leadership positions. Appendix 1 contains contact information for the associations mentioned.

The Dreaded Job Search

There are few things that are more demoralizing from a self-esteem perspective than a job search.[2] Key adjectives to keep in mind are proactive, assertive, upbeat, and strategic. Then, of course, we're also reminded of common "fortune cookie" sayings: perseverance brings success, or ninety percent of success is simply showing up. Stick with it. Don't let a week, or even a day, go by without a professional contact of some sort, whether it is a job interview, an informational interview, or a call to a colleague or friend requesting additional contacts. You just can't know which action will be the one that will lead to a job. One of our focus group participants sent out over fifty resumes and cover letters without success. Then he stumbled across a job announcement at the Peace Corps Office of Returned Volunteer Services and quickly secured a job.

We've watched a lot of people enter the job market with varying degrees of success. The results can be surprising. Sometimes someone has less experience than another, less training, fewer skills—but they'll get the job because they've been proactive. And not just today, they may have been building their networks over the course of their studies. They exercise the confidence and risk taking we talked about above and are very active in building their professional networks. As mentioned in Chapter 7, some organizations can be particularly difficult to break into. Starting as an intern and applying the general advice above— doing the grunt work, volunteering for things, in short, proving yourself and networking—can lead not just to mentoring but perhaps also to the creation of a full-time position or the identification and support for other opportunities in the organization.

Sadly, very competent people can sometimes be derailed because of their fear of failure. Even after graduation, some of our students choose to stay in the positions they had while in school, in part because the job search can be so daunting. Fear of failure can prevent you from making the necessary phone calls, and cultivating contacts. In their classic book on negotiation, *Getting to Yes*,[3] Fisher and Ury promote the idea of BATNA (the best alternative to a negotiated agreement), which prepares people to deal ahead of time with situations where they can't get exactly what they want. Similarly, we encourage you to think through the worst-case scenario. What if you call this person and he or she doesn't want to see you? What if you have the interview and nothing comes of it? Even worse, what if you commit a major blooper—arriving late, saying the wrong thing, or just leaving with the impression that you came across as really stupid? Okay, well, so what? This person probably wasn't in your network before, so what's the big deal? You didn't have a job before, and you still don't have one. So, really, there is nothing lost and, hopefully, you've learned something from the experience. As much as we'd like to think that we are very important, if you run into this interviewer a few years from now, chances are you will remember the blooper very vividly, but s/he won't.

Part of being proactive is moving beyond formal job announcements and seeking informational interviews.[4] You might identify appropriate people, for example, through your current work or internships. Our focus group stressed that it is often easier to pursue informational interviews when you are still doing something, whether working or in school. This way, there is less pressure on either you or the interviewee to find or provide a job, and you have something to talk about in the present tense. This is also a time when you can more easily ask quality-of-life questions related to the organization or the work the particular person is doing. As one focus group member noted, *people like to talk about themselves and it's a free thing to do.* This is a process you should start when you're still in graduate school. Often class assignments will provide a convenient entrée. And you should take every opportunity to pursue such interviews when you are overseas, whether traveling as a tourist, or serving with the Peace Corps or other volunteer organizations.

When going to interviews, whether for particular jobs or for learning purposes, don't just think about the job you want now. Consider each person you meet as part of your career network for the future. Each person you meet—whether on the job, as an intern, in an interview, or at a professional networking event—is someone you should cultivate as part of your professional network. You never know when they might be able to help you or you might help them. Remember David Yang's experience? After fifteen years with no contact, he ended up being hired as a political appointee by the director of his internship program. We also encourage you to always be honest. You should always focus on building long-term relationships. So when setting up informational interviews, you can tell them you hope for a job, but that if one is not available you would still like to meet to learn more about the organization, the field, the individual, etc.

International public service can be a very competitive field. You will need to assert yourself in order to build networks and identify and gain new opportunities. One member of our focus group advises, *you are doing yourself a disservice if you don't put everything out there. Use everything you have, including contacts from your family. Pull out all your "goods," no matter how uneasy it makes you feel.* Some career transitions can be particularly challenging. We discuss these below.

Making Significant Transitions

In every career, there are some transitions that seem more major than others. These are harder to face, fraught with bigger stakes, more conducive to fear that you'll make the "wrong" choice, and so on. Here we talk about the issues involved in several types of significant career shifts.

Getting the First Job

As we discussed in Chapter 6, it is commonly held that minimal entry-level requirements for a career in international public service are at least one year of relevant overseas experience and a graduate degree. There are exceptions. The first type is those who have extensive overseas experience, ten years or more. The second type is those who hold an undergraduate degree and work in purely administrative positions. The first type is increasingly rare. Especially if you aspire to working in the headquarters of international organizations, a graduate degree is expected, in some cases even a PhD. On the other hand, organizations working for change from outside of the international development industry may not hold the same expectations. Those working in the industry with a bachelor's degree tend either to remain in administrative work or to amass some experience and clarify their service visions before returning to graduate school. In terms of field experience, the onus is always on you to prove that your overseas experience is professionally relevant. We also encourage you to market yourself creatively, looking for ways to demonstrate the relevance of your domestic work experiences.

When you're just starting out, we urge you not to hold out for the perfect job, or even the one that is specific to your technical area of interest. In other words, don't consider your first job the be-all and end-all. Rather, you should think about it as the next "course" you need to take as you continue to build your skills, gain experience, and learn more about the field and where you fit in it. In the development industry, employers value skills and experience in contracting, budgeting, project management, and program evaluation—just for starters. You can gain all of these skills without working in the specific sector you may ideally seek. Remember Aaron Williams' encouragement to know your business and learn it from the bottom up. If you start that way, you will be stronger throughout your career. We also recommend that you look for potential mentors or role models when deciding among several options.

If you have been overseas in a volunteer service position (e.g., Peace Corps), or for whatever reason, you should seriously consider looking for a job on the ground before, and maybe instead of, immediately returning home. Once you're home, it is very difficult to convince people to send you back overseas. However, if you begin to knock on doors while in the country, you're a "bird in the hand." Those with whom you would work have an opportunity to interview you directly, and to witness your language skills and cultural understanding. They also don't need to make an investment in flying you in for an interview or moving you to the country. From these positions you can begin to network with home offices back in the United States. Many of our former students found interesting jobs immediately after Peace Corps with, for example, Save the Children, Care, and local NGOs.

If you're not already working while you are looking for a job, you probably still need to eat. If all else fails and you need to start bringing in some money while you conduct your job search; rather than work at McDonald's, we suggest you consider a temporary agency that supplies temporary workers to the kinds of organizations you'd like to learn more about. This can be risky as you might be typecast and not given serious attention. On the other hand, you never know if you might make a connection with someone, impress them in some way, and have them direct you to a bona fide position. Some organizations are really difficult to break into, so temping can offer other advantages. For example, the World Bank requires an identification card just to enter the buildings. If you are temping, you can more easily access information about who is doing what and you can attend the many, many lunchtime programs and use them for networking. If you're temping in such an organization, concentrate on networking beyond your placement. This can help you avoid the typecasting. You can introduce yourself as a recent graduate or Returned Peace Corps Volunteer, for example. Also, you never know when you might run into someone you know—literally. When Jennifer was working at the World Bank, she literally bumped into an old friend from graduate school who had just returned from the Peace Corps and was doing temp work. After some introductions of Stephanie and her skills, Jennifer's manager hired her into the program.

Entry-level jobs are usually project administration or research assistant positions. However, there are many job titles out there and they can be more or less representative of the actual job description, which often may not match what you actually do. This means that you will need to explore the particulars of each position before determining if it is the right one for you. And the same job title in different organizations may mean different things. Make sure you ask a lot of questions during your interview and when you are negotiating for a job. To advance from a junior project or research assistant position you will typically need a graduate degree or field experience. If you lack these, you will need to make an additional investment in graduate school or in overseas work, whether paid or volunteer, in order to move on in your career. Again, Peace Corps is a common path for those in such job slots.

The Second Job:
Moving Towards Greater Responsibility and Technical Work

There is a gap between jobs calling for a bachelor's degree and little experience for an administrative position and those requiring a master's and five or six years of experience. Such qualifications make you eligible for mid-level positions on USAID contracts, but acquiring the requisite experience can be a challenge, especially for recent graduates. In thinking about our curriculum and teaching, we see our primary challenge as preparing students to find not only the first job, but also the next job, and a steady progression towards more technical and leadership positions. In international public service, the job search consists, first, of "getting in," and then, of "getting beyond" junior project administration positions (typically based in the United States).

In many public service contractor organizations (both NGOs and private firms), the structure of employment often keeps young entry-level professionals in administrative and financial management jobs that can make it difficult to move to the kind of overseas technical or managerial work that most new entrants aspire to. Overcoming this hurdle is not impossible, however. For example, some organizations make a conscious commitment to put new entry staff on teams for overseas assignments to assist them in building their experience base. Working for a small firm or NGO may offer more opportunities to expand your experience quickly, as staff members may be expected to be involved in multiple projects and tasks.

In other cases, individuals may need to network within the international development industry and seek out opportunities that will provide them with the sector and country experience they want. This may entail taking an unpaid internship or a volunteer position as a strategic step in an individual's career path. One suggestion (and success story) from our focus group is to volunteer after hours on a project at your workplace. Once you've built your understanding of the project and demonstrated a contribution, when an opening comes up, you're likely to get it. Another suggestion, depending on your organization, is to generate your own project idea. Discuss your idea with others, see what related work is going on, and explore whether there are potential funders either within or beyond your organization. If you are working for a contracting organization, you should track the Requests for Proposals (RFPs) that your organization is considering pursuing and try to insert yourself into the proposals and the work as they evolve.

As with all aspects of your career path, we encourage you to be strategic. This means carefully evaluating lateral moves, rather than just vertical ones. You should move towards whichever position can help you acquire the next set of skills you think you need to advance toward your personal service vision. Your early jobs should be about discovery and skill building. This is your opportunity to explore what you enjoy and what you don't. Sarah Newhall recommends thinking about your job changes as two-and-a-half- to three-year experiences. *I thought of the first year as a learning year, mostly taking more than giving; the second year as a delivering year, giving more than taking; and the third year as a giving year, but also a transition year, if it seemed time for advancement. The second job should build on something specific that you discovered you loved on the first job.*

Transitioning to Fieldwork

It can be similarly challenging to transition from headquarters to fieldwork. This is in part because, most often, such a transition also entails moving from administrative to technical work, so the advice above applies here as well. Fieldwork may mean short-term overseas assignments (TDYs, or tours of duty, in US government-speak; missions in World Bank- and UN-speak), or a long-term placement. The latter is likely to come only when you have significant technical expertise and/or you have a long track record with your organization.

Most experienced professionals will advise you to get fieldwork as early as possible in your career. This may be for the simple reason that it is easier to make such commitments and changes in your lifestyle when you are single, without a spouse or dependents. There are growing numbers of married volunteers in the Peace Corps, but moving overseas with a partner can be challenging, requiring significant commitments and sacrifices—and that's not even accounting for the additional accommodations needed for children. Once you've had some field experience, you will have more options, whether in other field positions or in the headquarters of development organizations. As noted above, one way to acquire field experience early in your career is to go overseas as a volunteer and then find a professional job when your service is completed.

And to advance in your career, you may find it necessary to move between the field and headquarters. You may also choose to make such moves for personal reasons, as discussed in Chapter 9. As Jennifer Butz (Profile 6) warns, *if you only stay in the field, it's often hard to move to the next level up. So oftentimes you'll have to change organizations or at least come back—go into or out of the field. Sometimes a change of venue will result in a higher position.*

But how does one move to the field from a headquarters position? One of our colleagues identified three ways: 1) Peace Corps service, with follow-on professional work overseas; 2) parlaying a strong support role in headquarters into a field support role, for example, joining senior staff on a mission and developing necessary relationships and expertise; and 3) taking the really tough assignments where the demand for staff is perhaps greater than the supply. The third recommendation includes hardship posts in post-conflict countries, such as Afghanistan, Iraq, Liberia, Sierra Leone, or East Timor.

Transitioning from Domestic to International Work

Transitioning at mid-career from domestic to international work is one of the most challenging career changes. Regardless of your qualifications, you will likely need to make a significant investment to do so. This was true of Sarah Newhall, in taking her sabbatical. And it was true of Aaron Williams, who left a full-time, secure, high-paying job in international business to start as a consultant for USAID with no guarantees. Some of you might consider doing the Peace Corps. It's changed a lot from the early days, where volunteers were fresh out of college and lived in huts in remote villages. This model still holds, but both the volunteers and the service demands have become more sophisticated in many places in the world. More and more volunteers are older, at mid-career, or retired. And most volunteers have access to e-mail (though some only on visits to the capital city), and are working in technical areas. Today's Peace Corps volunteers do a lot of work in small business and NGO development—highly relevant skills to any international public service career. Some of you may opt, instead (or in addition), to return to graduate school to acquire international knowledge and skills.

If you are highly proficient in a technical area there may be organizations and programs that specialize in just your type of technical assistance. For example, health sector programs in many developing and transitioning countries call for expertise in modern health care management and systems development. Lawyers and municipal management specialists are other categories in demand. The American Bar Association has several international programs, as does the International City/County Management Association. You can begin to transition, for example, through short-term exchanges and study tours.

Unfortunately, you can have all the skills in the world, and very relevant experience, but breaking into the development industry may still be an uphill battle. You need to prove you can do the job, and you need flexible, creative employers to take a chance on you. For example, Sarah Newhall had to be screened by USAID in order to assume her first job with Pact, in Cambodia. *I was greeted by three people within USAID. It was really hardball. I walked into the room and they said, "You're completely unqualified for this job because you've only had less than two years' overseas work experience. You don't know anything about USAID's systems and processes." So in hiring processes, formal credentials get you through the door. I had to talk my way into the position.*

In the domestic-to-international transition, informational interviews and networking can really pay off. Any opportunity you have to discuss or formally present your domestic experience to an internationally oriented audience will push that door open a little further.

Final Thoughts

Despite our tendency to organize our career stories in a logical progression in retrospect, few, if any of us, can actually say in all honesty that we planned our careers and carried out the plans accordingly. The path your career takes will emerge from a combination of opportunities that present themselves, your own investments and proactive energy, and sheer luck. Fortunately, none of us move along the service-choice spiral (or the career path) in isolation. Through your networking, including your communities of understanding, you will both give and receive. As you make the many transitions from one job to another that are the hallmark of today's careers, you will take a large number of these relationships with you. Some of them will continue to support you; others you may lose touch with until another time when you find yourselves working together once more. So, in actuality, the phrase "career path," while conceptually convenient, is a misnomer. It implies a degree of intentionality and linearity that we rarely see in today's international public service careers, or any career for that matter. This is why we encourage you to think, instead, about the service-choice spiral, where your journey expands in both breadth and depth with time and experience. Jennifer Butz's profile is an example of such career evolution.

Notes

1. See recommended biographies to explore, Appendix 4.

2. Appendix 3 lists some sources for job announcements. The Internet is an increasingly important resource, especially if you are working overseas. For example, Jennifer Butz has found most of her jobs through Web sites and e-mail listservs.

3. Roger Fisher and William Ury, *Getting to Yes: Negotiating without Giving In* (Boston: Houghton Mifflin, 1991).

4. For an online guide to informational interviews, see: http://www.quintcareers. com/informational_interviewing.html.

Profile 6. Jennifer Butz:
Choosing the Overseas Life

Jennifer Butz is a self-described field junkie. *I prefer the field. Part of it is the intensity, always something different, something whacky or insane, or just wonderful. It's hard to find that full-on constant information overload here in the States. And I thrive on that.* Her path started at a very young age. *Social service or social action was always part of my family fiber. Coupled with that was a mantra of "always broaden your horizons." The two just sort of coincided. I always looked for, on the one hand, a social or political career, and on the other hand, something that was pretty far afield.* This explains how a young woman from Michigan ended up promoting democracy in Mongolia and Albania.

Jennifer Butz grew up in Ann Arbor, Michigan, where her father was an education professor at the University of Michigan. It was the late 1960s, early 1970s, and much of the country was demonstrating. She experienced her first political march, for civil rights, in Washington in 1968 and joined demonstrations against the Vietnam War in Ann Arbor in 1969. Her family was active in the Unitarian Church, where *instead of discussing the Bible, we'd talk about Emerson and Harriet Tubman.* Ann Arbor was one of the Northern transit points on the underground railroad that smuggled escaped slaves into Canada. *The whole environment of that community was about social action and change, particularly among the professors in the university community. And then there was the recurring mantra: "broaden your horizons, broaden your horizons." I remember when I called my dad the first time I was moving to Mongolia. He said, "Well, I guess I can't blame you. You were just listening to me. . . . But I never thought you listened!"*

At sixteen, Jennifer Butz was already traveling overseas on international exchanges. She had become active in Ann Arbor's sister city program with Tübingen in Germany, and also with a youth exchange program to Berlin. She continued that connection with a junior year abroad program in Freiburg, Germany, during her undergraduate studies, after which she stayed in London to work. *I wasn't ready to come home yet. So I added another country to the mix. When I did come home I stayed in the States for a while but was very restless. I was pretty much convinced then that I had to find a career outside of the United States. That's how I wound up in Monterey, California, attending the Monterey Institute of International Studies [MIIS]. The beauty there was all the practitioner faculty and students. They were people who had lived abroad, who were from abroad—it just reinforced all those interests and curiosities—"Ooh! I haven't been there yet!"*

As an undergraduate, she had wanted to have more than two languages—she was already fluent in German. *I saw a friend of mine at dinner one night practicing her characters, and I was just smitten. I just thought it was so cool. I immediately began Chinese classes. It was like a treasure hunt; every character took me deeper into this puzzle. So I studied it for ten years and wound up in China.* During her graduate studies, Jennifer Butz lived in China from 1988–1989—the year of democracy in China. *Most people think that only happened in Beijing, but it really happened all over the country. I was in a small city in Northeastern China, between the North Korean and Russian borders. I was teaching English at a teachers college. And the kids mobilized. They were running on the trains, which was fifteen hours one way to Beijing. They created a rotating circuit so that every day they had a live witness report on the events of the previous day from Beijing. All of a sudden, they turned from these northeastern farmyard kids into activists, with systems of communication and information sharing. It was amazing.* After the protestors in Tiananmen Square were attacked by the Chinese army on June 3, Jennifer had teachers in her living room comparing the cruelty to the Japanese occupation of China. *That sent chills through my spine. The whole Beijing Spring sensitized me to the importance of democratization.* This new appreciation for democracy was reinforced when the Berlin Wall fell shortly after she returned to the United States to complete her studies at Monterey.

Jennifer Butz had thought she would become a sinologist, a single-country analyst. *I realized after the Tiananmen shootings that I needed something broader, that I couldn't put all my eggs in one basket. So I started to look at regional issues.* Given her experience in Asia and her base in California, she was determined to work for the Asia Foundation, based in San Francisco. The Asia Foundation had been active in Asian democratization starting in the early 1950s. She was initially hired right away for a summer position. *I was the only person who knew what P-E-C-C stood for, which is fine, if that's what it takes.* She worked for The Asia Foundation but was seconded to the Pacific Economic Cooperation Council (PECC), the precursor to the Asia Pacific Economic Cooperation (APEC).

During that summer, she *decided that the Asia Foundation would be better with me, than without me. But I had a harder time convincing them.* She held out for a nearly a year, playing the waiting game so long that even the MIIS Career Development Officer, and now a friend, advised her to cut her losses and move on. *I said, "No, I'm pretty sure." And I really sweated it out. There were some very, very lean moments in that year. But finally, they did hire me and I stayed with them for six years. So, I was persistent. If it feels right, it's probably worth sticking with, even though it requires some sacrifices.* She began as a Program Officer for Economics and Trade, became a Regional Desk Officer for northeast Asia, and finally the Assistant Representative in Mongolia. *I was extremely lucky at the Asia Foundation to have three excellent bosses, each with different skill sets, and me in three different roles. They pushed me very, very hard, and I was always, sort of like that cat on the bar, just hanging in there. But I never fell. So, that gave me courage to be a pretty bold thinker programmatically.*

In her last assignment with the Foundation, among other things, she managed a grants program to women's NGOs promoting voter education for Mongolia's 1996 parliamentary elections, and a media/journalist-training program in support of media ethics consistent with democratization there. When the country program was facing budget cuts and her job was in jeopardy, a graduate school friend told her about a World Bank job she was vacating and put Jennifer Butz in touch with her boss. Jennifer Butz took the job at the Bank to work on a training program in support of social policy reform in transition economies, including Mongolia. *That was styling Mongolia as part of the Soviet Union, so it was sort of bringing me back into Europe, which is where my international awareness originated. So in a bizarre way, I kind of worked my way from East to West, taking whole chunks of the map, at one point all of the Pacific Rim, then Northeast Asia, then Mongolia, then Central Asia and the Former Soviet Union.* So she returned to Washington and brought with her a Mongolian husband.

When the World Bank contract ended, and because her husband needed to stay in the United States longer to obtain his green card, she took a US-focused job with a social innovations firm, then called the Harwood Group, whose aim was to explore ways that institutions, communities, and citizens all work together in America's democracy. Her clients included the Kettering Foundation, the Pew Charitable Trust, and the American Society of Newspaper Editors. *That reinforced some of the early tools that I had learned as a programmer and a grant-maker for the Asia Foundation.* One project for the Kettering Foundation involved conducting focus groups in eight bellwether cities around the country—including Philadelphia, Pennsylvania; Memphis, Tennessee; and Fresno, California—to explore citizens' perspectives on community renewal. *The experience reinforced for me the idea that democracy is a process and there isn't really an end point to it. It informed the notion that democracy lies somewhere between the very large and the very small, but it has to be crafted for each individual, and then transferred into a community setting.*

Following this experience, she returned to Mongolia under a USAID-funded program to strengthen civil society. This was a consortium program led by Mercy Corps and included three other organizations: Associates in Rural Development (her employer), to address the local governance component; Pact, managing the information side; and Land O'Lakes, responsible for the agricultural business program. *Those kinds of arrangements, which have become much more common now for USAID, really depend on personalities as much as on solid program designs.*

You can have a fantastic program design and if the chemistry isn't right or the institutional arrangements haven't been sufficiently thought out ahead of time, they start to be little mini-turf battles under the umbrella. After two years, Mercy Corps decided to focus on the information and economic development portion of the program and the local governance component was absorbed into the other sector components. Within a year, the remaining local government staff left to join other USAID projects in Mongolia.

Jennifer Butz left the Gobi Initiative and, after about three weeks, took a short-term consultancy to design a program and contribute to writing a grant proposal for community revitalization through democratic action in Serbia. Her client subcontracted to another organization and together they secured the $40 million project. She was offered the position to run the citizen-participation component of the project but at a salary that was forty percent less than what she had been earning in Mongolia. So she rejected the offer and moved back to the States to decide what to do next. *I was getting a divorce so I was coming back for that too. We thought it would be easier if we got married and divorced under the same legal code. So I gave myself three months to figure out what I wanted to be when I grew up, and within three weeks I was on a plane to Azerbaijan as an independent consultant conducting a final program evaluation for the same client.*

After returning to the States, after about three weeks—*because three weeks seems to work for me*—she came across the announcement, on an Internet site, for her next position as program director in Albania for the National Democratic Institute (NDI). She would again be running a citizen-participation program. *But this one was very different from the others. All of the previous ones were about NGO or institution building. Civic Forum is specifically targeted to individuals, and I really liked that. Because after about ten to twelve years, I decided that the international donor community really got it wrong. We had such a preoccupation with institutions—with NGOs—that basically we just facilitated a very tidy elite-to-elite transfer. So I very much appreciated the fact that this particular program was focused on citizens, on the individual.* While she was en route to Albania, NDI asked her to provide some support to Civic Forum in Kosovo. *They were facing budget cuts, so I went in and did a public relations analysis based on some very good survey work they had done. They hadn't done anything with the data because they hadn't had the time. There had been both sickness and death among the staff, so they kind of got frozen and they risked losing their funding. We got the additional funding and kept fourteen people employed for another year or so.* Once in Albania, it was agreed that NDI's presence in country required a higher degree of coordination than previously existed. She added the role of country director to her existing responsibilities of program director for Civic Forum. She has held both those positions now for about two years. Jennifer Butz was recently named the Chief-of-Party of a multi-institutional democratization program in Albania.

When asked, what's next? she responded: *Oh, God. I have no idea. I really have no idea. But you know, it will probably only take about three weeks to figure out!*

CHAPTER 9

Sustaining Motivation for International Public Service: Service in Balance

Remember Gloria Steinem's motto (which Sarah Newhall lives by)? Where your energy goes is what you become. For many of us, there is a fine line between professional and personal life. Your professional life is an expression of your being. Many of our profiled practitioners affirmed this perspective: *The work is the life*. But being dedicated to a life of international public service does not mean that it is all you are, or all that you do. As Sarah Newhall put it, *I don't see work and leisure as a dichotomy in my life. I think my work is my way of life. I want to work as hard at leisure as I do at my paid, professional work. But working is an orientation to an entire way of being, not just a job. My work is not my job.* And it's not just a question of happiness, though that is important. If all you do is pursue your service career, you're not likely to be able to sustain your motivation and passion. You're likely to burn out or, to some degree, become less and less effective.

In discussing burnout, Ram Dass and Paul Gorman put it this way: "Having started out to help others, we're somehow getting wounded ourselves. What we had in mind was expressing compassion. Instead, what we seem to be adding to the universe is more suffering—our own—while we're supposedly helping." As we discussed in Chapter 5, it is through your humanity that you connect with others and transform the world and each other together. Such connection to your own humanity requires that you embrace your emotional needs and lifestyle preferences. In other words, as you work to contribute to the quality of life of others, you should consider, too, your own quality of life.

In this chapter, we address how your career integrates with other aspects of your life. We touch upon challenges and choices regarding life partners and family. Our discussion considers how you can balance your personal and professional life in a way that can contribute to your happiness and sustained motivation. We again draw upon the experience and wisdom of our profiled practitioners, and recommend other sources of inspiration as well.

Having It All?

We can all draw lessons from evolving feminist perspectives and experience. Women were once relegated to the house and children. Then, starting in World War II, they entered the workforce in increasing numbers, and not just in "pink collar" jobs or the "helping" professions (e.g., nurse, teacher, librarian). For example, Derick's mother joined the US Navy and worked as an airplane mechanic during the war. The trajectory of women's experience has been a gradual expansion of options—today's dominant social ethos is having choices. This is not to say that women always have just the same choices as men, but women certainly have a vastly expanded range of possibilities available to them, which run the gamut from various types of family to diverse options for careers. With these emerging choices came an expectation, and some impressive role models, that we—both men and women—could have it all, that we could simultaneously have our careers and our families.

But this expectation masks a fundamental reality: there are always trade-offs. Having a family and a career does not mean that you "have it all," in the popular phrasing. It only means that you have some of each. And just because you have a career and a family doesn't mean that you will perform equally well in both. Finally, having both doesn't mean that you will be happy or satisfied. Are all of your needs met through these vehicles? When do you have time for yourself or time alone with your partner?

These considerations don't favor one set of choices or another. For example, an old friend recently shared, *Whoever says having children is always great, is lying. Being a mother is all of the best things in life. . . and all of the worst.* We encourage you to make your decisions consciously based on a healthy awareness of the trade-offs. We believe that the myth of having it all has led many to make decisions without thinking deeply about their implications, and to expect too much of themselves and others, setting everyone up for disappointment.

David Yang shared some wisdom on these challenges and making trade-off decisions. *I realized you can make certain choices for certain jobs, where you can turn down travel and long hours. And at this point in my life, I think I've forced myself to choose jobs where I still have some latitude. You can only give so many excuses to yourself or to your family, and your friends, that "I didn't know what I was getting into." Because I think it's important you do. You know the compromises professionally and personally and then you make clear-cut choices. Even though on certain days you might wake up bemoaning your choices, you made them for a clear reason.*

For some of you, the fundamental questions will be easy. Perhaps you already feel strongly that you don't want to have children. This is a decision Jennifer Butz made very early in her life.[1] *I put my nurturing and that sort of maternal instinct into my work. And so I nurture people, but they're not my own kin.* She and Sarah Newhall certainly demonstrate that you can have a very fulfilling life without having children of your own. (Sarah Newhall is very active in her stepchildren's lives). Aaron Williams and Najma Siddiqi (whose children are grown) and David Yang (whose sons are still young) all take great joy in their families. All three of them have naturally made career decisions that were in the best interest of their children, even when those jobs were not their first choice. Professionals living overseas, for example, often arrange to work in the United States when it's time for their children to start high school.

It's great when you know what you want from the beginning and plan accordingly. David Yang had a clear vision of what he wanted for his children: a sense of place, which was something that he, with his refugee roots, felt he had lacked. This led him to pursue a Washington-based career. Jennifer Butz knew she didn't want to have children and so worried less about the implications of pursuing a field-based career. She counts herself lucky for knowing what she wanted, but cautions others to show themselves compassion and to be flexible. *I have not been fraught with those doubts and questions like many people are. These decisions are very difficult to come to, because what you know today and what you are today, isn't what you know and will be five or ten years from now. And so the best that you can do is to allow yourself permission to make the decision of the moment. And then let yourself remake those decisions later on.*

You can find a lot of reward in nurturing many people through your work. As Najma Siddiqi's son once said to her about her job at NRSP, *You have 200 kids.* Each of you will find your own limits—and they will shift depending on the circumstances—in terms of how to balance this broader nurturing with the needs of your family members. Maintaining some balance between professional and personal life is essential to everyone, but is particularly challenging when family members, like children or elderly parents, need substantial care and attention. And these needs are not necessarily planned. Najma Siddiqi raced through her coursework at the Institute for Social Studies so she could be reunited with her son. She later abandoned her PhD plans to tend to her ailing mother. Aaron Williams gave up an opportunity to be an ambassador to be close to his sick mother and his college-age sons. When her contract at the World Bank expired, Jennifer Butz opted to stay longer in the United States so that her foreign-born husband could get his green card. There will likely be many times in the course of your career when family circumstances will influence, and maybe change, your career choices.

But before you can plan for children and family, many of you will first be concerned with finding a life partner. Or as one of our focus group members said, before cultivating a relationship, you have to first meet someone! Too often, when we spoke to single people about their personal lives, the response was *Personal life? What personal life?* No matter where you are, in the field overseas or in the United States, if you are a workaholic you will have difficulty meeting people. This same focus group member noted, only half-joking, *There are only so many hours in a day, and certain things happen at certain times during the day. Your lunch break, from 12:00 to 12:07, is not the best time to meet someone.*

These are challenges typical to people in any career, wherever they are. So let's concentrate a bit on the particular challenges of finding a partner while pursuing a career in international public service. Some, like the two of us, have found success in meeting someone profession-ally. But lest you think that's the best option, Jennifer originally told Derick that, although she was interested, she wouldn't consider dating him because his job at a private sector-consulting firm involved a lot of travel on short-term assignments; he represented a lifestyle she didn't want to share. Fortunately, he didn't listen beyond hearing that she was otherwise interested in dating him! Seriously, though, these are lifestyle issues you might want to consider. Life with a lot of time spent in air-ports can be lonely, as can waiting at home for those intermittent days and weeks when you and your partner can be together. And if you're both traveling, the chances for overlap can be minimal. We know of couples who take turns on whose career choice takes precedence, suc-cessively pursuing the best option for one and then the other. For exam-ple, one is hired for a great job overseas so the other one follows and finds a job related to his/her skills and interests, but perhaps not the ideal job. In the next move, the priorities will be reversed. The great thing about finding someone in the same field is that you share the same interests, understand the challenges, and may even find opportunities to collaborate. Professional collaboration doesn't work for every couple, but it has worked beautifully for us, as we hope this book attests.

As a single person in international public service, the greatest chal-lenges to meeting someone come from either traveling too much, espe-cially when it's short term, precluding you from developing relationships even in other countries; or living overseas. Everyone has a different tolerance for travel. Initially, you may be lured by the seeming glamor of international travel. But as you are likely to discover, it doesn't take long for the surface shine to wear thin. We encourage you to gauge your tolerance and commitments to travel both to prevent burnout and to enable you to meet people and nurture relationships. Some of you may choose, for example, to pursue longer stints overseas so you can be in one place.

In terms of living overseas, we've met people over the years who thought it was a good way to meet people, and others who considered it less than optimal. On the first count, it can be a good way to connect with others who share your interests. You may even meet and fall in love with a national from another country; this is a well-recognized pattern with Peace Corps volunteers. If this is your choice, we strongly encourage you to live in both of your home countries before committing to a life together. Cultural differences are always present and intensify when you undergo the periodic, though normal, stresses of life. You can save yourself a lot of heartache if you fully explore one another before you make choices that are difficult to change. Several (but not all) of our former students have returned from the Peace Corps with spouses in tow and found the challenges too great to bear. Initially, the ideals of love can obscure cultural differences that cannot be overcome. For example, before they decided to marry, Jennifer Butz and her husband agreed not to have children, but later found the social pressure and expectations of his culture were too great. They ended their marriage, but in their case, the friendship survives.

Living overseas can present roadblocks to meeting potential partners. This is true also of making friends. One of our focus group members was very clear that she doesn't want to live overseas right now. *As a single woman, I want balance in my life. And not just in terms of meeting someone. It's also about the friends and freedoms that you don't have as much of in developing countries.* You may find that there are cultural barriers or other issues that make it difficult to connect with and explore potential partnerships with local nationals. The expatriate communities can be small and rather confining in a lot of places. Many people will already have families or partners. Expatriate communities can be very insular, where it is difficult to explore relationships without being the subject of gossip. Jennifer Butz acknowledges, *being a woman does make it challenging. Sometimes the men think that you're there and available, whether they happen to be married or not. And it does actually create some tension. When I was the only woman, it was easy to be just one of the guys. Then recently another woman came, who is a chief of party. And since I was already one of the guys, that position was taken. She's had at least three or four men unwantedly ask her out. So it's kind of a drag.* In each country there is usually a club or association of expatriate women, primarily focused on the spouses of expatriate professionals. So if you are a professional woman, it can be difficult to be perceived as such and to be able to connect with others professionally.

Living overseas has its challenges, and balancing these with what is best for your personal life, including family, can be difficult.[2] Jennifer Butz stresses, *an international career is not an automatic sentence* [to lone-liness]. *But it does mean making choices, and often making hard choices.* Again, this is why we suggest that you get your field experience early in your career, as discussed in Chapter 8.

Sustaining Your Service Motivation

In discussing your service motivation, everything we've talked about so far comes full circle. Much depends on your self-awareness. This concerns both your preferences in terms of life choices and your ability to make them consciously and strategically with associated trade-offs in mind; and your capacity to recognize your personal needs—emotional and social—including when you are out of balance with them and may be headed towards burnout. Sustaining your service motivation also depends greatly on the quality of the service communities you participate in and have cultivated, including your professional and support networks. For example in balancing his personal and professional life, Aaron Williams relies on *a network of very good friends who are kindred spirits, who will allow you to step down and just relax and have moments of tranquility and peace in your life. And also reaching out to people who have an interesting perspective on moral leadership and a vision of the way the world should be. I find that to be invigorating.* You may reach particular points in your career when sustaining your service motivation requires cultivating new skills sets or seeking another environment in which to work, so you can renew your passion as you continue to grow and learn.

Balancing Your Personal and Professional Life

If there is anything consistent about careers, including international public service, it is the continuous challenge of trying to maintain a balanced life. From all of the people we talked with in putting this book together, we heard two persistent themes: 1) finding and maintaining balance is difficult; and 2) you have to work just as hard on your personal life, to maintain balance, as you do on your professional life. As GW student Jorge Baxter reflected, *As a development practitioner I wonder (as I become socialized) if I will become content with the perception that my colleagues respect and admire me, with the doors that open and close, with the feeling that I have lived a "respectable life," with the feeling that everything is under control, with the subtle feeling of power and pleasure that creeps into my brain when I have helped another, or even more subtly when I see the "other." Or will I have the strength to find my way out of my cave so that I can see and feel the sun?*

Balance is something Jef Buehler struggles with, as he candidly described. *I've got to be honest, it's very, very hard. It's almost impossible. Because when you're as deep into it as I am, on the personal side it's very tough. It's straining on family. I have a great community here where I live, but I don't spend nearly as much time in it actively participating in its community development like I used to when I first moved here, simply, because now I've branched out. If I think about it, there's probably about a thousand people in the State that I may have contact with in a given year for community development—a thousand people. And that takes a lot of energy. So, yeah, it's tough. You could ask my wife, it's tough.*

And it may be particularly difficult in the field, as Jennifer Butz describes. *That's one of the downsides of being a field person. It's very difficult to actually go home and not have work follow you, in part because often headquarters forgets that it's a six-hour or twelve-hour or sixteen-hour time difference. And their expectation is that their working day is also your working day, but you already did one of those. The other thing is that particularly in democratization, you're working with populations who already have full-time jobs so you have to get them after the normal workday, which means after your normal workday. So you're doing a lot of evening and weekend trainings, or traveling quite frequently. All of these things contribute to highly irregular and often completely overloaded schedules. So it's difficult to separate the personal and the professional. And even if you're hanging out with people, it's probably people who are also expats, so you might end up talking business and that feels a lot like working, not always, but sometimes. So it's hard.* Our focus group pointed out that Washington-based organizations with "flextime" can replicate this problem. Flexible schedules can remove the perceived standard work limits of 9 to 5, opening the possibility of working 24–7.

While it may seem counterintuitive, in creating balance in his life, David Yang draws on the notion that the work, or service, is his life, not just his job. *I make it clear that my job as a parent, my job as a community member, are part and parcel of my service, and that helps me say to my boss or to myself that "I'm leaving to coach [baseball] today" or "I have a sermon to give to my Unitarian Church this week, so I'm going to devote time to that." To me it's all part of the continuum of service. So it's not doing things that take away. I don't want to be sappy, but when I'm coaching Little League, I'm teaching leadership skills to my sons and their peers. Or when I'm part of*

*a lay-led service committee at my Unitarian Church—they're all fully inte-
gral expressions of my work. Not that my whole life is work. I have other
interests too. But it helps me to keep the office at the office because my other
pursuits in the community or my children, which I consider community work
also, are so much part of the ethic of service. I think it's helped to have a more
sort of integrated sense of work and play and leisure and work.*

Sometimes it is your partner or your family that will make sure you
maintain balance. This is Aaron Williams' experience. *I have to give my
wife Rosa a lot of credit because she demands balance in our life, and it's hard
for her to do that with a person who has the kind of energy level and the kind
of career I've had, with international travel and everything. But she's very good
at making sure I focus on that. It's important to me. It's also important because
of our two children—they're no longer children now, they're grown men. We've
always wanted to create a lifestyle and a family environment, where they were
valued and given a chance to be the best people they can be. And in order to
achieve this quality time, you have to be with your children. There's no such thing
as "I'm going to give you two hours of quality time between 7:30 and 9:30 at
night, so you better be ready for quality time!" Quality time only occurs when
you're around.* And Aaron provides an alternative perspective on the implications of living overseas for family life. *Being in the Foreign Service was
quite conducive to achieving this balance. Because people in other countries expect
the balance, more so than we do in America. Certainly that made it easier.* Living overseas can also mean less short-term travel away from your family.

Some of our focus group members make firm commitments outside
of work. Sometimes these entail service work, much like David Yang's.
In other instances, it may mean scheduling activities, such as classes
related to fitness or hobbies. Creating commitments and schedules can
help you to remain firm with yourself and your organization about
where your limits are with respect to working after hours.

Sarah Newhall has developed some routines to ensure some balance
in her life. *I have habits. For example, a habit of trying to have a midweek
date with* [my husband], *which is a sacred time where we go out and go to the
movies, have dinner.* For Jennifer Butz, it's about creating boundaries. *I
tend not to invite people over to my home, and while that might be antisocial,
it is in fact a strategy because it's the only place that I can call my own. And
while I'll do work there, I don't want it to become sort of an open space, because
it's a closed space in my opinion. Other people take the opposite tack. They open
their doors to everyone and it just becomes kind of a constant party. I find that
exhausting. I also have sort of quiet and individualized hobbies and interests,
like sewing, pottery, and reading, things that are slow and contemplative.
That's about as much private time as I get.*

Hobbies are important. Both David Yang and Jennifer Butz have
been involved in theater. In Mongolia, Jennifer Butz found support and

joy through an impromptu expatriate theater community. *We had an ambassador who was very much a devotee of the arts. He started a theater group and he and his wife would open up the Embassy recreation room. It started out just reading various plays and then reading was not enough. Then we had to actually start standing up and walking around. Well then that was not enough. So we had to memorize lines, do costumes and stage settings, sell tickets, bring the kids in. And it all culminated in what seemed like eight billion scene changes, with thirty costume changes. And I sewed them all. It was* The Sound of Music. *Who knew Maria wore eight dresses? I would never have signed up! It was great fun.*

Burnout and Rejuvenation

Burnout is integrally related to self-awareness and how we relate to our service communities. As Dass and Gorman discuss in their book, *How Can I Help?*, much of burnout is created by what we bring to service: our expectations, our fears and defensiveness, and our notions of personal responsibility. We begin to feel that without our doing the world will somehow end, or people will die. This is the subtle kind of "save the world" mentality that can begin to creep into your day-to-day work. As we discussed in Chapter 4, practicing self-awareness and maintaining a healthy vision for what development and success mean can help you to recognize those moments when you need to stop and remind yourself that, after all, it's not about you.

In her book, *The Rhythm of Compassion*, Gail Straub likens the service life to breathing:

> I've dedicated much of my life's work to teaching people about the rich and complex intersection between the inner life and the life of service. I've come to think of this relationship between soul and society much like following the in-breath and the out-breath, as in meditation practice. There's a natural time for the in-breath of caring for self and family, and a natural time for the out-breath of caring for the needs of the world. The challenge is to become skillful in following our rhythm—knowing when it's time to go inward and when to go out into the community.[3]

Carrying her metaphor forward, it's clear that we need both the in-breath, caring for the self, and the out-breath, caring for others, to live. Many treatments of burnout focus on sustaining effectiveness, but for those of us with a strong service ethic, the breathing—the balance—is about living and being.

Happily, none of our profiled practitioners indicated they had suffered from burnout. But they have experienced despair, stress, and frustration.

Sarah Newhall likens some of our work to the myth of Sisyphus. It may feel like each time we near the top as we roll that boulder, it comes sliding back down. So, she says, *you can experience temporary fatigue. Or you get sad, or disappointed, or tired, because you're trying to solve some incredibly complex problem. Then you can feel a sense of temporary despair because on a more cosmic level you're just outraged.* Aaron Williams shared, *I've experienced times, like everybody else, where you have too much work and not enough hours to do the work and wonder how you're going to do it. But not really burnout, where I've hit the wall and said, "I can't do this anymore."* After making this statement, he knocked on wood and chuckled.

This doesn't mean that he and our other profiled practitioners haven't seen burnout on the horizon. They have just learned to recognize the signs and to make changes to avoid it. Sarah Newhall has *learned how to watch the signals of my body so that I get sick less. Usually my way of getting sick is about being tired. So now I'm smarter about knowing when I'm feeling tired, and I can take a mental health day.* One of her habits is also to have a weekly massage. On his part, Jef Buehler practices and teaches Kundalini yoga. He even incorporates some yoga into his trainings for Main Street New Jersey in order to help community activists avoid burnout. Najma Siddiqi simply advises, *If you are frustrated, if you are burned out, if you are saying, "Why am I wasting my time here?" Try something different.* When Aaron Williams began to feel he was traveling far too much at IYF, he began to look for another job. *I decided to make a change. That's the other advantage of constructing a career where you have alternatives. You can look in other places to do something different. That's why it's so important to really learn your craft and become an expert at it and in lots of different areas, so people recognize you for having lots of different skills. And when you need to make a move people are interested in talking with you about the possibilities.*

Jennifer Butz relies on fostering a sense of joy to avoid burnout for herself and others. *Joy and humor keep cynicism at bay. It's very easy to become cynical or jaded. If you're not happy, it's not worth doing. And I don't mean giddy, "Ooh it's a wonderful morning!" But there has to be a certain zeal that goes along with what is done. I believe that laughter is extremely powerful. People often comment on the raucousness of the office that I keep. I just believe that it's energizing. Even if something's hard, I think that people take more courage if they laugh at it or find some way to see some humor or humorous elements in it, because then it's not so scary. Often what we do, and what we ask citizens to do, is scary. They're being asked to stand up and talk to a mayor that maybe fifteen years ago could have sent them to the labor camps. And we have to respect that. So oftentimes by encouraging them, or seeing the humor, or getting them to sort of engage in that, builds confidence and creates joy—and success, because then you get momentum.*

Paying attention to your service vision and the signs of burnout, and knowing some strategies for addressing them when they arise are important, because cynicism can hit you very early. Maybe even while you're still preparing for your career in international public service, as GW student Jennifer Villemez attests. *I'm beginning to feel uncomfortably disillusioned with the development field. Too much of what I am reading and seeing—in this class and in other contexts—seems uncertain. I am having trouble reconciling this impending skepticism with my want to believe that it can work, that all this discourse can play out effectively on the ground. I'm seeing that all of these theories and practices are fallible. Add to that, humans are unquestionably fallible. So, at what point is it likely that we can succeed? And if we do, how do we know? Then, once we know we have succeeded, how do we replicate that success?*

These feelings can be combated, in part, when you can identify change as a result of your work with others. When asked how he sustains his motivation, Jef Buhler responded, *I think a lot of it is through being inspired, reenergized by the wonderful work that the communities do as a result of what we've been able to teach them. You watch as they do all these incredible things to reclaim and enhance their community, whether it's social value, physical value, economic value, or political value. And they just make that one little corner of the earth a little bit better. And they do it using their ideas, and their vision, even if we teach them principles, techniques, and methodology. And maybe you inspire them, maybe you help them see their vision, and help them see their assets, and maybe you help them build on those assets. But they're the ones that are doing it. And when you see that happen— I just get chills right now thinking about it. It's an amazing thing.*

Of course, being inspired and reenergized by successes requires having reasonable expectations for what success means, and finding other ways to feel good and proud about your work when change cannot be measured. And it can be difficult to identify with successes when your work feels removed from the front line. There's a story about UNICEF Administrator Jim Grant's strong belief in the importance of connecting one's work, no matter what it is, to the larger service effort. It tells how with each shipment of goods to overseas children, he arranged for one longshoreman from the dock to accompany the containers to learn where they go and the difference they make in people's lives. This is one reason why we recommend, in Chapter 8, that you periodically visit the field, so you can stay fresh and recognize some of the fruits and meaning behind your labor. Najma Siddiqi rejuvenates this way: *traveling is always refreshing. I love to learn from others. Sometimes I meet very fantastic people and learn interesting approaches in this* [World Bank] *bureaucracy, but I can learn much more from my travels, wherever I am going, whether it's meeting with government or nongovernment people.*

For many of us, our service work and the nurturing of others that we do on the job are more than sufficient to feel we're living our vision. But when your work is far removed from the front lines, overly analytic or technical, or supportive but not explicitly linked to affected populations, you might opt for direct, frontline volunteer service where you live. David Yang does this in Washington, Jennifer Butz does it in Albania, and several of our quoted students and focus group members do so as well.

Staying Inspired

The subjects of this chapter are related to much of the discussion from other chapters. So, for example, sustaining your motivation is first and foremost about living your values, as GW student Kipp Efinger shared. *Understanding the values of the organization builds an employee connection with the organization. It brings pride and care to your work.* Being inspired by values does not mean that they are yours alone. You can also be deeply inspired when those values are shared and enacted in community. A huge source of inspiration also comes from our heroes.[4] As discussed in Chapter 8, we encourage you to read biographies and identify and explore other practitioners and social activists who can serve as role models. Not only will you be inspired by their vision and action, you can learn how they navigated the difficult choices and challenges in their service careers and personal lives, including how they managed cynicism, burnout, and balance.

Notes

1. For a wonderful resource on considering this option and also for making more conscious decisions about lifestyle choices, see Jeanne Safer's book *Beyond Motherhood: Choosing a Life Without Children* (New York: Simon & Schuster, Pocket Books, 1996).

2. To learn more from others' experiences, visit the Web site of Tales of a Small Planet: http://www.talesmag.com/index.shtml. The site includes personal stories, indexed by country, as well as topical essays and resources related to lifestyle issues.

3. As noted in Chapter 4, we recommend this book for exploring what service means to you as you develop your own personal service vision. See the complete reference in Appendix 4.

4. To expand your collection of heroes, visit http://myhero.com, an educational project that "celebrates the best of humanity."

Afterword:
The Practice of
International Public Service

Traveling the service-choice spiral combines both professional and personal development, which are intertwined in a life of international public service. Rather than an exercise in goal-setting and achieving milestones, we see a life in international public service as akin to the Buddhist notion that you don't "live" your religion, you *practice* it. The joy, and the beauty, is that we will never arrive. We will, hopefully, always be practicing and learning as we make our journeys along the service-choice spiral.

We close the book with a quote from George Bernard Shaw that James Grant, the visionary leader of UNICEF until his death in 1995, indicated was one of favorites. For us, this quote captures the essence of public service, the fundamental interpenetration between the individual and the community, and the notion of sustained commitment to a better world not just today, but for the future:

> This is the true joy in life, the being used for a purpose recognized by yourself as a mighty one. I am of the opinion that my life belongs to the whole community and as long as I live it is my privilege to do for it whatever I can. Life is no brief candle to me. It is a sort of splendid torch which I have got hold of for the moment, and I want to make it burn as brightly as possible before handing it on to future generations.

Appendix 1.
Selected Professional
Associations

- African Studies Association: http://www.africanstudies.org/
- Academy of International Business: http://aib.msu.edu/
- American Political Science Association: http://www.apsanet.org/
- American Society for Public Administration. See Section on International and Comparative Administration (SICA), and Conference of Minority Public Administrators (which publishes a newsletter with information on internships and job opportunities): http://www.aspanet.org
- Association for Research on Nonprofit Organizations and Voluntary Action: http://www.arnova.org
- Blacks in Government. See BIG Chapters: Department of State/Foreign Affairs Chapter: http://www.bignet.org/regional/foreign.affairs/index.html; and USAID Chapter: http://bigrxi.org/chapters/USAID.html
- Development Management Network (DMN): An informal, all-volunteer entity that organizes two workshops per year, one in conjunction with ASPA's national conference, and one in Washington, D.C. George Washington University's School of Public Policy and Public Administration hosts the DMN secretariat (it does not have a Web site).
- International Association of Facilitators: http://www.iaf-world.org/
- International Association of Public Participation (IAP2): http://www.iap2.org

- International Development Ethics Association: http://www .development-ethics.org/
- International Studies Association: http://www.isanet.org. See especially the Global Development Section: http://www. isanet.org/ sections/gd/.
- Latin American Studies Association: http://lasa.international.pitt .edu/
- National Forum for Black Public Administrators: http://www .nfbpa.org/
- Peace Corps Association, including a directory of country of service groups: http://www.rpcv.org/
- Society for International Development (SID): http://www.sidint .org. SID has individual chapters in various countries around the world. In the United States, the Washington, D.C., chapter is among the most active and organizes an annual conference, seminar series, job fairs, and networking events.
- UN Young Professionals for International Cooperation: http:// www.unausa.org. A program of the UN Association, UN YPIC provides professional development and networking opportunities across the country through local chapters.

Appendix 2.
Selected Degree Program
Information

Combining Peace Corps with Graduate School

- George Washington University's Teaching Corps Fellows Program: http://gsehd.gwu.edu/gsehd/viewarticle+254
- Peace Corps Fellows and Masters International Programs: http://www.peacecorps.gov/index.cfm?shell=resources.grads
- Rutgers University-Camden, Graduate Department of Public Policy and Administration, International Public Service and Development Program (a Peace Corps Masters International Program): http://camden-www.rutgers.edu/dept-pages/pubpol/concen/

Public Administration and Public Policy Programs

- Duke University, Terry Sanford Institute of Public Policy: http://www.pubpol.duke.edu/
- George Washington University, School of Public Policy and Public Administration: http://www.gwu.edu/~spppa/
- Harvard University, John F. Kennedy School of Government: http://www.ksg.harvard.edu/
- Indiana University-Bloomington, School of Public and Environmental Affairs: http://www.indiana.edu/~speaweb/
- Monterey Institute of International Studies, Graduate School of International Policy Studies: http://www.miis.edu/gsips-about-dean.html

- Princeton University, Woodrow Wilson School of Public and International Affairs: http://www.wws.princeton.edu/
- Syracuse University, Maxwell School: http://www.maxwell.syr.edu/
- University of Pittsburgh, Graduate School of Public and International Affairs: http://www.gspia.pitt.edu/
- University of Southern California, School of Policy, Planning and Development: http://www.usc.edu/schools/sppd/
- University of Washington, Daniel J. Evans School of Public Affairs: http://www.evans.washington.edu/

Business Administration Programs

- Carleton University, Eric Sprott School of Business: http://sprott.carleton.ca/index3.html
- Columbia University, School of International and Public Affairs: http://www.sipa.columbia.edu/
- George Washington University, School of Business: http://www.gwu.edu/~ibusdpt/
- Harvard University, Harvard Business School: http://www.hbs.edu/
- University of Pennsylvania, Wharton School of Business: http://mba.wharton.upenn.edu/mba/
- Stanford University, Graduate School of Business: http://www.gsb.stanford.edu/
- Thunderbird, The Garvin School of International Management: http://www.thunderbird.edu/
- University of South Carolina, Moore School of Business: http://mooreschool.sc.edu/
- York University, Schulich School of Business: http://www.schulich.yorku.ca/

International Relations/International Affairs

- Georgetown University, Edmund A. Walsh School of Foreign Service: http://sfswww.georgetown.edu/sfs/
- George Washington University, Elliott School of International Affairs: http://www.gwu.edu/~elliott/. See also: http://www.gwu.edu/~elliott/academicprograms/ma/ids/.
- Johns Hopkins, Paul H. Nitze School of Advanced International Studies: http://www.sais-jhu.edu/

- Tufts University, Fletcher School of Law and Diplomacy: http://fletcher.tufts.edu/
- University of California San Diego, Graduate School of International Relations and Pacific Studies: http://www-irps.ucsd.edu/

Specialized Programs

- American University, School of International Service: http://www.american.edu/sis/. Offers a Master's in Development Management.
- Brandeis University, Heller School for Social Policy and Management, Master's in Sustainable International Development: http://www.heller.brandeis.edu/sid/
- Clark University, Department of International Development, Community and Environment: http://www.clarku.edu/departments/idce/id/ba/
- Columbia University: Program in Economic and Political Development/Development Management Track: http://www.sipa.columbia.edu/func/epd/
- George Mason University, Institute for Conflict Analysis and Resolution: http://www.gmu.edu/departments/ICAR/
- London School of Economics, Development Studies Institute: http://www.lse.ac.uk/resources/graduateProspectus2004/departmentsAndInstitutes/developmentStudiesInstitute.htm
- School of International Training: http://www.sit.edu/
- University of Manchester, Institute for Development Policy and Management: http://idpm.man.ac.uk/index.shtml
- University of Notre Dame, Joan B. Kroc Institute for International Peace Studies: http://www.nd.edu/~krocinst/
- University of Sussex, Institute of Development Studies: http://www.ids.ac.uk/ids/

Appendix 3.
Selected Job/Internship
Resources

The following organizations are highlighted to provide a cross section of examples for each type of institutional base. The list is not at all exhaustive. Web pages for job search and internship opportunities are included, where available.

Internship Placement Services

- AEISEC (placement for paid traineeships or volunteer work): http://www.aiesec.org
- The Association for International Practical Training (AIPT), the International Association for the Exchange of Students for Technical Experience (IAESTE): http://www.aipt.org/subpages/iaeste_us/index.php
- Washington Center (see their program on international affairs): http://www.twc.edu/about/index.htm

Selected International Service Opportunities

- Alliance of European Voluntary Service Organizations: http://www.alliance-network.org/
- Canadian University Services Overseas: http://www.cuso.org/
- European Voluntary Service: http://europa.eu.int/comm/youth/program/sos/vh_evs_en.html

- Global Volunteers, Partners in Development: http://www.global volunteers.org/
- Habitat for Humanity, Global Village Program: http://www.habitat .org/GV/
- Idealist.org and Action without Borders: http://idealist.org
- International Urban Management Fellowship, National Forum for Black Public Administrators: http://www.nfbpa.org/Center LeaderShip.cfm
- International Volunteer Programs Association: http://www.volunteer international.org/
- Jesuit Volunteers International: http://www.jesuitvolunteers.org/
- Minority International Research Training Grant, National Institutes of Health: http://www.fic.nih.gov/programs/mirt.html. Sends minority undergraduates and medical students abroad to do health-related research.
- NetAid: http://www.netaid.org/volunteer/
- Rotary International: http://www.rotary.org/. Offers exchange and service opportunities, including a three-week professional exchange program.
- Sister Cities International: http://www.sister-cities.org/
- UN Volunteers: http://www.unv.org/
- US Peace Corps: http://www.peacecorps.gov/
- VolunteerAbroad.com: http://www.volunteerabroad.com/
- Volunteers for Peace: http://www.vfp.org/
- Volunteers in Asia: http://www.viaprograms.org
- Voluntary Services Overseas (Canada): http://www.vsocanada.org/
- Voluntary Services Overseas (United Kindgdom): http://www.vso .org.uk/
- World Volunteer Web: http://www.worldvolunteerweb.org/

Pre-service Opportunities for the Entrepreneurial and Research-oriented

- Echoing Green: http://www.echoinggreen.org
- Fulbright Grants for Educational and Cultural Exchange: http:// www.iie.org/
- National Security Education Program: http://nsep.aed.org
- US Institute of Peace: http://www.usip.gov/

General Job and Internship Search Information

Miscellaneous Sources

Visit the career development office of your university. It is likely to subscribe to many sources, including those listed here.

- Peace Corps offers a range of services for Returned Peace Corps Volunteers, through its Office of Returned Volunteer Services: http://www.peacecorps.gov/.
- See Interaction's newsletter *Monday Developments*, or register for their weekly e-mail job announcements: http://interaction.org/jobs/.
- See and subscribe to *International Career Employment Weekly* at: http://www.internationaljobs.org/.
- For additional tips, see Craig P. Donovan and Jim Garnett, *Internships for Dummies* (New York: Hungry Minds, 2001).

Relevant Web Sites

- The Development Executive Group: http://www.developmentex .com
- DevJobs: http://www.devjobsmail.com
- DevNetJobs: http://www.DevNetJobs.org
- Eldis Gateway to Development Information, job page: http:// www.eldis.org/news/jobs.htm
- Foreign Policy Association job board: http://www.fpa.org/
- Idealist.org and Action Without Borders: http://www.idealist .org
- Intern Abroad.com: http://www.internabroad.com/search.cfm
- International Jobs Center: http://www.internationaljobs.org/
- One World: http://www.oneworld.net/job/list/professional/
- Schwab Foundation for Social Entrepreneurship (lists selected jobs and internships in developing countries): http://www.schwabfound .org/jobs.htm

Job and Internship Information for Selected Organizations

International Donors

Regional Organizations
- African Development Bank: http://www.afdb.org/about_adb/ vacancies/opportunities_vacancies.htm

- Asia Development Bank: http://www.adb.org/Employment/
- Inter-American Development Bank (includes a Junior Profession-als Program): http://www.iadb.org/aboutus/
- Organization of American States: http://www.oas.org/

UN Agencies

- Food and Agriculture Organization: http://www.fao.org/VA/Employ.htm
- International Labor Organization (ILO): http://www.ilo.org/public/english/employment/
- UN Children's Fund (UNICEF): http://www.unicef.org/about/
- UN Development Programme (UNDP): http://www.undp.org/mainundp/jobs/
- UN Education, Scientific and Cultural Organization (UNESCO): http://portal.unesco.org/
- UN Fund for Population Activities (UNFPA): http://www.unfpa.org/about/employment/
- UN High Commissioner for Refugees (UNHCR): http://www.unhcr.ch/cgi-bin/texis/vtx/home
- World Health Organization (WHO): http://www.who.int/employment/en/

World Bank

- General information and links to Young Professionals Program, Junior Professionals Program, Junior Professionals Program for Afro-Descendants, Bank Internship Program: http://lnweb28.worldbank.org/hrs/careers.nsf

US Federal Agencies

General Information

- For information on jobs with the US Government, see http://www.usajobs.opm.gov.
- FedBizOpps also includes information on Personal Service Con-tractor (PSC) opportunities: http://www.fedbizopps.gov/.
- Entry-level programs available in most US Federal agencies include:
  - Student Educational Employment Program (you must be cur-rently enrolled in a degree program; can lead to permanent positions): http://www.usajobs.opm.gov/STUDENTS.asp
  - Presidential Management Fellows Program: http://www.pmi.opm.gov

- Partnership Fellows Program: http://www.ourpublicservice.org/aboutus/
- See also http://www.calltoserve.org.
- Bridges Internship Program, National Forum for Black Public Administrators: http://www.nfbpa.org/CenterLeaderShip.cfm

US Agency for International Development

- General employment information:
  - http://www.usaid.gov/careers or
  - http://www.usaid.gov/about/employment/ or
  - http://www.usaid.gov/about/employment/gscover.htm
- Contract award information for subcontracting opportunities is available from the "Current Technical Services Contracts and Grants Book" (W-443, better known as the *Yellow Book*) at: http://www.usaid.gov/procurement_bus_opp/procurement
- Personal Service Contractor (PSC) positions: http://www.usaid.gov/procurement_bus_opp/procurement/psc_solicit
- PSC opportunities in disaster assistance and emergency relief may be found at: http://www.globalcorps.com
- American Association for the Advancement of Science (AAAS) Diplomacy Fellows Program: http://www.usaid.gov/about/employment/fellows/fp_aaas.html
- Democracy Fellows Program: http://www.worldlearning.org/wlid/dfp/index.html
- Health and Child Survival Fellows Program (managed by Johns Hopkins University): http://jhuhcsfp.org/
- International Development Intern (IDI) Program (junior-level focus) and New Entry Professionals (NEP) program (mid-level focus), must be a US citizen:
  - http://www.usaid.gov/about/employment/nepanno2.htm
  - http://www.usaid.gov/about/employment/nepbro.htm
  - http://www.usaid.gov/about/employment/cpfaqn.htm

US State Department

- General Information: http://www.careers.state.gov, http://www.foreignservicecareers.gov/
- Current Job Postings: http://www.state.gov/employment/
- Student Programs and Internships: http://www.careers.state.gov/student/

Selected US Federal Agencies with International Programs

- Broadcasting Board of Governors, overseas non-military international broadcasting, including Voice of America, Radio Free Asia, and the Middle East Television Network: http://www.bbg.gov/bbg_aboutus.cfm
- Central Intelligence Agency: http://www.odci.gov/employment/
- Environmental Protection Agency, Office of International Affairs: http://www.epa.gov/oia/
- Health and Human Services, Centers for Disease Control and Prevention, Office of Global Health: http://www.cdc.gov/ogh/
- National Science Foundation, International Programs: http://www.nsf.gov/home/int/
- Nuclear Regulatory Commission, International Programs: http://www.nrc.gov/what-we-do/international.html
- Peace Corps: http://www.peacecorps.gov/
- US Department of Agriculture: http://www.fas.usda.gov/admin/jobs/jobs.html
- US Department of Commerce: http://www.commerce.gov/jobs.html
  - Bureau of Industry and Security: http://www.bis.doc.gov/internationalprograms/
  - International Trade Administration: http://www.ita.doc.gov/
  - National Oceanic and Atmospheric Administration: http://www.international.noaa.gov/
- US Department of Education, International Education Portal: http://www.ed.gov/about/offices/list/ous/international/
- US Department of Energy, Office of Policy and International Affairs: http://www.pi.energy.gov/
- US Department of the Interior, International Technical Assistance Program: http://www.doi.gov/intl/itap/
- US Department of Labor, Bureau of International Labor Affairs: http://www.dol.gov/ilab/
- US Department of Transportation:
  - Federal Highway Administration, Office of International Programs: http://international.fhwa.dot.gov/
  - Federal Transit Administration, International Mass Transportation Program: http://www.fta.dot.gov/initiatives_tech_assistance/imtp/2430_ENG_HTML.htm

US Congressionally Funded Organizations

- African Development Foundation: http://www.adf.gov/employment.htm

- Inter-American Foundation: http://www.iaf.gov
- International Republican Institute: http://www.iri.org/opportunities .asp
- National Democratic Institute: http://www.ndi.org/employment/ currentemploy.asp
- US Institute of Peace: http://www.usip.gov/jobs/index.html

US-based NGOs

Additional advocacy-oriented NGOs are listed below, under advocacy organizations. As discussed in Chapter 7, the NGO sector is extremely diverse. Some nonprofits operate little differently from private consulting firms; we've included these in the following section on US private consulting firms. Some NGOs are faith based and/or operate outside of the international development industry. And some of them resemble think tanks.

Overview Information

- A listing of PVOs that receive USAID funding can be found on the Web at http://www.usaid.gov/about/resources/.
- Interaction (an association of US-based international development and humanitarian assistance NGOs):
  - List and links to Interaction's 158 member organizations: http://www.interaction.org/members/
  - Jobs with Interaction: http://interaction.org/jobs/jobads.html

Specific Organizations

- Adventist Development and Relief Agency: http://www.adra.org/employ.html
- Africare: http://africare.org/contact/employment.html
- Ashoka: http://ashoka.org/involved/jobs.cfm
- Asia Foundation: http://www.asiafoundation.org/About/jobs.html
- Care: http://www.careusa.org/careers/
- Carter Center:
  - Careers: https://emory.hr.emory.edu/careers.nsf/vwEUVDept?OpenView .Scroll to "Carter Center"
  - Internship Program: http://www.cartercenter.org/aboutus/education _doc.htm
- Catholic Relief Services: http://www.crs.org/about_us/careers/
- Habitat for Humanity International: http://www.habitat.org/hr/

- International Youth Foundation: http://www.iyfnet.org/section.cfm/ 32
- Just Associates: http://www.justassociates.org/
- Land O'Lakes, International Development Division: http://www .idd.landolakes.com/ (Note: Land O'Lakes is technically not an NGO, but a cooperative.)
- Mercy Corps: http://www.mercycorps.org/jobs/
- Pact: http://www.pactworld.org/career/
- Path: http://www.path.org/about/jobs.php
- Save the Children: http://www.savethechildren.org/careers/
- Trickle Up: http://www.trickleup.org/getinvolved_wwtu.asp
- VSA Arts: http://www.vsarts.org/x205.xml
- World Learning: http://www.worldlearning.org/hr/jobs.html
- World Vision: http://www.wvi.org/wvi/employment/employment. htm
- World Wildlife Fund: http://www.worldwildlife.org/about/jobs. cfm

US-based Private Consulting Firms (for-profit and nonprofit)

- Abt Associates Inc.: http://www.abtassoc.com/
- Academy for Education Development: http://aed.org/employ .html
- Associates in Rural Development (ARD): http://www.ardinc.com/ htm/jobs/jobs.htm
- Bearing Point: https://bearingpoint.recruitmax.com/eng/candidates/
- Chemonics: http://www.chemonics.com/career/
- CH2MHill: http://www.ch2m.com/flash/Careers/careers_frame.htm
- Development Alternatives Incorporated (DAI): http://www.dai .com/
- Management Sciences for Health: http://www.msh.org/employment/ positions/
- Management Systems International (MSI): http://www.msi-inc .com/gral/afghan.html
- Pragma: http://pragmacorp.com/Employment_Opportunities/index .htm
- QED Group, LLC.: http://www.qedgroupllc.com/Company/ employment.htm
- RTI International: http://www.rti.org/
- Social Impact: http://www.socialimpact.com/
- Urban Institute: http://www.urban.org/content/About/Employment/ Employment.htm

University-based Consulting Groups

- American Indian Higher Education Consortium: http://www.aihec.org/
- Hispanic Serving Institutions, see the Hispanic Association of Colleges and Universities: http://www.hacu.net/
- Historically Black Colleges and Universities: http://www.hbcu-central.com/
- Eastern Mennonite University, Institute for Justice and Peacebuilding: http://www.emu.edu/ctp/ijp.html
- Harvard University, Center for International Development: http://www.cid.harvard.edu/
- Johns Hopkins University School of Public Health (JHPIEGO): http://www.jhpiego.org
- University of Maryland, Center for Institutional Reform and the Informal Sector (IRIS): http://www.iris.umd.edu
- University of Maryland, Center for International Development and Conflict Management: http://www.cidcm.umd.edu
- Mississippi Consortium for International Development: http://www.mcid.us/
- Rutgers University, Local Democracy Partnership Program: http://www.rci.rutgers.edu/~crcees/ldp.html
- State University of New York at Albany, Center for Legislative Development: http://www.albany.edu/cld/index.html
- University of Wisconsin, Land Tenure Center: http://www.wisc.edu/ltc

Think Tanks

Many of these have internship and fellowship programs as well as listed job opportunities.

- American Enterprise Institute: http://www.aei.org/about/
- Aspen Institute: http://www.aspeninstitute.org/
- Brookings Institution:
  - Employment: http://www.brookings.edu/admin/employment.htm
  - Fellowships: http://www.brookings.edu/admin/fellowships.htm
  - Internships: http://www.brookings.edu/admin/internships.htm
- Carnegie Endowment for International Peace:
  - Employment: http://www.ceip.org/files/about/about_employ.asp
  - Junior Fellows Program: http://www.ceip.org/files/about/about_Junior.asp

- Center for Global Development: http://www.cgdev.org/About/
- Center for Strategic and International Studies:
  - Employment: http://csis.org/employment/
  - Internships: http://csis.org/intern/
- Heritage Foundation:
  - Employment: http://www.heritage.org/About/Careers/
  - Internships: http://www.heritage.org/About/Internships/
- International Center for Research on Women: http://www.icrw.org/html/jobs/jobs.htm
- World Resources Institute: http://joblist.wri.org/

Private Foundations

- General information: http://fdncenter.org
- Bill and Melinda Gates Foundation: http://www.gatesfoundation.org/AboutUs/Employment/
- Ford Foundation: http://www.fordfound.org/employment/
- John D. and Catherine T. MacArthur Foundation: http://www.macfdn.org/announce/jobs/
- Kettering Foundation: http://www.kettering.org
- Rockefeller Brothers Fund: http://www.rbf.org/about/employment.html
- Rockefeller Foundation: http://www.rockfound.org/

Advocacy Organizations

- Bank Information Center: http://www.bicusa.org/bicusa/issues/misc_resources/628.php
- Bank Watch: http://www.bankwatch.org/overview/memployment.html
- Bread for the World: http://www.bread.org/jobs/
- Citizen's Network on Essential Services: http://www.servicesforall.org/
- Development Gap: http://www.developmentgap.org/intern.html
- Freedom House: http://www.freedomhouse.org/aboutfh/empopp.htm
- Gender Action: http://www.genderaction.org

Sources for Canadian and UK Citizens

Canada

- Canada Online: Click on "international development careers" at http://canadaonline.about.com/od/careers/.
- Canadian International Development Agency (CIDA): http://www .acdi-cida.gc.ca/workin-e.htm

United Kingdom

- BOND (network of UK NGOs working in international development): http://www.bond.org.uk
- Department for International Development (DFID), United Kingdom: Click on "Recruitment" at http://www.dfid.gov.uk.
- University of Edinburgh Career Service: http://www.careers.ed .ac.uk/STUDENTS/Careers/B6.html
- World Service Enquiry: http://www.wse.org.uk/

Appendix 4.
Selected Reading

On Service

Beckmann, David, Ramgopal Agarwala, Sven Burmester, and Ismail Serageldin. *Friday Morning Reflections at the World Bank.* Washington, DC: Seven Locks Press, 1991.

Block, Peter. *Stewardship: Choosing Service Over Self-Interest.* San Francisco: Berrett-Koehler, 1993.

Dass, Ram, and Mirabai Bush. *Compassion in Action: Setting out on the Path of Service.* New York: Bell Tower, 1992.

Dass, Ram, and Paul Gorman. *How Can I Help? Stories and Reflections on Service.* New York: Alfred A. Knopf, 1988.

McSwain, Cynthia J. "A Public Service Life." *Journal of Public Affairs Education.* 8, no. 1 (January 2002): 5–8.

Rimmerman, Craig A. *The New Citizenship: Unconventional Politics, Activism, and Service.* Boulder, CO: Westview Press, 1997.

Shea, Margo, and Kevin Mattson. *Building Citizens: A Critical Reflection and Discussion Guide for Community Service Participants.* New Brunswick, NJ: Walt Whitman Center for the Culture and Politics of Democracy, Rutgers University, 1998.

Smith, Stephen C. *Ending Global Poverty.* New York: Palgrave, 2005.

Straub, Gail. *The Rhythm of Compassion: Caring for Self, Connecting with Society.* Boston: Journey Editions, 2000.

General International Development

For Development Ethics, see the International Development Ethics Association: http://www.development-ethics.org

Rahnema, Majid with Victoria Bawtree, eds. *The Post Development Reader.* London: Zed Books, 1997.

Rist, Gilbert. *The History of Development: From Western Origins to Global Faith.* London: Zed Books, 1997.

Sachs, Wolfgang, ed. *The Development Dictionary: A Guide to Knowledge as Power.* London: Zed Books Ltd., 1992.

Sen, Amartya. *Development as Freedom.* Oxford: Oxford University Press, 1999.

Simon, David, and Anders Narman, eds. *Development as Theory and Practice.* Essex, United Kingdom: Addison Wesley Longman, 1999.

Development Management

Brinkerhoff, Derick W. *Improving Development Program Performance: Guidelines for Managers.* Boulder, CO: Lynne Rienner Publishers, 1991.

Brinkerhoff, Derick W., and Benjamin L. Crosby. *Managing Policy Reform: Concepts and Tools for Decision-Makers in Developing and Transitioning Countries.* Bloomfield, CT: Kumarian Press, 2002.

Brinkerhoff, Jennifer M. *Partnership for International Development: Rhetoric or Results?* Boulder, CO: Lynne Rienner Publishers, 2002.

Bryant, Coralie, and Louise White. *Managing Development in the Third World.* Boulder, CO: Westview Press, 1982.

Cooke, Bill. "Participation, 'Process,' and Management: Lessons for Development in the History of Organizational Development." *Journal of International Development* 10, no. 1 (1998): 35–54.

Esman, Milton. *Management Dimensions of Development: Perspectives and Strategies.* Bloomfield, CT: Kumarian Press, 1991.

Kaplan, Allan. *The Development Practitioner's Handbook.* London: Pluto Press, 1996.

Thomas, Alan. "What Makes Good Development Management?" *Development in Practice* 9, nos. 1 and 2 (February 1999): 9–17.

Community Development and Empowerment

Alinsky, Saul. *Rules for Radicals: A Primer for Realistic Radicals.* New York: Random House, 1972.

Berryman, Phillip. *Liberation Theology: Essential Facts about the Revolutionary Movement in Latin America and Beyond.* New York: Pantheon Books, 1987.

Burkey, Stan. *People First: A Guide to Self-Reliant, Participatory Rural Development.* London: Zed Books, 1993.

Campfens, Hubert, ed. *Community Development Around the World: Practice, Theory, Research, Training.* Toronto: University of Toronto Press, 1997.

Freire, Paulo. *Pedagogy of the Oppressed.* New York: Seabury Press, 1968.

Kahn, Si. *Organizing: A Guide for Grassroots Leaders.* New York: McGraw-Hill, 1982.

Macy, Joanna. *Dharma and Development: Religion as Resource in the Sarvodaya Self-Help Movement.* West Hartford, CT: Kumarian Press, 1983.

NGOs

Edwards, Michael, and Alan Fowler, eds. *The Earthscan Reader on NGO Management.* London: Earthscan, 2003.

Fowler, Alan. *Striking a Balance: A Guide to Enhancing the Effectiveness of Non-Governmental Organisations in International Development.* London: Earthscan, 1997.

Lewis, David. *The Management of Non-governmental Development Organizations: An Introduction.* London: Routledge, 2001.

Lindenberg, Marc, and Coralie Bryant. *Going Global: Transforming Relief and Development NGOs.* Bloomfield, CT: Kumarian Press, 2001.

Selected Biographies to Explore

Addams, Jane. *Twenty Years at Hull House.* The founder of Hull House—a settlement house for young women to live and work with local, primarily poor immigrant residents that became an innovation center for social programs—describes her life and work.

Ariyaratne, A. T. See: http://www.sarvodaya.org/Library/AriBiography/Index.htm.

Carter, Jimmy. *Living Faith.* New York: Random House, 1996.

Clinton, Bill. *My Life.* New York: Alfred A. Knopf, 2004.

D'Agnes, Thomas. *From Condoms to Cabbages: An Authorized Biography of Mecha Viravaidya.* Bangkok, Thailand: Bangkok Post Books, 2001. See also the Population and Community Development Association Web page: http://www.pda.or.th.

Durrani, Tehmina. *Abdul Sattar Edhi: An Autobiography. A Mirror to the Blind.* Islamabad, Pakistan: National Bureau of Publications, 1998. See also: http://myhero.com/myhero/hero.asp?hero=as_edhi.

Eppsteiner, Fred, ed. *The Path of Compassion: Writings on Socially En-gaged Buddhism.* Berkeley, CA: Parallax Press, 1988.

Freire, Paulo. See: http://www.unomaha.edu/~pto/paulo.htm.

Gandhi, Mahatma. See: http://www.mkgandhi.org.

Horton, Myles, Judith Kohl, and Herbert Kohl. *The Long Haul.* New York: Doubleday, 1990. A biography of the founder of the Highlander Folk School, started in the 1930s to educate people for participation in community and social change initiatives.

Ingram, Catherine. *In the Footsteps of Gandhi: Conversations with Spiritual Social Activists.* Berkeley, CA: Parallax Press, 1990.

Jolly, Richard, ed. *Jim Grant: UNICEF Visionary.* New York: UNICEF, 2003.

Jones, Ken. *The Social Face of Buddhism: An Approach to Political and Social Activism.* London: Wisdom Publications, 1989.

Khan, Akhtar Hameed. Founder of the Orangi Pilot Project in Pakistan and of the Comilla Rural Academy in East Pakistan (now Bangladesh). See: http://www.yespakistan.com/ahkhan.asp and http://akhtar-hameed-khan.8m.com/.

King, Martin L., Jr. *A Testament of Hope: The Essential Writings of Martin Luther King Jr.* San Francisco: Harper and Row, 1986.

Leonard, David K. *African Success: Four Public Managers of Kenyan Rural Development.* Berkeley: University of California Press, 1991.

Mandela, Nelson. See: http://www.anc.org.za/people/mandela.html.

Sivaraksa, Sulak. *Seeds of Peace: A Buddhist Vision for Renewing Society.* Berkeley, CA: Parallax Press, 1992.

Terkel, Studs. *American Dreams: Lost and Found.* New York: New Press, 1999. Americans of different generations and places discuss their personal experiences with community service.

About the Authors

Derick W. Brinkerhoff

Derick Brinkerhoff is Senior Fellow in International Public Management at RTI International (Research Triangle Institute), a nonprofit research organization headquartered in North Carolina, and has an associate faculty appointment at George Washington University's School of Public Policy and Public Administration. He holds a doctorate in public policy and administration from Harvard University and a master's in public administration from the University of California Riverside. Derick has published extensively, including six books and numerous articles and book chapters.

As an undergrad, he studied anthropology at the University of California Riverside and then served three years in the Peace Corps in Chad, teaching English in secondary school. His doctoral program at Harvard University's School of Education, in administration, planning, and social policy, allowed him to combine an international policy focus with study in organizational development (OD) and public management. While at Harvard, he worked with Rosabeth Moss Kanter (then at Yale, currently at the Harvard Business School), spending two years doing US-focused OD and research. He also consulted with the Harvard Institute for International Development, working in Mali.

Following graduation in 1980, Derick began taking international development assignments as an independent consultant, which led him to Portugal, Zaire, and Washington, D.C. He then accepted a job with USAID in the Office of Rural and Institutional Development. There, he managed an applied research project and traveled to USAID Missions to work on project designs, implementation start-ups, and evaluations. It was during this period that Derick and a core group of like-minded colleagues founded the Development Management Network.

After nearly three years in Washington, Derick became an advisor to the planning ministry in Haiti, where he worked for four and a half years, as a staff member of the University of Maryland's International Development Management Center (IDMC), which was founded in cooperation with USAID and USDA. He then returned to the College Park campus and served as IDMC's Associate Director for Research for six years, pursuing research, training, and technical assistance work with USAID, the World Bank, and WHO in institutional development, policy implementation, program evaluation, and administrative reform. During this period USAID established a program in democracy and governance, and Derick began a close collaboration with that office through the Implementing Policy Change (IPC) project.

Derick completed his IPC research program as a Principal Social Scientist with Abt Associates, where he worked for ten years on a wide variety of public policy, governance, democracy, anticorruption, and service delivery issues. He managed Abt's governance portfolio with USAID's Democracy and Governance Office, codirected an analytic support project for the White House Initiative to End Hunger in Africa, directed a USAID/World Bank project to improve performance and sustainability of African agricultural research and technology systems, directed studies of the role of NGOs in health service delivery and of accountability mechanisms for health systems performance improvement, and continued to conduct research related to good governance and democratization. Derick traveled extensively during this decade, working in Africa, Asia, Latin America, Eastern Europe, Central Asia, and the Middle East. In addition, he taught as an adjunct professor at Johns Hopkins School of Advanced International Studies and at George Washington University, gave numerous conference and seminar presentations, and found the time to woo and marry Jennifer.

In the fall of 2003 he joined RTI International where he is currently pursuing research and analytic support focused on democracy and governance in fragile states, post-conflict reconstruction, decentralization, and strategies for strengthening local government. Recent travel has taken him to Iraq, Bulgaria, Ghana, and Madagascar.

Jennifer M. Brinkerhoff

Jennifer Brinkerhoff is an Associate Professor of Public Administration, International Affairs, and International Business at the George Washington University. She holds a PhD in public administration with an emphasis on development administration from the University of Southern California in Los Angeles, and a master's of public administration from the Monterey Institute of International Studies. She teaches courses on international development policy and administration, development management, and organizational behavior; and keeps a foot in the practitioner world through consulting with the World Bank, USAID, and NGOs. Her book, *Partnership for International Development: Rhetoric or Results?*, combines her research with this work. She has also coedited three journal issues and published over twenty articles on topics ranging from evaluation, to NGOs, failed states, governance, and diasporas. She cofounded an interdisciplinary working group at GW that focuses on the role of NGOs in development, and serves as the coordinator for the Development Management Network.

Jennifer earned her BA in business economics and French literature from the University of California Santa Barbara, where she also completed a Global Peace and Security Certificate, conducting research on international development. While in Monterey, she worked for the County Chapter of the American Red Cross, implementing the chapter's minority outreach initiative, and serving as a family caseworker and assistant shelter manager after the 1989 Loma Prieta earthquake. She later used her training in post-traumatic stress disorder while working with her South Central Los Angeles community in the aftermath of the Los Angeles civil unrest of 1992.

After completing her PhD, Jennifer took a job with a small international development consulting firm in Alexandria, Virginia. There, she worked on some of the original contracts for the establishment of USAID's democracy programs. As a member of the civil society team, she traveled to Tanzania, Morocco, and Egypt exploring programming opportunities in response to Mission needs. She later worked with the USAID Mission to Mali, helping them to articulate their democratization strategy, and providing training on democracy, governance, and civil society, as well as on USAID's re-engineering planning requirements. Also, during this time, she began working for the World Bank's Economic Development Institute (now the World Bank Institute), where she conducted training for Vietnamese government officials from the Ministry of Finance and the Ministry of Transportation, and worked with the China Health Economics Network. For three years she worked as a Bank staff member with the Social Policy Reform in Transition Economies (SPRITE) program, providing training and institutional development to capacity building teams in twelve countries of the Former Soviet Union and Mongolia.

In the fall of 1996, Jennifer left her full-time position at the World Bank to begin an academic career as Director of the International Public Service and Development MPA/Peace Corps Masters International program at Rutgers University-Camden. She redesigned the program, including the formalization of a local service learning component, and began work to establish partnerships with universities in Namibia and South Africa. She is now an Associate Professor in the School of Public Policy and Public Administration at George Washington University. She also serves on the advisory board for the International Development Studies master's program in the Elliott School of International Affairs, and has an appointment in the International Business Department.

Index

Also from Kumarian Press...

International Public Administration, Corruption

Better Governance and Public Policy
Capacity Building for Democratic Renewal in Africa
Edited by Dele Olowu and Soumana Sako

Building Democratic Institutions: Governance Reform in Developing Countries
G. Shabbir Cheema

Culture, Development, and Public Administration in Africa
Ogwo J. Umeh and Greg Andranovich

Fighting Corruption in Developing Countries: Strategies and Analysis
Edited by Bertram I. Spector

Governance, Administration & Development: Making the State Work
Mark Turner and David Hulme

Managing Policy Reform
Concepts and Tools for Decision-Makers in Developing Countries
Derick W. Brinkerhoff and Benjamin L. Crosby

Reinventing Government for the Twenty First Century
State Capacity in a Globalizing Society
Edited by Dennis A. Rondinelli and G. Shabbir Cheema

Where Corruption Lives
Edited by Gerald E. Caiden, O.P. Dwivedi, and Joseph Jabbra

Humanitarianism, Civil Society, Peacebuilding

Human Rights and Development
Peter Uvin

Nation-Building Unraveled? Aid, Peace and Justice in Afghanistan
Edited by Antonio Donini, Norah Niland and Karin Wermester

Ritual and Symbol in Peacebuilding
Lisa Schirch

The Charity of Nations: Humanitarian Action in a Calculating World
Ian Smillie and Larry Minear

Kumarian Press, located in Bloomfield, Connecticut, is a forward-looking, scholarly press that promotes active international engagement and an awareness of global connectedness.